Counseling Women in Prison

Women's Mental Health and Development

Series Editor: Barbara F. Okun, *Northeastern University*

Women's Mental Health and Development covers therapeutic issues of current relevance to women. This book series offers up-to-date, practical, culture-sensitive, professional resources for counselors, social workers, psychologists, nurse practitioners, family therapists, and others in the helping professions. Volumes in this series are also of significant value to scholars in gender studies and women's studies.

This series is designed to deal particularly with those issues and populations underrepresented in the current professional literature. Particular attention is paid to the sociocultural contexts of these issues and populations. While some of the volumes of this series cover topics pertinent to all women, others focus on topics applicable to specific groups. The series integrates material from established models, emerging theoretical constructs, and solid empirical findings in a format designed to be applicable for clinical practice. Professionals and trainees in a variety of mental health fields will find these readable, user-friendly volumes immediately useful.

Authors of volumes in this series are selected on the basis of their scholarship and clinical expertise. The editorial board is composed of leading clinicians and scholars from psychology, counseling, and social work.

Editorial Board

Counseling Women in Prison

Joycelyn M. Pollock

Women's Mental Health & Development, Volume 3

SAGE Publications
International Educational and Professional Publisher
Thousand Oaks   London   New Delhi

For information:

SAGE Publications, Inc.
2455 Teller Road
Thousand Oaks, California 91320
E-mail: order@sagepub.com

SAGE Publications Ltd.
6 Bonhill Street
London EC2A 4PU
United Kingdom

SAGE Publications India Pvt. Ltd.
M-32 Market
Greater Kailash I
New Delhi 110 048 India

Printed in the United States of America

Library of Congress Cataloging-in-Publication Data

Main entry under title:

Pollock, Joycelyn M., 1956–
    Counseling women in prison / by Joycelyn M. Pollock.
       p. cm. — (Women's mental health and development; vol. 3)
    Includes bibliographical references (p.   ) and index.
    ISBN 0-8039-7330-6 (cloth: acid-free paper). —
  ISBN 0-8039-7331-4 (pbk.: acid-free paper)
    1. Women prisoners--Counseling of—United States. 2. Women
prisoners—Mental health services—United States. 3. Mental health counseling—
United States. 4. Correctional psychology—United States. 5. Social work with
criminals—United States. I. Title. II. Series: Women's mental health and
development; v. 3.
HV9276.P58 1998
365'.66—dc21   97-33903

98 99 00 01 02 03 10 7 6 5 4 3 2 1

Acquiring Editor:	Jim Nageotte
Editorial Assistant:	Fiona Lyons
Production Editor:	Michele Lingre
Production Assistant:	Denise Santoyo
Typesetter:	Christina M. Hill
Print Buyer:	Anna Chin

Contents

Series Editor's Introduction   vii

Acknowledgements   ix

1. Change Efforts and the Female Prisoner   1
   Rehabilitation and Counseling in Prison   2
   Who Are the Women in Prison?   7
   Implications for Counselors   20

2. Women's Prisons   23
   More Prisons, More Prisoners   24
   The Prison World   26
   Change in the Prison World   40
   Implications for Counselors   43

3. Criminality and Classification   45
   Theories of Criminality   45
   Criminology and Corrections   53
   Assessment Issues   56
   Needs Analysis   65
   Implications for Counselors   71

4. Drug Abuse, Criminality, and Treatment   73
   Drugs and Crime   73
   Theories of Addiction   77
   Treatment Programs in Prison   83
   Implications for Counselors   92

5. Family Issues and Treatment Approaches   95
    Childhood Abuse   96
    Prisoners as Partners and Parents   100
    Children   102
    Family Programs   108
    Implications for Counselors   117

6. Prison Programs   120
    Personality Disorders in Prison   121
    Selected Prison Programs   123
    Elements of Intervention Programs   138
    Implications for Counselors   140

7. Life Skills: Making It on the Outside   143
    Women and Work   144
    Life Skills: Personal Development   152
    Implications for Counselors   159

8. Counseling in Prison: Issues and Concerns   165
    Choosing Corrections   165
    Counseling in Prison   177
    Implications for Counselors   186

9. The "Black Box" of Prison—Feminism and Cultural Issues   187
    Rehabilitation, Recidivism, and Research   188
    Feminism, Ethnocentrism, and Correctional Counseling   192
    Empowerment   200
    Conclusion   201

References   203

Resources   212

Index   213

About the Author   219

Series Editor's Introduction

Within the past two decades, the number of women in prisons has increased dramatically, about 202% from 1980 to 1989 (Bureau of Justice Statistics, 1991). While women still comprise less than 10% of the prison population, this growth overshadowed the male population increase by 90% and brought with it numerous questions and complications for the criminal justice system and society as a whole. The needs of female inmates are significantly different from those of male prisoners, for whom most of the existing institutional programs and policies were developed and implemented. For example, the repercussions of a woman's incarceration differ from those of a male, particularly when there are children. Less than half of the incarcerated women in state systems were employed prior to their incarceration, and many were unmarried and had received welfare assistance (American Correctional Association, 1990). They appear to have fewer opportunities upon release than do males, and their recidivism rate is over 66% (Bureau of Justice Statistics, 1991).

Thus, in order to work effectively with these women, counselors and human service workers must become more familiar with their characteristics and the multitude of issues affecting their development and behaviors prior to, during, and post incarceration. It is futile to attempt to understand these women out of the context of their environments, their families, and available resources. It is important to emphasize that substance, physical, and sexual abuses as well as poverty and gender oppression are major issues in the lives of a majority of this population. These factors need to be known and integrated into individual, family, and systems programs.

In Volume 3 of the Women's Mental Health and Development series, Joy Pollock brings her wealth of research and work with criminal justice systems to address these issues. She provides us with a comprehensive overview of the multiple factors contributing to women's criminality, the special issues they present during incarceration, and the types of planning and services required for them to progress to a satisfactory post-release experience. Not only does this volume contribute to our empathic and cognitive understanding of this special population, but it provides suggestions for ecologically based treatment planning and intervention.

Effective services and interventions for women in prison benefit their community and society as a whole, as well as the inmates and their families. Without meaningful treatment and rehabilitation, their children are at risk for truancy and delinquency, and the likelihood of recidivism is high. Pollock helps us to consider where te individual has come from, what she will be returning to, and how we can provide sound resources and treatment.

The editorial board and I are pleased to offer the professional community the opportunity to learn more about this unique population which is underrepresented in the mental health literature.

Barbara F. Okun, Ph.D.
Series Editor

Acknowledgements

As is usually the case, this book benefited from the contributions of many individuals. Much of the material for the book was obtained while working with a small group of individuals who produced a PBS documentary ("Mom's In Prison—Again," Forest Glen Productions, Box 101823, Fort Worth, TX 76185) on drug programs for women offenders: Annabella Chan, Ellen Halbert, Glen Ely, and Mary Willis Walker were a wonderful group to work with and allowed me the opportunity to participate in a worthwhile project. I also need to thank the Wackenhut Corporation for awarding me a small grant to conduct a needs assessment of women inmates in Texas. Their financial support, combined with a faculty-development grant from the School of Applied Arts and Technology, Southwest Texas State University, helped to support a needs assessment using a sample of close to 200 women inmates. Sue Williams and Verna Henson, faculty members at Southwest Texas State University, and Sherry Schroeder, a graduate student, helped with the interviews. Daisy Sartor, a graduate assistant, assisted with the final report. The Texas Department of Criminal Justice—Institutional Division—was helpful in providing information for sampling purposes and approving and clearing my visits to the prisons. Staff at the various prisons were helpful in organizing the interviews. Barbara Okun, the series editor, and Jim Nageotte, at Sage, conceived of the idea and guided development every step of the way. The reviewers improved the book's content with their advice and suggestions. Finally, of course, I must acknowledge all the women in prison who shared their lives with me.

Change Efforts and the Female Prisoner

> Imprisoned women tend to be marginalized women. A significant proportion of the female prison population shares characteristics devalued by society such as minority status, little education or work experience, and significant histories of personal and substance abuse.
>
> *Owen & Bloom (1995, p. 180)*

It has been said that the criminal justice system, especially the subsystem of corrections, is a system of men, for men. Women certainly are in the minority—as offenders and as professionals in the corrections system. Yet recently there has been a tremendous increase in imprisonment of female offenders. Between 1980 and 1995, the average annual increase in incarceration was higher for women (12%) than for men (8.5%); and whereas women still make up only 6% of the total inmate population in the United States, this represents three times the number of women in prison from the early 1980s. Even more troubling, there is every sign that the probability of a female offender being sentenced to prison will continue to increase (U.S. Department of Justice, 1995). This means that correctional counselors and other professionals will increasingly find themselves working with female offenders. Female and male offenders share many of the same problems, but women also have unique life experiences and present different counseling concerns. It is important for those who work with female offenders to recognize and understand these differences.

This book focuses on the female offender in prison and issues related to counseling female prisoners. It has been written for those who work with female offenders in an institutional setting. The reader may be an institutional counselor, a correctional officer, or a psychologist or psychiatrist engaged to provide either individual or group counseling to female offenders. Though much of the discussion concerns elements unique to the prison environment, community treatment professionals (for instance, those in probation and parole settings) who work with female offenders also might find the content helpful. The book is not designed as a technical guide for counselors or as a textbook in counseling; rather, it touches on some sociological and organizational issues that have relevance to counselors who work with female offenders. The goal is to provide the correctional professional or the student who plans to enter the field with some understanding of criminological theory, the nature of the prison environment, some familiarity with selected prison programs, and background characteristics of the female offender. Each chapter closes with a section titled "Implications for the Counselor" that highlights the relevance of the chapter's subject matter to concerns of the counselor.

We begin in Chapter 1 by discussing the topic of rehabilitation in prison and the appropriate focus of counseling. A profile of the female offender is offered, including demographic information, criminal history, and personal history. Chapter 2 describes the prison world—for inmates and the correctional professionals who work there. Classification and assessment are covered in Chapter 3. In the second section (Chapters 4 and 5) of the book, two dominant themes in the lives of female offenders are focused on—drug use and family issues. The following two chapters (Chapters 6 and 7) briefly describe selected prison programs. The final section (Chapters 8 and 9) presents some common concerns for those engaged in counseling female offenders.

Rehabilitation and Counseling in Prison

Can individuals change? What constitutes rehabilitation? Who are the women in prison? These are the questions we will consider in this first chapter. Individuals are in prison because they broke the law. Many in prison also have problems with drugs, alcohol, anger management, or display other dysfunctional behavior patterns. The goals of imprisonment are to punish, deter, and rehabilitate. The emphasis placed on these three goals, respectively, has shifted from time to time. Sometimes rehabilitation has been emphasized, such as during the so-called "rehabilitative era" of the late 1960s and 1970s. In other time periods, punishment and deterrence have been the dominant goals. We are in a "punishment era" when there is very little rhetoric or resources directed toward the goal of rehabilitation. Yet even now, when the dominant paradigm is punishment, rehabilitation and individual change efforts continue.

Rehabilitation may be defined as "restoring to a previous state of wholeness." In corrections, this means restoring to some previous state of noncriminal behavior. It has been criticized as a misnomer in correctional treatment, because it is questionable whether some offenders have ever fallen within the boundaries of "normality," at least as far as attitudes and behavior regarding lawbreaking are concerned. The term rehabilitation is commonly applied to many forms of correctional intervention. In fact, practically all available programs or opportunities in prison—education, vocational training, religion, volunteer services—typically fall under the rubric of rehabilitative services. More specific definitions of rehabilitation include the following: "a programmed effort to alter attitudes and behaviors of inmates which is focused on the elimination of their future criminal behaviors" (Senese & Kalinich, 1992, p. 223). Or rehabilitation includes those programs that have specific goals, a specific structure and method, a history of success, are based on a clear concept or theory, are intense and require time, run by trained counselors, and offered to inmates who can benefit from them (Gottfredson, 1979).

For the last 10 years or so, administrators of correctional institutions have been concerned with such management issues as overcrowding, equal protection litigation, and court-mandated change, whereas little attention has been given to rehabilitation, counseling, or other forms of "treatment." Part of the disillusionment with rehabilitation efforts was due to the spate of research findings that concluded that "nothing worked" in corrections, that is, nothing affected recidivism (subsequent criminal behavior). Part of the shift in emphasis was due to the changing political climate that included less tolerance toward the criminal offender and a nostalgic attitude toward the days when a prison sentence meant hard labor and deprivation rather than treatment programs (Pollock, 1997c). The result of the shift in public and political opinion has been that many rehabilitative efforts in prison have been discarded or eliminated. Although basic education and vocational training can be found in virtually all prisons today, there are fewer rehabilitative programs than there were in the late 1970s and early 1980s. Treatment professionals may find that they have other responsibilities, including classification, supervision, a variety of record-keeping assignments and diagnostic tasks, and ongoing casework management. Despite the lack of emphasis on rehabilitation today, the many correctional professionals who work in drug and alcohol-treatment programs and life-skills programs, and those who interact with female offenders in groups for survivors of incest, or are involved in casework counseling, continue to facilitate the occurrence of positive change.

Counseling Female Offenders

Counseling can be defined as "a relationship with a helping professional, with a goal of improving the individual's coping, interpersonal skills, or addressing a specific personal problem." The goals of prison counseling have been defined as "to assist the offender to establish a lifestyle that is personally satisfying and conforms to the rules and regulations of society, and . . . to protect the community from harmful activity by offenders placed under correctional supervision" (Kratcoski, 1994, p. 1). In prison, counseling may be done by a range of treatment professionals with varied backgrounds—through an individual casework relationship, through general or specific-issue groups, or in a therapeutic community setting.

There has been criticism that "counseling" female offenders or, indeed, all "mental health services" to female prisoners, have more to do with controlling their behavior than helping them achieve personal fulfillment and that counseling efforts deny offenders dignity and respect by taking away the right to make personal lifestyle choices (Kendall, 1994b). To be sure, treatment professionals in prison are called on to intervene in situations of "acting out" and counselors often deal with the inmates' confrontations with prison officials and maladaptive coping patterns in prison. Interestingly, though, female offenders don't seem to see counseling efforts as intrusive or oppressive; in fact, when prisoners themselves are asked how they feel about treatment and treatment professionals, their responses are almost uniformly positive. Indeed, one of the strongest findings to emerge from surveys of female offenders is how favorably they respond to treatment programs. Although female offenders complain a great deal about prison itself and characteristics of prison life, their complaints regarding prison treatment programs and treatment professionals center on lack of availability, not goals or objectives (Pollock, Williams, & Schroeder, 1996).

What are the proper goals of treatment or intervention efforts? Should treatment professionals be concerned solely with a reduction in criminal behavior? If so, how does one move toward the goal of reducing criminal behavior in a prison where opportunities for criminal behavior are obviously limited? Should treatment professionals have more inclusive goals, addressing other problems and concerns of the offender? Unfortunately, the prison is an abnormal environment filled with stressors that the real world does not have but without many responsibilities that most of us must deal with, such as working and providing food, shelter, and clothing for ourselves and dependents. Therefore, counseling in prison is unique in many respects. The issues often dealt with in counseling, such as dealing with families of origin, are somewhat removed from the immediate lives of the clients, and the immediate concerns of the client are often prison-related, which, by their nature, are somewhat aberrant. Prison is not like the "real world," and problems that one has in prison will not be the same as those that the women will face on release.

Thus, it may be the case that counseling in prison simply acts to reduce the negative effects of the prison environment. The fundamental problems the female offender will continue to struggle with when she leaves prison and returns to street life can be addressed, but it calls for extra effort by the female offender and the counseling professional to get past the prison world.

What Is Success?

Typically, correctional intervention efforts address aspects of behavior or personality that may lead to criminal behavior, such as drug addiction or anger management. The goals of treatment are related to the criminal behavior that brought the women to prison, but the actual criminal behavior may not necessarily be directly addressed. Should one be concerned, for instance, if a female offender, after some form of counseling or program participation, progresses in measurable indices of mental health (for instance, she has more self-esteem, she is less depressed, and she has no suicidal ideation) but she still professes to be committed to a criminal lifestyle? Is it the therapist's or counselor's job here to try to change the offender's views regarding lifestyle choices? Is a program a success if it accomplishes the above-described individual improvement or a failure if the offender is released only to be caught again committing another crime? In the past, the practice has been to judge treatment programs solely on their ability to affect recidivism rates (the rate of reconviction or rearrest). Although a good argument can be made that a program should be judged a success if it moves an individual to a higher level of functioning either cognitively or emotionally, or in some other way improves his or her mental health, an equally persuasive argument can be made that, if the public is paying for the program, it has a right to expect the offender to be not only more "healthy" but also more law-abiding. What about an offender who, after completing some form of counseling in prison reoffends, but does so in a less socially harmful way, perhaps is arrested for simple drug possession rather than robbery? Would the program be a success or a failure in this case?

Meta-analyses of prison programs have reported fairly dismal results, if success is measured solely by recidivism. There are no evaluations that specifically target prison programs for female offenders. Martinson's (1974) meta-analysis is the best known. After reviewing over 200 separate prison program evaluations, he concluded that "nothing worked." Others have also reported that, overall, prison programs do not seem to affect recidivism (Logan & Gaes, 1993). Nevertheless, others point to flaws in the design of these studies. For instance, when all programs are collapsed into one data set, small "pockets" of success in certain programs or for certain offenders are eclipsed by the negative results overall. Palmer (1994) and others contend that results do support the success of some programs for some offenders. Matching offenders with appropriate programs is an essential component of success according to Palmer, and certain programs seem to show more success than others. The debate continues whether prison programs can affect recidivism or not. Certainly, one thing has been shown and that is the difficulty of defining, much less measuring, "success" in intervention efforts.

What can be said for intervention that succeeds in reducing law-abiding behavior but reduces mental health? Actually, prison itself might be an example of this. Many authors can provide evidence that the prison experience does little to enhance mental functioning and does a great deal to retard growth and/or provides the impetus for deterioration of mental health. If it could be shown to be a deterrent to future criminal offending, does this justify the emotional damage it does to its inhabitants or should we even care? Treatment professionals working in the prison probably have pondered the above questions. Day-to-day concerns, however, are more immediate. Counselors in a prison typically address the real problems of female offenders as best they can, in the time they have, with the tools they have available.

Types of Counseling

Counseling in prison might be divided into three categories, not necessarily mutually exclusive. Crisis counseling addresses current events in a woman's life that cause stress and threaten her ability to cope. Examples might be such family concerns as losing parental rights, adaptational or coping problems to prison life, or specific traumas, such as finding out one has AIDS. A second category of counseling is directly related to the criminal behavior that brought the woman to prison. Examples of this type of counseling are guided groups for women who killed their children, drug-treatment groups for drug offenders, and interventions for shoplifters. Finally, a type of counseling that addresses personal development issues can be distinguished from the other two categories. This type of counseling also can take place in a group setting or through a standard casework approach, and includes issues of incest and sexual abuse, communication patterns, life scripts, family problems, goal setting, and self-esteem.

The needs of women in prison obviously change depending on the stage of imprisonment. On entry, a woman may need crisis counseling to help her adjust to the prison environment. Many offenders are extremely frightened and traumatized by the imprisonment and need help to adjust to the loss of family and the structure and impersonality of prison. During the middle phase of imprisonment, counseling may address the second two foci of counseling described above—either a direct treatment of the criminal behavior or a more holistic approach to the woman's personal development. Finally, as the offender nears release, counseling may take on some elements of crisis counseling, again, to deal with the emerging fears and problems of release. Goal setting, planning, problem solving, and contingency structuring may be the focus of the counseling relationships in the final weeks of incarceration.

Women in prison present a multitude of issues for counselors. Many of them have had lives marked by trauma and suffer from drug, alcohol, or both abuses, depression, self-esteem problems, and an inability to achieve healthy intimate relationships. In the second part of this chapter, a profile of the female prisoner will be presented.

Who Are the Women in Prison?

Female prisoners represent all socioeconomic classes, races, and backgrounds. Nevertheless, there are groups that are disproportionately represented in prison populations, and certain types of offenders predominate. The following is a demographic profile of the female prisoner: She is a black woman, in her early 30s, she has one or more children, but probably has not been their primary caregiver, instead lives a life centered around dysfunctional relationships with men, drugs, and alcohol. She may have dropped out of school because of a pregnancy. She has probably held a series of low-paying jobs, primarily nurse's aid positions and fast-food, but other income has come from welfare programs, men, family, and crime. She has had a succession of boyfriends, one of whom probably introduced her to the drug culture. Her crimes may have started with helping a boyfriend or friend in a credit card scam, shoplifting, or passing bad checks, but she probably ended up getting caught for something she did herself. She has low self-esteem, which may stem from a childhood marked by sexual abuse, physical abuse, and/or neglect. As an adult she has had few, if any, good relationships with men. She wants to change, to be a better mother to her children and to have a decent job and home life, yet she can't seem to make the change to a different lifestyle on the outside. She says she is going to stay away from "trouble," yet she plans to go back to living with her family or other relatives, in her same neighborhood. When asked how she will avoid the old patterns of behavior, she has no good answer.

The description above represents a composite of female prisoners in this country. The first issue to note is that the profile of women in prison is not necessarily the same as that of female offenders. Women who end up in prison are more likely to be members of a minority group, more likely to have a history of drug use, more likely to come from family backgrounds characterized by alcoholism, drug use, and a criminal history. They are also more likely to be without skills or education and, to a great extent, without hope for their future. Because of these differences we must be careful not to assume that a prison population is representative of all female criminals. White women in suburbia commit crimes too, typically embezzlement and shoplifting, and some do end up in prison; but proportionally, they are much more likely to be sentenced to probation and community service.

The other issue to note is the differences between men and women in prison. Whereas only rough generalizations are possible, it is true that women in prison tend to be a bit older and more educated than men. They tend not to have as extensive criminal histories, they are more likely to be parents, and they are more likely to come from dysfunctional backgrounds (Fletcher, Shaver, & Moon, 1993). In the pages to follow, four sources were used to provide the reader with a demographic profile of female offenders. All were surveys of female prisoners. All used random samples and all covered a multitude of issues, including criminal history, drug use patterns, history of victimization, children and custody issues, and other background characteristics. The national study was the "Survey of State Prison Inmates, 1991" (Snell, 1994). The other three were surveys of Oklahoma (Fletcher et al., 1993), California (Bloom, Chesney-Lind, & Owen, 1994; see also Owen & Bloom 1994, 1995) and Texas (Pollock et al., 1996). Although there are some differences in results among the states, such as the percentage of certain ethnic or minority groups in prison, the state surveys show remarkably consistent results, especially in reporting incidences of childhood victimization and drug use. Combined with the national survey, these sources give us a good description of the women in prison and their problems. Women in prison will be discussed according to their age and race, family background, income status, and typical crimes.

Age and Race

Women in prison are most likely to be in their early 30s. This is slightly older than the average age of male prisoners (late 20s) (Fletcher et al., 1993;

Owen & Bloom, 1994). Slightly more women than men in prison report being married. About 27% in the Oklahoma and Texas samples were married, compared with only 20% of men in a national sample (Fletcher et al., 1993; Pollock et al., 1995).

Black females are overrepresented in this nation's prisons—even more so than black males. Nationally, about 46% of all female prisoners are African American (Snell, 1994). In California, more than half of the women in prison are either African American (35%) or Hispanic (17%) (Bloom et al., 1994, p. 3). In the Texas sample, 41.9% were African American, 39.8% were white and 13.4% were Hispanic. In the Oklahoma study, 37% of the women were black and another 11% were Hispanic or American Indian (Fletcher et al., 1993).

By all accounts, race is becoming the single greatest correlate of imprisonment. The U.S. Department of Justice (1994a) reported that the number of imprisoned black males increased 186%, whereas the number of imprisoned white males increased by 143%, between 1980 and 1992. Actually the rate of increase for females was even higher. The rate of increase for black females was 278%, compared to the increase of 275% for white females. In 1992 the rate of incarceration for the entire population was 344 per 100,000. The rate for white males was 372 per 100,000, but the rate for black males was 2,678 per 100,000. The rate for white females was 20 per 100,000, but the rate for black females was 143 per 100,000. Thus, the rate for African American males and females was roughly seven times that of whites (U.S. Department of Justice, 1994a). Similar patterns were found for other minority groups. What this means is that our prisons are increasingly seen as evidence of oppression and discrimination by those who are sent there, as well as others in minority communities. Whether the criminal justice system discriminates against minorities is a complicated question, but what cannot be ignored is that in prison, minorities are quickly becoming the majority, and race is an issue that is hard to ignore in institutions where African Americans and other minorities predominate in numbers grossly disproportional to their percentage of the national population.

Family Background

More than half of the women in prison have grown up in a household without both parents present, although the likelihood of having both parents at home varies by race. Whereas 55% of white women grew up with both parents, only 31% of African American women and 40% of Hispanic women grew up with both parents in the home. In the national sample, 42% of female prisoners had lived in a single-parent household—39% of the total sample had lived only with mothers and 16% grew up with neither parent present (Snell, 1994). Female inmates are twice as likely as the general population to have grown up in a single-parent household (Snell, 1994). African American women were most likely to have grown up in a home with only their mothers (46%) compared with whites (29%) and Hispanics (41%) (Snell, 1994).

Women are more likely than male inmates to have had family members incarcerated (47% compared with 37%). They are also more likely to have had a family member with a drug or alcohol problem (about 33% compared with about 25% for males) (Snell, 1994). In the California sample, almost three quarters (71%) reported that at least one family member had been arrested and 63% reported at least one relative with a prison or jail sentence. Slightly more than half who had a current partner reported that the partner had a history of incarceration and one quarter were currently incarcerated (Bloom et al., 1994).

In the Texas sample of female inmates, almost three quarters (71.5%) had a family member who had been arrested and 59.1% had a family member that had been in jail or prison. Forty-five percent of the women's partners or spouses had been incarcerated. About one quarter (22.6%) of their former or current partners were currently incarcerated (Pollock et al., 1996).

The Female Offender and Poverty

In an average city, 80% of all African American families living below the poverty line are headed by single women (Taylor, 1993, p. 192). Single-parent families now account for one out of three American families; nearly 4 out of 10 are headed by a parent who has never been married (McLeod, 1995). The likelihood of single parenthood varies by race: Whereas 25% of all white families are headed by one parent, 65% of African American families and 33% of Hispanic families are headed by one parent. Most often the single parent is a woman (McLeod, 1995).

Women in prison are likely to be single parents of small children, and they are also likely to have been raised as a child in a single-parent household. One effect of being a single parent is poverty. In recent national statistics, households headed by women earned about half as much as married-couple families earned. Black women heads of households earned the least of all groups: $239 weekly family earnings compared with $290 for white women heads of households, $302 for black male heads of households, $410 for white males, $457 for black married couples, and $567 for white married couples (McLeod, 1995).

Women in prison are more likely than males to be unemployed before arrest—47% of women worked at the time of arrest compared with 68% of male inmates in the national sample of prisoners (Snell, 1994). In the California sample, 37% of women reported working at a legitimate job and in the Texas sample, about 42% of the women reported working at a legitimate job before incarceration. Jobs tended to be unskilled, minimum wage positions in service occupations. In the Texas sample, the jobs mentioned, in descending order of frequency, were nurse's aid, housekeeper, waitress, fast-food, and office or clerical (Pollock et al., 1996).

Women's Crimes

Women's crimes are typically prostitution and fraud, especially those frauds that involve some level of acting or artifice. More recently, drugs have become part of the picture—both drug crimes *per se* (sales and possession) but also drugs as related to other crimes: assaults, homicides, and crimes committed for money to purchase drugs.

Women are responsible for 32% of all larceny or theft arrests, 34.6% of all forgery arrests, 44.2% of all fraud arrests, and 41.2% of all embezzlement arrests (Federal Bureau of Investigation, 1990). In the last 10 years, women's contributions to homicide have decreased, but there have been modest increases in some property crimes. Women's contribution to fraud arrests was 35% in 1976 and 40% in 1992; their contribution to embezzlement went from 29.5% to 39%, and other property crimes show some increases. For personal violent crime, the results are mixed; for homicide the change was downward, from 13.8% to 8.8%, but for robbery it went up from 6.7% to 8% (Federal Bureau of Investigation, 1993).

Juvenile History. Typically, female offenders do not have an extensive criminal background. More women than men in the Oklahoma study, for instance, were serving their first prison term (32% versus 19%) (Fletcher et al., 1993). In the California study, more than half (54.6%) of the imprisoned women were serving their first prison sentence and another 21% reported having only one prior commitment (Bloom et al., 1994).

Forty-seven percent of the Texas sample were serving their first prison term. Another 21.5% reported having only one prior term. Nationally, about 28% of female inmates reported no previous prison or probation sentences (compared with only 19% of men) (Snell, 1994). About 51% of women had only one or no prior offense, with an additional 66% having only two or fewer offenses, compared with 39% and 55% of male inmates respectively (Snell,

1994). Nationally, about 2 out of 10 women have a juvenile record, compared with 4 out of 10 men (Snell, 1994). Slightly less than half of a California sample had any juvenile-arrest history (Bloom et al., 1994). In the Texas sample, less than half of the women (39.8%) had been arrested as juveniles (Pollock et al., 1996).

Property Offenses. Steffensmeier (1993) has found that the greatest difference in arrest profiles of women between 1960 and 1990 is the greater involvement of women in such minor property crimes as larceny and fraud. Women's percentage of total arrests for larceny increased from 17% to 30% between 1960 and 1975 but has held fairly steady since. Nevertheless, their percentage for fraud and forgery continues to rise (Steffensmeier, 1993, p. 26). The increase has come about in offense categories such as shoplifting, passing bad checks, credit card fraud, theft of services, welfare fraud, and small con games (Steffensmeier, 1993).

All evidence seems to indicate that women are committing the same crimes they have always committed and often doing so for economic reasons. As Steffensmeier (1993) points out,

> Rising rates of divorce, illegitimacy, and female-headed households, coupled with continued segregation of women in low-paying occupations, have aggravated the economic pressures on women and have left them more responsible for child care than they were two or three decades ago. Growing economic adversity increases the pressures to commit consumer-based crimes such as shoplifting, check fraud, theft of services, and welfare fraud. (p. 17)

Changes in society that have contributed to the rise of female property crime are not necessarily due to female "liberation" or the entry of women into all occupations but, rather, changes in the market economy, such as the expanded use of credit cards, increases in shopping malls and self-service marketing, and the proliferation of small portable but expensive items. Opportunities for fraud exist in the misuse of student loans, social security, Medicaid, ADC (Aid to Dependent Children), insurance, and so forth (Steffensmeier, 1993).

A different view of the increase in property crimes by females was offered by Albanese (1993) who presented statistics that compare women's entry into white-collar occupations and their increase in "white-collar" crime. Albanese showed that in 1970 women constituted only 31.7% of managerial positions and accounted for roughly 25% of white-collar crime (fraud, forgery and counterfeiting, embezzlement). In 1989 women accounted for 44.7% of all managerial positions and committed roughly 40% of white-collar crimes. The parallel increases in entry to the managerial workforce and contributions to white-collar crime are supportive of the idea that women are using their employment opportunities for crime. What is needed is a deeper look at the types of crimes committed within the fraud, forgery, and embezzlement categories. Steffensmeier (1993) and others believe that the types of crimes are not necessarily related to employment in managerial capacities, although other researchers believe they are.

The percentage of total arrests for burglary rates has inched up for women, largely because of a decrease in male arrests. With more women working, houses are left empty and female offenders are perhaps more likely to attempt burglary now that there is little chance of detection. Steffensmeier (1993) provided a quote from one female burglar.

> My involvement came from selling real estate. A couple of the homes I was showing left money laying around. I was very short of money at the time. I had the keys, so I went back later. Did it twice and got caught. It amounted to $844 in all. (p. 24)

Violent Offenses. In the late 1970s Freda Adler (1975) ignited a huge interest, on the part of academics and journalists, by her thesis that female criminals were becoming more violent; in effect, equal opportunity had hit the illegitimate occupations as well, and women were entering such previously all-male criminal occupations as robbery and burglary in increasing numbers. The only problem with this thesis was that there was no evidence to back it up—women continued to represent about 10% of all arrests for violent crime. Whereas it was true that the percentage increase of female crimes was larger than that for males, part of the reason was because of the minuscule base numbers. It is not difficult to show a 200% to 300% increase when working with a small base number. The raw numbers, however, gave a different picture and it was abundantly clear that violent crime was still the bastion of the male criminal, and most of the increase in female criminality was taking place in such traditionally female areas as larceny.

Although women account for about 10% of the arrests for violent crime, 41% of the women in prison are there for a violent offense. This is a reduction from years past when it was closer to 50% (U. S. Department of Justice, 1991). This percentage varies from state to state. In California, for instance, it was reported that only 23.9% of female prisoners were serving time for a violent crime (Bloom et al., 1994, p. 3). The percentages seem to be influenced by arrest patterns for drug crimes. For those states that aggressively prosecute drug crimes and use mandatory and/or long sentences, there is a correspondingly higher percentage of inmates incarcerated for drugs as compared with other types of crimes.

Serial murder is a crime that is almost exclusively associated with male perpetrators. Some dispute the conclusion that a minuscule proportion of serial murderers are female and believe their participation to more closely approximate their representation in all violent crimes (closer to 10%) (Keeney & Heide, 1994). Because the crime is so rarely committed, and difficult to detect if the homicides are not connected in some way, it is impossible to verify which of these opinions is closer to the truth. Studies of identified serial murderers indicate that differences exist between male and female offenders (Hickey, 1991; Keeney & Heide, 1994). Keeney and Heide (1994) reported that there were differences in the amount of damage inflicted on the victim, the presence of torture during the criminal episode, the method of targeting the victim (women "lured" whereas men "stalked"). Men were more likely to kill with their hands or use objects other than guns to kill, whereas women were more likely to use poison (Keeney & Heide, 1994). Males were more likely to have affective motives (emotional or psychological reasons for killing) whereas women in the sample were about equally divided between affective and instrumental motives for killing their victims. Women and men were likely to have come from dysfunctional families and to have suffered physical and sexual abuse. The majority of the sample was diagnosed with some form of pathology (antisocial personality, schizophrenia). Women were more likely to stay in one location, whereas male offenders often were mobile (for example, Ted Bundy moved from the Pacific Northwest to Florida before he was captured) (Keeney & Heide, 1994). Although the study sample was small and the authors used secondary sources to arrive at their conclusions, it is instructive to note that even in the most extreme violent crime, there are substantive differences between male and female offenders.

A third of all family murders are committed by a female perpetrator (Dawson, 1994). Females were the killers in 41% of spousal murders and 55% of killings of children. Among African Americans, women were almost as likely to kill as be killed by their partner (53% of spousal victims were wives), but white women were less likely than males to be the killers in spousal killings (62% of white spousal victims were wives) (Dawson, 1994). More than one third of the women incarcerated for a violent offense had assaulted or killed a relative or intimate (U.S. Department of Justice, 1991). A later U.S. Department of Justice study reported that female inmates were more likely to have killed relatives or intimates (49%) than nonrelatives (30%) or strangers (21%). They were almost twice as likely to have killed a husband, ex-husband or boyfriend as any other relative (Snell, 1994). These statistical studies do not indicate whether or not the homicide was related to battering; nevertheless, other evidence indicates that battering plays a large part in homicides of intimates when women are the perpetrators (Browne, 1987; Ewing, 1987). In New York, 59% of the women committed to prison in 1986, for killing someone close to them, were being abused at the time of the offense (Huling, 1991).

Actually, the female percentage of homicide arrests has decreased since 1960 from 17% to 10% (Steffensmeier, 1993, p. 22). A large part of this decrease has been the reduction in spousal or intimate homicide. The latest U.S. Department of Justice study (1994b) on homicide reported that

> In 1977, 54 percent of the murder victims who were killed by intimates were female. By 1992, the ratio of female to male victims had changed, with 70 percent of the victims being female. In other words the number of male victims fell from 1,185 in 1977 to 657 in 1992 and the number of female victims increased from 1,396 to 1,510 during the same period. (p. 3)

It has been speculated that the increase in shelters and services for battered women has helped to reduce the numbers of women who kill their abuser, by providing alternatives for them (Browne, 1987). On the other hand, the number of men who kill their spouses has not decreased.

In a New York study of female homicide offenders, it was found that in two thirds of the cases (other than when the subject was not present at the crime), there were elements of victim precipitation. Drugs played a large role in homicide; 4 out of 10 were high on a drug at the time of the offense, most commonly alcohol or crack. The researchers rated more than half (57%) of the homicides as "psychopharmacological drug-related," 12% as "economic-compulsively drug-related," and 11% as "systematically drug-related." Only about one third were not related to drugs in any way (Spunt, Brownstein, Crimmins, & Langley, 1994). These authors disputed the views of those who describe most female homicide as usually an escape from abuse.

> Our findings show that while it is unreasonable to generalize that women kill in moments of abuse, it is fair to say that most women who have been convicted of murder or manslaughter have experienced abuse at some point in their lives. The lives of the women we studied were complex and filled with patterns of pain, prolonged abuse, and isolation. There does not seem to be any one factor to which we could point and say, this is what led them to become involved in violence. Instead, a host of factors, including abuse, contributed to the wear and tear these women experienced with violence as an integral part of their everyday lives. To intervene in that cycle requires programs that address multiple needs and deficits of living. (p. viii)

Mann (1993) also presented a more multidimensional view of the female homicide offender than as a woman who kills her abuser. In a description, for instance, of women who kill other women, she had the following to say:

> It was found that women who kill other women basically resemble the portrait depicted over the past two decades by previous researchers: they are young, black, undereducated, and unemployed. Anger, arguments, and fights which could take place at any time or any place were most often the precipitating factors that led to the killing of another woman, who, in many instances, instigated her own death. Possibly because of the victim's contributory role in her homicide, prison sentences were assigned in only 41.1% of the cases, and time to be served in prison averaged only 6.4 years. (p. 219)

Most research indicates that when women commit robbery, they are often playing a passive or accomplice role; nevertheless, at least one study disputes the passivity of women in robbery. Sommers and Baskin (1991) reported that, in their sample of violent female criminals, there were two apparent groups— an early-onset group who started offending as early as 10 years of age and a late-onset group who were more likely to be situationally violent or became violent after they left school. For both groups, Sommers and Baskin reported that members were likely to have been raised in single-parent families with little supervision, to have experienced physical and sexual abuse, and to have witnessed abuse between parents or guardians. They were also likely to have come from poverty and to have had guardians who were substance abusers or incarcerated. Women in the early-onset group could be distinguished by the severity of early childhood problems.

Gangs: The New Female Criminal? Recently we have seen a resurgence of the idea that female criminals are becoming more violent. The current thesis is that girls are forming gangs similar to those of young males or, alternatively, joining male gangs. The activities of these girls are similar to their male counterparts in terms of violence and criminality. Only a few researchers have actually gathered evidence to support this thesis and much of their work has been phenomenological—conducting interviews with girl gang members. (These "girls," by the way, often are in their early 20s.) There is little evidence that females contribute much to the "gang problem" in any substantial way. Joe and Chesney-Lind (1993) reported, for instance, that Hawaii police figures indicate that only about 7% of gang members in Oahu were female. Because they also reported that more than one third of the women in this group were over 26 years old and one woman was 52 years old, it is obviously stretching the definition of youth gangs to even arrive at the 7% figure. Their research also indicated that female gang members tended to commit fewer crimes and less serious crimes than male gang members. In fact, the most typical activity for their sample of female gang members was getting together, talking and dancing. As reported in much earlier gang research in the 1950s, Joe and Chesney-Lind (1993) indicated that girls might act to suppress the violence of the male gang members. Using a quote from one of their sample, "If we not with the girls, we fighting. If we not fighting, we with the girls." Although their girl gang members did report fighting, the authors cautioned that this behavior needed to be understood in the context of the youths' lives, which were commonly marked by familial violence and cultural proscriptions against seeking help from school or authority figures. Gangs, for these girls, became substitute families and havens from abusive families. Fighting to resolve interpersonal conflicts was part of the tradition in which they had all been raised.

Taylor (1993) also conducted numerous interviews with female gang members in the Detroit area. According to Taylor, their formations, called "posses," were more criminal organizations than the teenage gangs that one normally thinks of, but he documented their attitudes toward violence (necessary in their business), men (nice to have around but not necessary), and the straight life (only for jerks and "honkies"). Taylor used the typology of "scavenger gangs," which drift in and out of crime as opportunity presents itself; territorial gangs, which hold power over geographic boundaries; commercial gangs, which have a product and an organization to sell it; and corporate gangs, which have an infrastructure not unlike any business in corporate America. Of these types, women were involved in all types, even the corporate—female offenders ran drug rings and displayed the signs of wealth that comes from this type of corporate success, including expensive cars, clothes, and houses. According to Taylor, they displayed their success a little less blatantly than did the male drug kingpins and were known and respected for their ability to "take care of business." Taylor (1993) described them in the following way:

> Structurally, these gangs are a cross between "Amway-type" distributorships and covert guerrilla operations. Females have emerged as key players in this model. The product in this case is illegal dope. Women have found joining corporate gangs and covert operations to be rewarding. Despite public perception, most gangs are not drug-crazed terrorists. Women in corporate gangs as well as those who decide to branch out on their own do not, generally speaking, use drugs. (p. 199)

Drugs. As reported earlier, drugs account for a substantial amount of the increase in women's imprisonments. For instance, it is reported that the percentage of women admitted to prison for drugs increased from 14.2% of total admissions in 1982 to 42.2% of the total in 1992 (Bloom et al., 1994, p. 6).

It is also clear that women's involvement in the drug trade is rarely on the same order as males. They often serve only as assistants to a male partner. Often the drug business is a part of the household, from which they could not escape even if they wanted to. Huling (1995) reported on a particularly vulnerable group of women—the so-called "mules" who bring drugs into this country. These women, often from Third World countries, are usually poor, uneducated, and completely oblivious to what consequences may result from their actions. They often are coerced or duped into carrying the drugs, only to be caught and face severe punishments in states like New York, which have mandatory sentences for some drug crimes. For instance, a conviction for 4 ounces of a narcotic drug would carry a mandatory minimum of 15 years to life in New York (Huling, 1995, p. 5). In a catch-22 worthy of Joseph Heller, what occurs in sentencing is that these women are not able to take advantage of an exception to the mandatory laws that provide reduced sentences if the offender offers material assistance to the prosecution of crime partners, because they usually have so little knowledge of the operation and are ignorant of anything that may be of use to the prosecutor. Because their peripheral involvement provides no material assistance, they will be sentenced to the same Draconian sentences as would be imposed on the top kingpin (Huling, 1995; Raeder, 1993). Case studies illustrate the situations of the many women who are in New York prisons for smuggling drugs (Huling, 1995).

- Marie, a 40-year-old black woman, carried with her on a plane from Haiti a small wooden statue filled with cocaine. She said she did it at the behest of a village police chief who told her he would blow up her mother's house with a grenade should she leave the country without the statue.
- Blanca was a mother of two and wife of a Colombian bartender who left her pregnant and ill with a gallbladder problem. Denied welfare benefits because she had a house, she tried factory piecework to make ends meet, but she soon fell behind in the mortgage payments. When she was approached by someone from her neighborhood who knew of her problems, she agreed to carry a package of cocaine back from Colombia in exchange for $3,000.
- Delia, a divorced mother of four with a seventh-grade education, traveled outside of Greensboro, North Carolina, for the first time to meet her future husband in Nigeria, the brother of a businessman she knew. The businessman, who paid for her plane ticket, had invited Delia to meet his brother, a doctor in Nigeria who

was looking for an American wife. Delia's fiancé sent her home from Nigeria with a gift: a quilted suede coat, the lining of which she was told upon her arrest contained 15 oz of heroin. (p. 16)

Huling reported that 96% of the women arrested at JFK airport and sentenced to *life terms* for drug smuggling had no prior record (p. 17). Most (95%) used a public defender and agreed to a plea bargain. She also reported that race appeared to play a part in the decision to imprison inasmuch as 52% of African American and 50% of white women were sent to prison, but 83% of Hispanic women were sent to prison.

There has been a huge increase of women drug offenders sent to federal prisons. For instance, from January 1989 through September 1990, 39% of all women sentenced under federal guidelines committed drug offenses (Raeder, 1993, p. 22). About 8% of female federal prisoners were drug offenders compared with about 6% of female state prisoners. Nevertheless, these percentages are likely to go up, considering that drug crimes now account for more and more crimes of conviction for women sentenced to prison. For example, in 1989 drug crimes accounted for 64.3% of all crimes for which women received a sentence longer than 12 months (Raeder, 1993, p. 22). The sentence lengths in the federal guidelines system were computed as an average of typical sentences for each crime, which means that women, on average, are serving longer sentences than they would have before guidelines went into effect, because in the past they often received less severe sentences than men. This sex neutral sentencing approach seems fair on the surface, but when one explores the realities of women's lives, this equality seems less just. There are real differences in offense characteristics and family responsibilities, as well as differences in recidivism rates and culpability factors between men and women that are not taken into consideration in current federal guidelines. For example, one criterion for a downward adjustment of federal guideline sentences is duress, but courts have usually excluded personal relationships as an example of duress. Thus, a woman who entered drug trafficking through a relationship with a male drug trafficker would not be able to use the relationship as a mitigating factor. Battering would be evidence for a duress exception to guidelines sentencing, but it evidently must require physical abuse or at least the threat of physical abuse in relation to the criminal event. The cultural and psychological influences that compel some women to stay with a criminal male partner are not accepted as meeting the legal definition of duress. It is clear, however, that for many women, their role in criminal drug conspiracies is minimal and occurs because of their relationship with the male crime partner. According to Raeder (1993),

The women typically are married to, living with, or intimately involved with males who are described as having central roles in the conspiracies in question. The women are likely to be aware of the males' criminal endeavors, and their familial actions may even promote those activities. However, the women's roles in the conspiracies are usually relatively minor and may include facilitating drug deals by answering the telephone, opening the door, or acting as couriers for their male intimates. (p. 60)

To say that these women knew that the activities they engaged in were criminal and should now pay the price for their criminal activity is to negate the reality that it is still the practice in this culture for women, especially women in lower socioeconomic classes, to accept male direction in where to live, what to do, and who to socialize with. Fewer men follow their wives or girlfriends to a new city, engage in activities to please them, have a financially dependent relationship on the partner, especially with the additional burden of children, or have cultural prescriptions of "standing by your man." The fact is that very few men enter into criminal endeavors through a relationship with women, whereas that is very often the vehicle of women's entry into crime.

Implications for Counselors

Women are being sent to prison in ever increasing numbers. Counselors in prison may find that their caseloads are growing and their time is being divided between more and different types of female offenders. Female offenders are likely to be sent to prison for drug crimes and homicide. Whereas most crimes committed by women are typically in the larceny or theft category, women receive prison sentences more often if they have committed more serious crimes, so one should be careful never to interpret crime percentages of prison populations as representative of their participation in crime commission. On the whole, although we have seen an increase in women's criminality in the last few decades, this increase is eclipsed by the increase in the rate of imprisonment. That is, women are being sentenced to prison in far greater numbers than any corresponding increase in crime rates. Counselors will be seeing women in prison today who wouldn't have been there 10 years ago. They are probably also experiencing women's anger and frustration at the prospect of prison sentences that may be perceived as comparatively more severe than those of male counterparts.

Women in prison are likely to be poor and without a record of employment. They have few, if any, skills and lack education. They are likely to be members of a minority group. They are likely to have family members with criminal records. Women in prison are likely to have abused drugs, alcohol, or both, whether or not their crime of conviction was drug-related. In other words, crime is only one issue in these women's lives. Typically, there are a multitude of problems, including dysfunctional families, a lack of skills, an inability to set goals, and poor self-image.

The correctional professional may need to resolve the question of what is the ultimate goal of counseling in prison—is it to make the woman a better prisoner or to help her achieve personal goals that may or may not be consistent with the institution's needs? For instance, many women could improve their ability to assert their needs and establish their autonomy, yet that wouldn't necessarily be helpful to the smooth functioning of the prison. Some professionals believe that the best prisoners are the worst risks for release. If one becomes too comfortable in a prison setting, then it is more difficult to survive on the outside. It may be true that as women grow emotionally and become stronger in their self-image and personal autonomy, prison becomes more painful because of its impersonality and lack of freedom.

Any formal program will have to measure success using some form of recidivism, because that is about the only measure of success generally accepted for prison programs. Counselors who interact with inmates in such programs may feel that other measures of success more accurately chart the effect of the program on the individual and may be surprised to find that recidivism figures do not reflect what they feel to be successful intervention. All measures should be part of any evaluation effort, including such changes as in educational level achievement, drug use pattern shifts, and changes in standard scoring devices measuring such traits as self-esteem, values, autonomy and other measures addressed by the change effort.

Some counselors involved in casework or with established programs will interact with inmates under less scrutiny or expectation of measurable success, but there still should be efforts to measure progress. A counseling relationship should have a goal—whether it be short-term crisis management to help the woman get through the adaptational problems when entering prison, or to help her improve various aspects of her behavior or personality, or parole planning.

Correctional professionals today may hear criticism about what they do and the perceived ineffectiveness of rehabilitative efforts. All correctional professionals should have thought about, and come to terms with, the widespread belief that criminals can't change and "nothing works." Those who believe that probably shouldn't be working with offenders.

In the next chapter I will describe the prison world. Any counselor who works with female offenders in prison will quickly become familiar with this world and how it influences those who live within. The prison world sometimes provides an opportunity for some women to avoid drugs, sexual relationships, and dysfunctional behavior for a period of time that then enables them to "take stock" and address individual issues they have been avoiding, perhaps all their lives. Nevertheless, many aspects of prison life exacerbate problems that individuals had on the outside, and very often the counselor spends more time dealing with issues of prison life than those issues that would make a difference in success on release. It is ultimately possible for the prison experience to result in productive change but only for those inmates who are willing to accept change and for those inmates who are fortunate enough to encounter a caring, helping professional along the way.

2

Women's Prisons

This is for some women almost a vacation . . . they have three meals a day, they
get away from abuse, they don't have to go out and perform acts of prostitution
in order to keep their boyfriend or themselves on drugs. [An inmate]

Pollock et al., (1995)

Prisons for women have undergone fairly substantial changes in the last 20
years, positive and negative. There are more programs for women and many
programs have the potential to provide skills that will earn a living wage; on
the other hand, female offenders are more likely to be sentenced to prison than
ever before. There are now over 100,000 women incarcerated in state and
federal facilities (U.S. Department of Justice, 1995). Facilities for women are
being built at a rapid pace, yet many suffer from overcrowding. Existing
programs are not sufficient to meet the needs of the increasing numbers of
women sent to prison, so many have no access at all to vocational and
counseling programs.

In this chapter, we will look at some of the features of women's prisons.
Today's prisons bear the legacy of the past. Programming and architecture,
especially, are influenced by the historical factors that influenced the creation
and development of women's prisons. Sentencing practices have an impact
on who ends up in prison; thus, we also spend some time discussing sentencing patterns. Counseling in prison is different from counseling outside of a
prison. For instance, every staff person in a prison must be concerned with
security issues. Every staff member knows or comes to learn the unique prison
language and procedures for calling an inmate out, the importance of "count,"
and which rules can be circumvented and which rules are inviolate. Prisoners will also exhibit behavior patterns and experience stresses unique to
the prison. It is important to understand the prison if one expects to work
within it.

Women's prisons tend to be built in rural areas of the state. Very few are large. Whereas prisons for men may hold over 5,000 inmates, rarely do women's prisons hold more than 1,000 and many states have only facilities housing 500 or fewer. Women's prisons bear a historical legacy that has more in common with juvenile facilities; thus, they may be built according to the "cottage plan," with separate, small housing units, rather than the tier blocks more commonly associated with penitentiaries for men. Women's prisons are more likely to have living units with kitchens, fewer perimeter security measures, and what has been described as a "softer appearance." They tend to reflect commonly held beliefs about differences between men and women. For instance, older facilities may not have gymnasiums or sports facilities because of the belief that women do not enjoy active recreation in the same manner that men do; instead, they are likely to have "beauty salons." Historically, women's institutions were built to shield female offenders from the evil influences of men (Pollock-Byrne, 1990; Rafter, 1985). It was believed that good female role models were necessary to teach female offenders how to act "like ladies." Therefore, prisons were built separate from the institutions for men, they were managed by women, and activities included learning such feminine skills as laundering, cooking, and cleaning. It has only been fairly recently that prison programming for women has responded to the fact that most women will need to support themselves and perhaps their children on release. Many of the differences between prisons for men and women are disappearing, and in the recent building boom of prisons, facilities for men and women are sometimes indistinguishable.

More Prisons, More Prisoners

The increase in the rate at which we incarcerate women is staggering. The rate of growth for females, for instance, exceeded that for males in every year since 1981. The percentage increase of female prisoners was double that of males between 1980 and 1989 (U.S. Department of Justice, 1991, p. 1). Since 1980, the number of women imprisoned has tripled (Bloom et al., 1994, p. 1).

Increases in female prisoners in certain states are even more shocking. Oregon reported a 154% increase in the number between 1985 and 1991 (Oregon Department of Corrections, 1991). Texas experienced a 61% increase in the number of women prisoners in *one year* between 1992 and 1993 (U.S. Department of Justice, 1994a, p. 5). There were 6,700 women imprisoned in Texas in March 1995 and closer to 9,000 at the end of 1995. A partial explanation for this huge increase is that the state had finished building several new facilities for women inmates and took custody of thousands of state inmates who had been backed up in county jails (Lenhart, 1995). California, with the dubious distinction of incarcerating more people than any other state and, indeed, more than most countries in the world incarcerate, experienced a 450% increase in female inmates between 1980 and 1993, going from 1,316 to 7,232 imprisoned women. In 1995 this number surpassed 8,000 (Bloom et al., 1994. p. 1).

Increasing crime rates are not the reason for the increased number of women in prison. Simon and Landis (1991) found that, in a study of women sentenced in California, New York, and Pennsylvania comparing 1987 sentences to 1982 sentences, the percentage of women sentenced to prison increased in every crime category. For instance, in 1982 only 9.8% of women who were convicted of theft were sent to prison in 1987 that percentage almost doubled to 18.4%. The percentage of women convicted of felonies who were sentenced to prison increased from 54% in 1978 to 79% in 1987. Whereas the number of women arrested for felonies in California declined between 1989 and 1991, the rate at which they were sentenced to prison increased by 289%! (Bloom et al., 1994, p. 3). Nationally, between 1986 and 1991 there was a 23.5% increase in adult arrests for women but a 75.2% increase in commitments to prison (Snell, 1994).

These numbers mean that there has been a building boom in women's prisons. Rafter (1990) reported that between 1930 and 1950 only three or four prisons for women were built in each decade. In the 1980s, 34 prisons for women were built. The numbers for the 1990s are not in yet, but it seems safe to say that all states have built, are building, or are planning to build more women's prisons. States that have until this point managed with one institution for women are now building several. Ironically, those advocates who embraced the idea of new building to ensure better program opportunities now wonder if their goals haven't really hurt female offenders, rather than helped them (Chesney-Lind & Pollock, 1994). States that have built new, larger facilities for women have filled them, arguably with women who might have received a community sentence before the prison was built. It is hard to see this as a better solution.

Today one observes that through determinate sentencing, mandatory sentencing, guidelines, and judicial practices, women are being treated more like men. But are they the same as male offenders? Demographics indicate that they are not. Women are less likely to have juvenile records and they are more likely to be serving a first term in prison, they may have played a subservient role to a crime partner, they are often poor and responsible for small children, and they often come from dysfunctional family backgrounds and are struggling with a host of issues, very often including drug addiction.

The Prison World

Women's prisons are typically isolated in rural areas of a state. There may be only one facility for women in the state, necessitating that all classification levels be in the one institution. In the most recent survey of women's prisons, 23 states reported having fewer than 300 women prisoners, 18 states reported having between 301 and 999 women prisoners, and seven states reported having more than 1,000 women incarcerated. Thirty-five states had only one women's facility (two of these housed both men and women), and 13 states had more than one facility (Burke & Adams, 1991). What this means is that all women, even those classified as minimum custody, live under higher security to accommodate those inmates with higher security classifications.

The "pains of imprisonment" for women are many. Even though for some women prison is a relief from the danger and economic reality of poverty on the outside, there are also deprivations and punishments inherent in prison life. Faith (1993) presented the most comprehensive list of these "pains of imprisonment." Elements of the prison world that will be discussed here include stress, the lack of autonomy, monotony, discipline, correctional officers, and the prisoner subculture.

The "Pains of Imprisonment"

The stigma of incarceration
The claustrophobia of confinement
The boredom
Anxiety about one's children
Loneliness for family
Withdrawal from alcohol and street drugs
The lack of privacy
Abuses of power
Little or no choice of diet
The cacophony of radios, television, [and] people
The uncertainty of when you will be released

Adapted from *Unruly Women: The Politics of Confinement and Resistance* (Faith, 1993, pp. 151-153).

Stress

The world of prison is filled with stress. It remains just under the surface most days and frequently erupts with shouting, pushing and shoving incidents, or self-mutilation. Women report various sources of stress, but the three most commonly perceived are the arbitrariness of rule enforcement, assaults on self-respect endemic to prison life, and loss of children (Fox, 1990).

Rule Enforcement. There are a multitude of rules in prison, not all of which make any sense. Rules are created to deal with certain incidents and then the incidents are forgotten, as is the reason for the rule. For instance, one prison had a rule about red fingernail polish, even though any other color was acceptable. The best explanation seemed to be that the state was "protecting" the women in passing such a rule during a time when Red Dye #2 garnered a lot of press coverage for being toxic. It is by no means clear whether this was the reason or not, the point was that no one—even the administrators—seemed to know the original purpose of the rule.

Lax enforcement of some rules is essential to the smooth running of the tier, but at any given time what was overlooked one day can be sanctioned the next day. Almost every activity in prison is governed by rules: An inmate must wear certain clothes, take only one piece of bread in the food line, have only a certain number of pictures on the wall, only put up a curtain when she is using the toilet in her cell, line up to go to eat, buy only a certain amount at the commissary even if she has the money for more, get up in the morning whether she feels like it or not, and so on. Obviously, prison is not a hotel and offenders should not expect it to be comfortable; nevertheless, living in such an environment creates a great deal of internal stress. Being told what to do seemingly every minute of every day is difficult, especially for adults who are used to making their own decisions about what to wear, what to eat, and whether to get up or not. Some inmates handle this type of stressor better than others. Some develop maladaptive behavior patterns, such as acting out and receiving disciplinary reports.

Assaults on Self-Respect. Women in prison are extremely sensitive to how they are treated. The very fact of incarceration and banishment can be perceived as an attack on self-respect. Prison staff can exacerbate the situation in the way they treat women in prison. In the female prisoners' words, they are "no less a woman" because they are on the wrong side of the bars in a prison and demand to be treated with respect. According to a report by Fox (1990),

Some of these officers don't know how to talk to you as a woman. Sure, some women don't demand respect, but I do. Like the way some of them talk to you, like, "Do this, do that." All nasty like. Who in the hell do they think they are? They're no better than me. Just because they are a C.O. [Correctional Officer] and I have a number, they are no better than me. I'm no less a woman than they are. I get so aggravated, so angry. I just go right into anger, and they feed right into it. (p. 23)

One inmate related the story of being on a yard crew supervised by a young male officer who was having problems getting the women to perform the task in the way he expected. Finally, in frustration he yelled at them, "Y'all ain't shit. You're nothing." Telling the story brought tears to her eyes, indicating the impact it had on her and perhaps the other women, even though the male officer probably didn't think twice about his frustrated outcry. The story also illustrates the conundrum of corrections. How can helping professionals facilitate personal growth and positive change if every message inmates receive—from the first disinfecting shower and rectal search, the barbed wire, and officers yelling at them that they "ain't shit,"—tells them that they are unworthy and unwanted?

Loss of Children. The third major source of stress that was cited by Fox (1990) was loss of children. Even those women who were absent or neglectful parents on the outside feel the loss acutely, because they blame themselves for the hurt they have inflicted on their children. In prison, free from drugs, alcohol, or both, the women have time to reflect on their actions toward their children, and many feel very guilty about their neglect and abandonment. Other women in prison were good mothers despite their criminal behavior and feel that no one can take care of their children as they did. In addition to the fear of what is happening to their children when they are inside, many women experience anxiety about reentry and whether their children will accept them or not. Fear and anxiety, as well as guilt and remorse about their children, cause a great deal of stress for female inmates and can lead to "acting out" behaviors, even escape.

Effects of Stress

One result of prison stress is a fairly high rate of self-mutilation. Ironically, some prison staff approach "cutting up" as a discipline problem rather than a mental health problem. Female inmates are more likely to mutilate or hurt themselves, whereas males are more likely to respond to prison stress by violent acting out against guards or other inmates (Dobash, Dobash, &

Gutteridge, 1986; Fox, 1975). This activity has been explained as "internalized anger." Another explanation is one of control: The woman has so little control in her life that the ability to control her own pain is empowering. Yet another explanation is that the prison experience is so dehumanizing that it is a way for the woman to feel something (Morris, 1987). Faith (1993) presented a quote from Pollack that described how mutilating one's body is a coping strategy to "reconnect."

> The woman may cope with feelings of powerlessness by disassociating, or psychologically separating herself from her body, a tactic often used to survive the actual abuse during childhood. Self-injury may be a desire to reconnect with one's own body—a desire to ensure that one can feel. In this sense it is a life-preserving measure. (p. 244)

Pollack described a peer-counseling program for women in a Canadian prison. After 6 weeks of training, these women were used for crisis counseling of other female prisoners. The majority of women who received counseling felt that they were helped, specifically, that they felt "less alone," "less depressed," "more optimistic," and "less angry" (reported in Faith, 1993, p. 245). Whereas suicide attempts and "cutting up" are extreme reactions to the stressors of prison life, all incarcerated women exhibit some forms of coping behaviors. Some women overeat and gain a great deal of weight in prison or use whatever drugs are available, including those prescribed by prison medical staff. Some retreat into a private world, restricting their contacts with prison inhabitants to the minimum necessary. Some women adopt a loud, abrasive, and threatening demeanor, in effect assuming the position of "a good defense is a good offense." Those women who do not have a criminal outlook, nor come from an antisocial subculture before prison, probably have the most difficult time adjusting to prison life. Those with existing psychological problems are especially at risk when faced with the stresses of incarceration.

Because of the stress induced by entry into and adaptation to prison, many women have little energy or inclination to deal with personal issues. Just surviving in prison, without succumbing to depression or serious mental distress, is sometimes a triumph. Many women resist helping professionals' attempts to address individual issues, because their immediate problems seem so much more important. Often the initial entry period is the most stressful and after the woman achieves some level of stability in her living arrangements and comes to terms with how to live with inmates and work with correctional officers, she can turn to other issues. For other women, prison creates a level of stress that leads to mental illness or breakdown. Still others survive in prison quite well; nevertheless, they are likely to be enthusiastic participants in the antisocial prisoner subculture. These women are unlikely to benefit from counseling efforts, because their outlook is similar to that of one with antisocial personality disorder—they do not see anything wrong with how they see the world, and they are quite content to continue their egocentric and predatory behavior.

Helping professionals can help troubled women through the initial entry into prison. Many women spend time in administrative segregation before being placed in the general population, and this would seem to be a good time to assist them through more frequent contacts with a counselor or with a group approach. Counselors also can help to identify those who seem particularly vulnerable to the stressors of prison life and provide them a more sheltered living and/or job assignment if possible. Early intervention might prevent suicide attempts, mutilations, and psychotic breakdowns.

Lack of Autonomy

One of the elements of prison life that has long been identified as a barrier to rehabilitative efforts is the lack of control prisoners have over any decision regarding behavior. If responsible citizenship is leading one's life in a manner in which one makes rational choices regarding behavior, it is hard to see how these characteristics can be developed behind prison walls. Prisons create dependence, encourage irresponsibility, and restrict autonomy. Inmates are said to be "infantilized," because the prison is omnipotent. Prison staff control all movement and are responsible for the provision of all resources. In every aspect of life, from asking for toilet paper to being told to get up in the morning, adults have been firmly put in the place of children again. Many make comparisons to the army. Because soldiers are told what to do, when to do it, sleep in uncomfortable surroundings, and so on, the argument goes, why should prisoners complain? The difference, of course, is that to join the army is a choice (until the next draft anyway) and, perhaps even more important, pride and an *esprit de corps* exist in the military compared with the stigma and banishment that come with a prison sentence.

Effects of Lack of Autonomy

Much of prison behavior can be interpreted as a perfectly natural attempt to create some control over one's life. The previous section described how mutilating one's body and suicide attempts have been explained as an attempt to gain control. Other forms of acting out can be explained in the same way. Why, for instance, would an individual refuse to come out of her cell when there is no doubt whatsoever that prison staff will eventually win, and the female inmate will be removed forcefully and perhaps painfully? Very often prisoners will engage in such battles when there is no way to win. It seems clear that these incidents can only be interpreted as attempts to gain control, if only for a short period of time, rather than a rational response to the environment. Why do inmates destroy their own cells and living units? They are the ones who suffer afterward by having to live with broken windows and overflowing toilets. This destruction is not rational; it can only be understood as an emotional release that creates, for a very short period of time, a feeling of power in a world of powerlessness.

Prisoners attempt autonomy in healthy ways. For instance, some methods are finding a niche, "programming," or creating a circumscribed life in their cell, rarely coming out except for necessities; or they may pursue autonomy in less healthy ways, such as using drugs to create a different reality, grouping together in gangs or cliques for strength and power that is then used against other prisoners, or they "act out" in irrational and violent ways to induce the prison authorities to incarcerate them in segregation, thereby eliminating any vague impression of control. Faith (1993) provided a quote from a perceptive correctional officer who explained how the prison environment strips the individual of all autonomy.

> We controlled every moment of the lives of the women we guarded. We told them when and where they could go, when they could eat, shower, sleep, when and with whom they could talk. We strip-searched them after an afternoon visit with their children. We made them work to acquire skills, but told them they were capable only of sewing, mopping floors, or preparing food. We confiscated their personal belongings. We read their mail. We threw them in the "quiet room" for punishment. We were the ones who took away their dignity. . . . [W]e were disempowering them and setting them up for failure once back on the street. (p. 162)

This lack of autonomy may result in a number of different reactions on the part of women prisoners. Some welcome the retreat from the adult world and "act like children." With these women, a counseling professional must guard against dependency. Some will seek in the counselors either "mothers" from whom they will seek nurturance and act out against, or "fathers," whom they will attempt to manipulate. Many women in prison exhibit a great deal of passivity, in regard to their own personal growth as well as the world around them. They may get agitated over day-to-day concerns, but in a larger sense they accept the status quo, including negative labels and low expectations for their future. Many women in prison have low self-esteem and tend to look for direction from others. Many can be described as codependents and have had a succession of relationships with controlling men. Those women who do exhibit assertiveness usually have not learned how to resolve conflict without aggression. They have a great deal of trouble accepting authority and following rules. Women with stronger needs for autonomy may say "no" to a relationship with a helping professional as one small exercise of personal power. Accepting their right to make the choice gives them the opportunity to freely choose to participate in a program or engage in a counseling relationship with a caseworker. The very act of making such a decision will help bolster their own power of self-direction.

Monotony

Another element of prison is the dreariness of existence; that is, each day is virtually the same as the previous day and there is little to look forward to. Some women tend to gain weight in prison, partially due to the diet and partially due to the fact that about the only thing to look forward to is eating. Visits, telephone calls, and letters take on monumental importance, and when something happens to thwart them, there is an extreme reaction. Women who take advantage of programs suffer less from this aspect of imprisonment; indeed, some women in prison juggle work, education, and leisure activities at the same frenetic pace that those of us on the outside sometimes do. One woman, living in a therapeutic community program in prison, described her day as follows: she wakes and goes to eat at 5:00 a.m. to get to her job in the kitchen by 6:00 a.m.; from 6:00 to 9:00 a.m. she works; at 9:00 she attends a group session until 12:00, then works again until 3:00 p.m.; at 3:00 she attends another group session until 5:00, then she has an hour before dinner; after dinner she goes to college classes and studies until 11:00 p.m.

For the women who have no programs, classes, or work to look forward to, the day stretches interminably. There are large populations of prisoners who are idle, owing to their choice but more often owing to lack of programs. Many women would attend any type of class or program just to fill the time, but owing to limited resources prisons must restrict entry. As a result, women who have high school diplomas are not allowed into life skills classes in one state system; women have been barred from college courses, unless they can pay for them personally; and in one newly opened prison there was one vocational program available—a commercial floor cleaning program that had slots available for 10 women in a prison of 600.

Effects of Monotony

At least one positive effect of the monotony of prison life is the eagerness with which women in prison embrace new treatment programs. Whether they are vocational programs, life skills classes, parenting programs, or groups for "survivors," female inmates participate and express appreciation for them. Even if their commitment may be at times superficial, female prisoners attend and enjoy programs. Many have expressed the view that more programs are needed, and in some prisons this is certainly true. Some women may experience several prison sentences before arriving at a point when they are ready to change. Some female inmates relate stories indicating that a program or something they learned in counseling did not "hit home" or have meaning for them until years later. This illustrates, again, the difficulty of measuring the effect of prison change efforts. It may be that the woman who attends a program solely to relieve boredom may nevertheless absorb some messages that affect her decision making when she is ready to act on the messages.

Discipline

A number of studies have documented the phenomenon of seemingly more discipline "problems" in institutions for women. McClelland (1994a) summarized the research with the following points: (a) There are more rules in women's institutions and they are more likely to be petty in nature, (b) women are more likely to be strictly supervised than men and cited for behavior that would be overlooked in an institution for males, (c) women receive a greater number of disciplinary infractions than men, (d) these infractions are more likely to be nonserious in nature than those of male inmates, and (e) women are not punished as severely as men.

She then went on to research the issue with samples from Texas prisons. Her two samples were composed of 271 males (all from one prison) and 246 females (from two women's institutions). These inmates were followed for one year, and information was collected from numerous sources, both from central computerized files and "travel" cards that record demographic and case history information and disciplinary infractions, as well as the individual institution's records, such as "hall cards," disciplinary reports and reprimand slips (McClelland, 1994a, p. 73). The sample of men and the sample of women were roughly comparable on all demographic and crime history factors, except that males were more likely to be African American (51% versus 41%), women were more likely to be younger (average age 32 versus 39), and women were more likely to have shorter sentences (p. 75).

McClelland (1994a) found that one disciplinary option—a "reprimand"—was used only in the prisons for females. These reprimands were recorded on hall cards and affected such things as telephone privileges. A number of reprimands would equal a minor discipline case (p. 74). In fact, a majority of women received reprimands (87% of the sample) whereas the men received none, because the sanction did not exist in the prison for men. Her other findings included the following:

1. Females committed more disciplinary infractions (almost 90% of the female sample were cited for disciplinary infractions at least once whereas 57% of the males were cited). Close to 30% (28.6%) of the women received 21 or more citations, compared with only 2.2% of the men.

2. Females received an average of 16.7 citations, compared with males who received an average of 5.1.

3. The most frequent offenses for women were "violation of a written or posted rule" and "refusing to obey an order."

4. Women were much more likely than men to be cited for "threatening or striking an officer" (66 offenses versus 12). Many of the women were cited for this on two or more occasions.

5. Women's infractions were more likely to be nonserious in nature than men's (43% of the women's total were nonserious, versus 11% of the men's total).

6. If "violation of written or posted rules" were removed from the analysis there would be much less divergence in the rule-breaking behavior of men and women; it would eliminate 83.4% of all female Level 3 (nonserious) offenses. This rule seems to be used for a multitude of such minor offenses as drying undergarments on radiators, "excessive art work" in the cell or "failing to eat all the food on their plate."

7. Sanctions seemed to be more severe for women than for men, even though the offenses were less serious.

McClelland (1994a) concluded by saying that the philosophy of rule enforcement seemed to account for a large part of the difference in disciplinary infractions between male and female offenders. Whereas the prison for men was run by a warden who had a philosophy of informal resolution of minor offenses, the female wardens of the two prisons for women seemed to espouse a philosophy of rigid and formalistic rule compliance (pp. 86-87). McClelland (1994a, b) went so far as to propose that the discipline system is the origin of the greater number of "acting out" incidents among women. She cited Dobash et al., (1986, p. 85) who concluded that " 'incidents' may be the results of such a policy of close control of female behaviour" and she stated (McClelland, 1994b) that

> Faced with implacable patriarchal authority, a female inmate's seemingly irrational opposition behavior becomes a mechanism for re-establishing her nature, for resisting the alienation experienced when she is denied traditional expression of both her personal individuality and her collective responsibility. (p. 12)

McClelland's (1994a, 1994b) study is important in a number of ways. First, she confirmed and replicated earlier studies that found that the objective number of disciplinary infractions is higher in women's institutions. Second, she identified the nature of such infractions as largely nonserious, minor, and, some would say, even trivial. Infractions of such rules as "not cleaning one's plate" would never be enforced in a prison for men and harks back to the reformatory era in its pervasive control of women's behavior, far outside the purview of what might be subject to control for male offenders. Third, she identified a situation in at least one state system in which the philosophy of discipline held by the respective wardens probably has more to do with the objective numbers of disciplinary infractions than any objective behavior on the part of inmates. This called into question any quantitative analysis that does not explore the action of defining infractions as well as the behavior itself that is defined as an infraction. Finally, she reminded us that the way female prisoners are treated may influence the way they behave. That is, the very nature of the formalistic and pervasive social control found in these two women's prisons may lead to "acting out" behavior occasioned by the stress of constantly being scrutinized in every aspect of one's day.

This research on discipline is important for the helping professionals who work in prisons and are routinely called on to intervene in "discipline problems." It continues to be the case that many behavior problems that are labeled as discipline problems are evidence of seriously disturbed individuals who cannot cope with the prison environment. For these women, the sheltered environment of an isolated living unit or mental health ward is probably necessary. Other discipline problems are presented by women who have temporary or situationally specific crises. Nevertheless, for some women, it may be that discipline problems are nothing more than expecting the female inmates to conform to an impossibly high standard of behavior and to petty rules.

Counselors in prison are criticized by some prisoner advocates for seeking conformity and helping the woman become a "better prisoner." One might respond to this criticism by pointing out that as long as the counselor follows ethical guidelines for establishing treatment goals and relating to the prisoner or client, there is nothing wrong with the goal of helping the woman develop better skills for dealing with authority figures and learning to "play by the rules." On the other hand, if McClelland (1994a, 1994b) and others are correct, that the prison for women is unduly petty in its rule making and enforcement, then perhaps the system needs adjusting rather than the people who have to live in it. All those who work with women should examine their behavior and expectations. Are women treated differently from male offenders? Are there higher expectations regarding dress, appearance, and demeanor? If so, are these differences fair or remnants of sexist socialization that demand women to be "nicer" than men?

Correctional Officers

In the last 20 years women have made great strides in attaining equal employment, including working in prisons for men (see Zupan, 1992). In January 1993, 16.7% of correctional officers were female, and 33% of new officers hired were women (Camp & Camp, 1993). The consequence of this has been that male correctional officers have demanded and won the right to work in women's prisons. In fact, the percentage of women officers in women's prisons is getting smaller. The percentage has been reduced from 83% to 65.2% from 1978 to 1993 (Camp & Camp, 1993). Thus, there are now more men working in female institutions than women working in men's institutions.

In cases such as *Gunther v. Iowa State Men's Reformatory* (1980) and *Timm v. Gunter* (1990), courts considered the privacy needs of male and female inmates and typically found that the employment opportunities for officers outweighed the privacy interests of the inmates. Nevertheless, some courts have recognized that female inmates may be different from males, considering the potential for sexual exploitation and abuse that may occur with men guarding women.

Jordan v. Gardner (1993) ruled that it was a violation of the Eighth Amendment to permit male officers to pat search female inmates. In a similar case, this same court ruled against male inmates proposing a privacy claim against female correctional officers conducting pat searches on male prisoners. The different ruling evidently was based on the fact that female inmates have often been victims of sexual abuse. In this case a new superintendent of the Washington Prison for Women ordered that pat downs could be conducted by male officers on the female inmates. These pat downs included breast and crotch areas. The prison's mental health staff advised the superintendent that this would be extremely traumatic to the women who had suffered sexual abuse as children and as adults, and this group was a large portion of the women imprisoned. One of the first women searched by a male officer reportedly had a severe reaction, which included crying, holding on to the bars, and having to be carried back to her cell. The 9th Circuit Court at first allowed the practice and then, in a rehearing by the full panel, ruled that the searches violated the women's Eighth Amendment rights (right to be free from cruel and unusual punishment) basing their holding on the traumatic effect these searches would have on those women who were incest and rape survivors. The ruling (*Jordan v. Gardner,* 1993) stated that

> There should not be male guards at a women's prison. There should not be a male superintendent of a women's prison. Our statutes should not be construed to require such mechanical suppression of the recognition that in our culture such a relation between men in power and women in prison leads to difficulties, temptations, abuse, and finally cruel and unusual punishment. (pp. 1544-1545)

Recent news stories indicate that the court may have a legitimate point in recognizing the potential for abuse. Allegations in Texas, Hawaii, and Georgia have surfaced that female inmates have been coerced into having sex with male officers (Dayton, 1991; Faith, 1993; van Ochten, 1993).

Female prisoners will react differently to male and female correctional officers (Pollock, 1986). Some women "overreact" to any physical touching by male officers. Some react negatively to male officers' commands with an attitude of "Don't tell me what to do." It is probably true that, for some of these women, "flashbacks" occur to assaults and intimidation by male partners or parents. Then, their hostility, abrasiveness, or outright defiance of the authority of a male correctional officer escalates into a serious incident and the woman may hit or shove the male officer and be restrained and sanctioned in turn.

Another reaction to male officers and staff occurs because some women in prison do not know how to interact with males other than on a sexual basis. That is, they have spent their lives with males who are interested in them only for sexual gratification and have come to see all men as "users" and to be used. Of course, if male correctional officers do react to female inmates in a similar manner as men have in the past, this sets the scene for unethical and illegal behavior. On the other hand, if he can develop a healthy relationship with the female inmate, he could provide a model for successful, nonsexual, nonexploitive relationships with men.

Helping professionals could be very useful in training programs for male officers in prisons for women. Part of such training could alert them to the potential meaning of interactions with female inmates and help them understand the dynamics of incidents when a female inmate reacts seemingly irrationally to the situation.

Prisoner Subcultures

Early studies of prisoner subcultures were all conducted in prisons for men and described the prison world of men. Except for a unique study of women's reformatories done in the 1930s by a Dutch lawyer (Lekkerkerker, 1931), only in the 1960s did any studies in prisons for women become available. Giallombardo (1966), Heffernan (1972), and Ward and Kassebaum (1965), were some of the first to study women prisoners' subcultures. Later authors added to and summarized what we knew about women's prisons (Pollock-Byrne, 1990), but recently there have been very few studies conducted on prisoner subcultures for either men or women in prison.

Studies identified the presence of "pseudo families" that were kinship systems in which women would take on roles of father, mother, daughter, and so on, in an extended family network. Their relationships were characterized by the same elements one might expect in such a relationship on the outside: mother-daughter dyads would be nurturing; father-child relationships would be more paternalistic, with the "father" providing protection and guidance; and siblings would be friendly rivals for parents' attention.

Homosexual relationships also formed part of the inmate subculture, including marriages and divorces, jealousy, and promiscuity. Giallombardo (1966), for instance, provided a detailed list of the role types in prison, oriented around prison sexuality. For example, "jailhouse turnouts" were women who entered homosexual relationships in prison; "commissary hustlers" engaged in relationships for material gain, and so on. The true extent or nature of prison homosexuality remains unclear. At least one author believes that early researchers exaggerated or misidentified the family systems and nature of personal relationships (Faith, 1993). Some object to defining sexuality in prison as homosexuality, because those engaged in the practice do not maintain a lesbian identity once released. In fact, some lesbians who enter prison do not participate at all in the sexual liaisons in prison and scorn the artificial game playing that takes place.

Although it seems clear that women do form affectional ties that have some similarity to familial relationships, it is not clear that the extensive kinship networks were or are anywhere near as defined as one might believe reading the early studies. Certainly, they have dissipated in more recent years. According to Fox (1990),

> In 1973 the idleness within the prison tended to foster a heavy reliance on "kinship" relationships as solutions to prison adjustment problems. The kinship network, consisting of numerous loosely structured "family" units, routinely gave interpersonal comfort, shared limited resources, and provided crisis intervention for acute adjustment problems lying outside the scope of prison services. During 1973, 52 percent of the Bedford Hills prisoners held membership in a kinship unit, and 45 percent had formed a close personal relationship with another prisoner in an attempt to deal with the impersonal nature of confinement. By 1978, the proportion of prisoners holding membership in the kinship system had fallen to 27 percent, and only 25 percent of the Bedford Hills prisoners were involved in a personal relationship with another woman. (p. 210)

In the 1980s and 1990s, prisons became even more permeable with more programs and outsiders coming into the prison; thus, Fox's (1990) observation of the late 1970s would probably hold true even more so today. Owen (1994) filled the nearly 30-year gap between the earliest studies of women prisoner subcultures and today with her recent study of the prison life of women in California. She found that the social world of imprisoned women still has commonalties with those described by the research nearly 30 years ago—she did find some elements of pseudofamilies, and homosexuality evidently still has many similar elements to those described by Giallombardo (1966) (for instance, lack of coercion, presence of commissary hustlers, relationships that are more "social" than sexual, etc.).

Owen (1994) used the phrase "in the mix" to describe the participation in the prison culture, which includes ties to a pseudofamily, homosexual relationships, or both, as well as interacting in the social life of the yard. Whereas Owen found that the majority of her sample spent a great deal of time in their cells, one of the differences between those heavily involved in the subculture and those who did not participate was their presence in the yard. It is clear from Owen's work that there may be differences between women who are "in the mix" and those who are not, in their willingness and inclination to take advantage of treatment programs. Those heavily involved in the subculture are distrustful of staff and less apt to see anything in their own lives that needs improvement. They are not inclined to introspection and continue to involve themselves in relationships, drugs, and other distractions to divert their attention away from looking at their own behavior.

As with those studies done 30 years ago, race does not seem to be the divisive feature of women prisoners as it is in prisons for men. Women tend to interact across racial boundaries, and there is less racial violence, actually less violence overall, than is found in prisons for men. Although Owen did note that there is a gang presence, it was small and did not seem to influence the prisoner subculture in the same way as it had in prisons for men.

The subculture of a women's prison is not as intense, nor is it as antisocial as the one found in prisons for men. Nevertheless, it is true that it serves as a barrier to treatment goals. Most women who adapt well to prison and enthusiastically participate in the social world are those women who are committed to their preprison lifestyle. For them, prison is a minor inconvenience, although one shared by friends and relatives. Programs are only to be used for privileges or other such benefits as to meet friends from other living units, break up the monotony of prison life, or receive visits. Some women admit that, although they feel successful and committed to a treatment program, this may be their third prison term. "I wasn't ready," is the typical response when asked why other programs didn't seem to work. For these women, the subculture was too powerful and too tempting, until age, children, or general dissatisfaction with their lives made them realize the deficiencies of that world.

Change in the Prison World

Legislation has worked to eliminate many of the differences that existed in the past in the way men and women were treated by governmental authority, such as social security, insurance, employment, and so forth. Some feminist scholars hail this "equality" approach as the only way to eliminate the paternalistic treatment that has kept women from empowering themselves and maintaining an equal footing with men in social and economic spheres. The alternative argument, which we might call the "difference" approach, takes into account women's differential needs. This would allow different treatment as long as it did not put women in a more negative position than males, and it allows recognition of special needs, such as those related to pregnancy and child rearing (Chesney-Lind & Pollock, 1994).

A "difference" approach runs the risk of handicapping women by identifying special needs, and some legal scholars believe that difference will always mean "less" than males, but it does have the advantage of accepting the biological and social realities that exist in women's lives. To assume that the law can establish equal treatment depends on a supposition that the groups in question are equal in larger issues such as needs, abilities, and opportunities.

If larger social realities create inequalities, legal rights are irrelevant. The special needs or "difference" argument accepts the fact that women live a different reality than men and that this must be taken into account when evaluating legal "equalities." As Eisenstein (1988) pointed out, "Legal equality is only part of the issue of sex equality, because laws are only a partial expression of the relations of power that shape sex equality" (p. 42). For instance, having equal opportunity laws to protect employment is important, but no less important is the social reality of having the burden of childcare. The legal right to prosecute a battering husband ignores the social reality of economic and psychological dependence on a man in a society that defines a woman's success by how well she "holds onto her man." Finally, the legal right to equal sentencing is a bad joke when the woman's participation in drug enterprise is as an ignorant "mule," either coerced or tricked into participating, but her sentence is *equal* to that of the drug kingpin.

Historically, the "difference" approach was used in female corrections. Women were less likely to be incarcerated for any crime (unless they violated stereotypical views of women). Women's prisons were built for the specific purpose of treating women differently from incarcerated males. This difference didn't extend to all women—African American and older criminals were still sent to custodial prisons (Rafter, 1985). Nevertheless, the reformatories and even custodial prisons for women operated with different policies and procedures that resulted from a belief that women were different from men and should be treated differently. Policies regarding visitation, privacy, and personal clothes were often more lenient for women. On the other hand, fewer vocational programs, stronger social controls on such trivia as language and hairstyles, infantilization, and a greater concern for women's sexuality were also the effects of the difference approach (Chesney-Lind & Pollock, 1994).

Today, prisons have more programs but women are sent to prison more often. State systems have publicly stated that they intend to run the women's prisons as part of the system rather than as a "stepdaughter" to the system. Of course, what this means is that they intend to run it as they do prisons for men and treat women with the same policies and procedures that have been developed for men's prisons. Today, one observes that through determinate sentencing, mandatory sentencing, guidelines, and judicial practices, women are being treated more like men. But are they the same as male offenders? Demographics indicate that they are not. Women are less criminalistic (fewer have juvenile records and they are more likely to be serving a first term in prison), they have reduced roles in crimes in which they have crime partners, they are often poor and responsible for small children, and they often come from dysfunctional family backgrounds and are struggling with a host of issues, very often including drug addiction.

"Women-Based" Corrections

By emphasizing parity and then using a male standard, women will always lose. Equality in sentencing has led to staggering increases of women in prison, equality in prison programming has led to more vocational programs, but it has also led to more security measures, more formalistic approaches to supervision, and arguably a more "prisoners first, women second" approach to supervision. The idea of gender differences in justice applications has captured the interest of several writers; the so-called masculine ideal of justice that emphasizes fairness, equal treatment, and rationality, is contrasted with the female version of justice, which emphasizes needs, motives, and relationships (Daly, 1989; Eisenstein, 1988; Gilligan, 1982; Heidensohn, 1986; Resnick, 1987). Heidensohn (1986) described what a justice model might look like under a caring feminine model: There would be a greater concern for needs of all concerned, victim, offender, and others. There would be a recognition that the lines drawn between victim and offender are sometimes arbitrary. There would be a concern that what is done in response to an offense should compensate and, when possible, improve the lives of all concerned. Sometimes this might involve punishment, sometimes it may not. This approach may be more typical of the juvenile system, and it used to be represented by the rehabilitative ideal, but since the mid-1970s we have been firmly entrenched in the just-desserts "male" model of justice, which is concerned with punishment and little else.

These authors are struggling to define a correctional (and justice) approach that can recognize and respond to the special differences of females in a way that would make the system more positive and productive than it is currently. We know that paternalistic (or maternalistic) treatment is not helpful—women are not children and do not benefit from being treated as such. We know that women are not helped by a blind equality approach—they are not men, do not live with the same social realities of men, and have different goals, needs, and desires. One solution is to pay attention to the voices of the women inside. In most situations in which they have been allowed to tell us what they need, the response has been a desire for more treatment programs, parenting classes, and the opportunity to learn skills to earn a decent wage. Many recognize the various elements in their lives that led them to commit crime, many would like to avoid criminal patterns in the future but they need help to do so.

Implications for Counselors

The prison world is one filled with stress. Petty rules, strict and arbitrary enforcement, staff who are burdened by their own problems, and a lack of meaningful opportunities to fill the day, all combine to make the prison experience painful. Prison may be a respite for some. Those who experienced incredibly harsh conditions on the street—violent pimps, homelessness and addiction, or poverty with the burden of children—are somewhat released from those problems on entering prison; nevertheless, prison life has its own "pains." The reaction to these pains is to involve oneself in programming opportunities or the "life" of prison, meaning the subculture. Those who are heavily involved in the subculture engage in fewer programs; those who are heavily involved in programs participate less in the subculture.

Any counselor who works with female offenders in prison will quickly become familiar with this world and how it influences those who live within. The prison world sometimes provides an opportunity for some women to avoid drugs, sexual relationships, and dysfunctional behavior for a period of time that then enables them to "take stock" and address individual issues they have been avoiding, perhaps all their lives.

Nevertheless, prison also creates special problems for treatment. Stress, sexual exploitation, and subcultural pressures all compete against any positive change. As McClelland (1994a, 1994b) indicated, the manner in which rules are enforced may create behavioral problems that are due entirely to the prison experience. The counselor or helping professional may consequently be forced to spend an inordinate amount of time "putting out fires" rather than working on long-range goals with female inmates. Some programs can insulate female residents from some of these stressors to a certain extent but they are always present.

The prison world also may be unpleasant for treatment staff. Women prisoners may be unwilling, unfriendly, and unforgiving of the limited ability of the professional to effect any changes needed or desired by the inmate. Although there is not as much general inmate hostility toward treatment staff as there is toward correctional officers, there are those inmates who will dislike a person solely because of their position. For these women, all those connected to the prison in any capacity are discounted and detested. These women can be extremely hostile and difficult to deal with. Some women have an inflated view of the counselor's ability to "get things" for them, such as extra telephone calls, housing reassignments, special visiting privileges, and the like. Further, counselors are often asked to intervene in situations occurring outside the prison, for instance, disputes with social services over child custody issues, schools, relatives, and others involved with the woman. Problems always are multifaceted and involve bureaucratic snafus that take incredible amounts of time to sort out, and the prison inmate is virtually powerless to help herself. Some helping professionals never fully resolve the issue of mixed goals; that is, the counselor must pay allegiance to the public's safety, as well as be committed to the individual needs of the offender. Because many correctional security staff believe treatment goals are unnecessary, ineffective, or improper for a system that should do more to "punish," some respond to treatment staff and helping professionals with a degree of aloofness, disdain, or hostility that can be hard to deal with. The bureaucracy of a prison often becomes the central lament of those who work inside—it often seems as if there are four forms required to do something as simple as open a door or let an inmate make a phone call. The wise professional knows when to circumvent rules and how to "get things done," but that takes time to learn and cooperation on the part of other staff. Also, the fact that the prison has bureaucratic goals may greatly influence treatment goals. It may be the case that a program is closed owing to lack of staffing, an inmate is transferred 3 days before being certified as having completed a vocational course, an inmate is put into segregation and loses the opportunity to start a life-skills course that includes how to deal with one's anger, and so on. Some, perhaps many, helping professionals will never be comfortable in the prison world; these individuals would be happier in almost any other kind of setting. For those who do find the challenges rewarding, the remainder of this book addresses issues that concern them. In the next chapter, we take a closer look at the women who are sent to prison and what happens to them when they get there.

3

Criminality and Classification

> In order for women offenders to receive justice, it must be recognized that men and women inhabit different social realities and that women are not necessarily best served if they are treated in ways that assume their needs are identical to their male counterparts.
>
> *Chesney-Lind and Pollock (1995, p. 170)*

Why do women commit crime? Criminology has been largely silent in answer to this question despite the fact that the sex differential in crime rates has been one of the most significant and long-standing of all correlates of crime. A complete answer to why women commit crime must also address the question, "Why do women commit so many fewer crimes (especially violent crimes) than men?" Interestingly, most traditional theories of criminality addressed only male criminality and entirely ignored the sex differential in crime rates. In this chapter we will first explore theories of criminology. Then we will move to a discussion of how assumptions of female criminality affect the correction system's treatment of women offenders. The second half of the chapter will look at classification and assessment issues concerning female offenders.

Theories of Criminality

Early theories of female criminality in the late 1800s and early 1900s postulated that women offenders possessed more masculine traits than "normal" women. Normal women's criminal tendencies were suppressed by their qualities of "piety," "maternity," and "weakness." The relatively fewer number of female criminals was explained by "sexual selection." Female criminals supposedly exhibited masculine tendencies and also exhibited masculine features that made them less attractive. Being less attractive to males, they could not pass on their criminal tendencies (because they could not find mates to have children with)! In the late 1800s Cesare Lombroso believed that about 14% of all criminal women were "born criminals." Other types included the "occasional criminal" who was led into crime by a male, the "hysterical criminal" who exhibited mood swings and destructive behavior, and the "passion criminal" who committed crimes for love or material riches (Lombroso & Ferrero, 1894/1920).

Later writers pointed to psychological theories of female criminality, that is, criminal behavior derived from a "feminine" desire for new experiences or need for affection (Thomas, 1923/1969). Others pointed to "feminine rage," "deceitfulness," and the female's "lack of willpower." Most of the writers of this time period viewed criminality as an inherent trait and the criminal woman as psychologically or biologically compelled to commit crime. Some researchers pointed to the woman's role in the genetics of criminality and traced a criminal line through women, portraying women in the process as "breeders" of criminality (see review in Pollock-Byrne, 1990).

An alternative view was offered by such female researchers as Frances Kellor. In the early 1900s, Kellor and others took extensive life histories of women prisoners and concluded that their lower scores on intelligence and physical skill tests could be attributed to poverty and deprived backgrounds. Kellor pointed to the difficult financial circumstances of women, especially those women in domestic service (see review in Pollock-Byrne, 1990). Even these researchers, however, saw women as little more than errant children easily swayed by men. As Pollock-Byrne (1990) reported,

> Thus, women's criminality was explained by either biological or social causes. Some women were still thought to be born criminal, either because of defective strains they inherited (and could pass on to their children) or because of mental defectiveness or stupidity, which created a propensity to commit crime. Social causes involved the environment women were raised in. If a woman had poor parental models, or if she was corrupted by evil males, then she was only weak and not inherently defective. These women could be saved. Separate institutions for women were supported by both trains of thought. (p. 15)

Sheldon and Eleanor Glueck (1934) studied women and men in their massive case history projects in the 1930s. They concluded that social and hereditary factors played a role in female criminality. They tended to focus on the sexual histories of their women subjects much more so than they did on their male subjects and concluded that 86.4% had "bad" sex habits. Prostitution was divided into categories from the "professional" to the "doubtful good girl." The Gluecks supported sterilization or indefinite terms of imprisonment to prevent criminal women from becoming pregnant. This was during the same time period that theorists had turned to the environment and societal factors to explain male criminality.

Pollak (1950) echoed earlier theorists in his emphasis on biological explanations for female criminality but also added the "chivalry" hypothesis, which proposed that women really did commit as many crimes as males, but their crimes were hidden and less detectable. Even within the same crime category, Pollak believed that women's choice of weapon or method hindered detection. For instance, he believed that women were more likely to use poison, whereas males were more likely to use firearms to commit murder. He also believed that women were more often "instigators" of crime and pulled strings behind the scenes of criminal enterprise. Of course, the supposition that women are responsible for unreported crime ignores the probability that males are also responsible for a large amount of unreported crime, which when added to the existing crime rates would not necessarily change the sex ratio of male to female crime. Self-report and victimization studies show no support for the proposition that females commit the majority of unreported crimes. Pollak provided a comprehensive review of early theories of female criminality but largely accepted stereotypes as fact and gender differences as immutable.

Theories developed to explain female criminality concentrated on pure biology or psychology even after most theories of male criminality had progressed to socioeconomic or sociopsychological elements. Even recently, theorists have used biological factors in crime causation. Menstruation, lactation, and pregnancy have all been used to "explain" certain crimes by women.

In the 1970s theorists predicted that women's liberation would encourage greater involvement in criminality as an extension of women's entry into legitimate job markets; Adler's (1975) "masculinity thesis" postulated a new, violent female criminal, and Simon's (1975) "opportunity thesis" postulated more white-collar crime as women entered previously male-dominated banking and business professions. Neither theory received much support in crime statistics. Women continued to commit such traditionally "feminine" or "consumer" crimes as larceny and forgery.

Another theory that proposed to explain female criminality could be called a structured opportunity theory. In this explanation, a woman's role in society and expectations regarding her activities and responsibilities insulate her from criminal opportunities. Hoffman-Bustamante (1973) pointed to five major factors that influenced women's reduced criminality.

1. Differential role expectations for men and women—for instance, girls are expected to be "nice." Role expectations for women include motherhood and responsibility for family, and women's role responsibilities are inconsistent with a criminal identification.

2. Sex differences in socialization patterns and application of social control—for instance, girls are still more likely to have afterschool family responsibilities and are usually expected home after school, whereas boys have more freedom of movement. These differences continue through early adulthood and girls typically spend a great deal of time around home or friends' homes, whereas boys are more mobile.

3. Structurally determined differences in opportunity to commit particular offenses—part of this element is included in the opportunity and mobility described above; but also, one can point to different skills learned by males and females. Males are more likely to have some type of experience that exposes them to physicality (football or other sports or playground fighting); males are more likely to be exposed to firearms and mechanics (allowing them to learn how to hot-wire a car or pick a lock).

4. Differential access or pressure toward criminally oriented subcultures and careers—because most young women have felt social pressure to marry (especially in lower socioeconomic classes), there is less pressure to acquire material goods through her own enterprise.

5. Sex differences built into crime categories—for instance, until fairly recently, prostitution has been a crime almost exclusively prosecuted against women without attention to the "john." Rape, on the other hand, was historically a crime that, by definition, could only be committed by a man. Since the 1970s when this theory was proposed, most laws have been rewritten and become "sex neutral." Women are now being prosecuted for sexual assault (usually as a participant in an assault against another female), and men are prosecuted for soliciting prostitution as "johns" and as male prostitutes. In other words, whereas women and men may have different crime patterns today, there are fewer examples of differential legal definitions of male and female crime.

Finally, the "economic marginalization thesis" explains that when women lose the economic supports of earlier time periods through no-fault divorce, the reduction or elimination of alimony, and an increase in the number of children out of marital relationships, but make no great strides in attaining economic parity with men, they will resort to property crimes to support themselves and their children. Surveys indicate that most often female prisoners are the sole supporters of children and typically come from extremely limited economic circumstances (Snell, 1994). Further, their crimes are not ordinarily committed through opportunities created by employment positions in nontraditional fields, such as banking; rather, they typically commit the same type of low level fraud and forgery that have characterized women's criminality for decades (Steffensmeier, Kramer, & Streifel, 1993). Thus, the economic marginalizaton thesis seems to be supported. Note that this theory does not explain other types of female crime, only the property crime that derives from being financially responsible for oneself and one's children.

Current Theories

The latest criminology theories are integrated theories in the sense that they include a number of factors in the explanation of criminality. For instance, Wilson and Hernstein (1985) used such elements as genetic makeup, intelligence, and body build. They believed that crime is a result of biosocial makeup, personality structure, rational choice, and social process. An individual chooses criminality after weighing potential gains. Immediate rewards of crime will outweigh distant threats unless the person's socialization has taught him or her guilt. The individual is the key element though, in that it is the person's ability to learn, his or her intelligence and personality that moderate socialization factors.

Gottfredson and Hirschi (1990) also postulated an integrative theory to explain crime. Individual factors, such as impulsivity, combined with poor self-control from poor parenting and lack of supervision, lead to a weakening of social bonds and criminal opportunity (through free time, association with gangs, and exposure to drugs). The result is a range of behavior including delinquency, smoking, drinking, and sexual behavior.

These theories have been criticized for ignoring regional and geographic differences in crime occurrence, economic factors in the temptation to commit crime, and the concept of morality (instead, defining it as self-control). Nevertheless, the most obvious criticism, once again, is that these theories fail to explain the differences in the crime rates between men and women. Despite the scathing criticism of feminist researchers in the 1980s toward traditional criminology, criminologists still seem unwilling or unable to explain the gender differential in crime.

Crime pattern differences are probably attributable to a combination of biological and socialization differences. It seems obvious that, despite the rapid social changes we have experienced in the last 30 years, men and women continue to be socialized differently. One might look to these differences to explain different behavior patterns. One potentially interesting avenue is to use the work of Chodorow (1978) and others who proposed that socialization differences between men and women result in women holding stronger values of "responsibility, care, and promotion of peace and love." According to this theory, during the development of one's identity, a woman maintains a connection with her mother, but the male's identity development derives from separation from the mother. This explains women's tendencies to "connect" rather than disengage, to be sensitive to others, and to be nurturing; and the ideal of masculinity as autonomous. The practice of having the primary responsibility of caring for children also may enrich these values. The theory proposes that women develop the capacity to empathize with others and to "love" because of their responsibilities of providing daily care. They feed, clothe, and comfort, and a loving relationship develops through these responsibilities. Note that this theory is one that is based on identity development differences between men and women whereas Hoffman-Bustamante's theory is sociological, focusing on differential opportunity patterns and skill acquisitions of men and women.

Of course, many questions still remain. The theories that point to women's identity development and socialization as nurturers cannot explain those women who are violent toward their children and/or others. These theories seem to be less relevant to property crimes, because there is almost gender parity in some types of economic crimes. There are those who propose that biological differences are overstated and socialization differences are disappearing, reducing the power of theories that are based on sex and gender differences. Yet one can see that our culture still has strong stereotypes that support the notion of the woman as a nurturer. This is why there is such extreme social condemnation toward a mother who kills or abuses her children (an example would be the incredible national spotlight on Susan Smith after she was found guilty of killing her two children by driving her car into a body of water and letting them drown). Public antipathy toward such women is remarkably stronger than that toward the more frequent offenders of this type of crime—fathers or stepfathers.

Motivations for Crime

Women in prison are not a representative sample of all female criminals, because they are more likely to be poor, members of a minority group, and without resources to avoid criminal prosecution. Nevertheless, discussions with them about their lives and how they got into trouble are enlightening in the patterns that recur—they very often come from homes in which parents are deviant, abusive, or neglectful. Even when the woman describes her parents as "all right," there seems to be little love or affection, or the parent is a strict disciplinarian and the woman seems to have absorbed the message that she has always been a disappointment (Pollock et al., 1996).

One such woman was a young African American in her early 20s. She had a record of juvenile delinquency, including membership in a female gang. When discussing her family, she took the blame for her criminality, explaining that she came from a "good" family; that they had clothes to wear and were made to go to school. With further discussion of her upbringing, however, she described a mother who was totally under the control of a strict, authoritarian husband. The father controlled the household with fear and intimidation and the girl was punished severely for not living up to his standards in dress, academic performance, or behavior. One incident she recalled was when she was 10 years old and went to a friend's house after school, instead of coming home. When she did return, her father beat her, called her a slut and locked her out of the house, telling her she was no longer his daughter. She was let back into the house, but her childhood became a pattern of engaging in increasingly more delinquent behaviors with consequential beatings and punishments from the father. She has now lived up to his expectations of her and is estranged from the family.

Another pattern is the overburdened parent, who, although loving, is also struggling to make ends meet and works at several jobs, spending little time with the children and leaving them to other relatives or the street. Many women explain that they left home at a very young age because "their momma had too many mouths to feed." Alcohol and drug addiction are part of the fabric of life—present in parents or uncles and aunts, brothers and sisters, and others. It is not a rare occurrence to have several or all family members who are addicts or alcoholics. It is also not a rare occurrence to have lost loved ones to homicide, gang-related or otherwise. The women who described getting into trouble at an early age usually came from the most abusive homes and left them to live on the street or escaped to a marriage or relationship that turned even more abusive than the caretakers they left behind. Those who entered crime relatively late in life (mid or late 20s) were more often situationally induced to sell drugs or get involved in other crimes to support a drug habit that originated because of a death, depression due to losing a loved one, or a change in economic circumstances. For instance, one woman recounted a life relatively unmarked by trouble through her teen years and early 20s. She got married, they both worked, and had a "good life." Then when she was 28, her husband died of cancer. She described how, to deal with her grief, she began to use drugs (crack cocaine) with a neighbor in the apartment complex where she lived. She quickly became dependent, and this dependency led to her helping to sell the drugs to others and then to using stolen checks with the other woman and her male crime partner (Pollock et al., 1995). This woman was fairly unusual in her lack of criminal history and lack of exposure to drugs or alcoholism until she was almost 30. Most women in prison describe childhoods when drug and alcohol use began, often to cope with grief, abuse, or sexual exploitation. The presence of low self-control in delinquent and criminal populations, as discussed by researchers (Gottfredson & Hirschi, 1990), seems almost a rational response to a life in which joys are few and tragedy seems always just around the corner.

Theories of female criminality typically point to some elements of opportunity, need, or both, in women's entry into crime. Arguably, because social structure puts more barriers in front of women's criminal opportunities, criminal women's lives may be different from those of law-abiding women. This would explain, for instance, the fact that criminal women seem to have histories of sexual, physical, or both abuses—far from being *insulators* against delinquency, these families are *instigators* of delinquency, addiction, and criminality. So too in their relationships with men; whereas personal relationships (marriage, family) may ordinarily serve to prevent lawbreaking by females and reduce recidivism for male offenders, the relationships of women offenders with men are often abusive, exploitive, and/or the mechanism by which they start drug use and related criminal activity.

In the Texas survey described in Chapter 1 (Pollock et al., 1996), one of the open-ended questions asked women respondents what led to their involvement in the criminal justice system. Their answers were interesting in that they reflected the attributions individuals define as their motivation to crime. The most common reason was the "wrong crowd" explanation. Women described their desire to "fit in" with a group, usually during teenage years, and the group was engaged in shoplifting, drinking, and/or using drugs. The next most often cited category was need (or want) for money. This was further explained as a need for money to buy drugs or to support children. Another category that was mentioned by a significant number was abuse (either physical or sexual) at home that led to running away and life on the street that led to prostitution and drug dealing. Some women described, in almost the same manner, how someone died (husband, brother, father, mother, or boyfriend) and that this death made them "go crazy" or become so lonely that they started using drugs to "belong" or to "feel less pain." Other reasons given were that they liked to "live on the edge" or that a boyfriend or husband started them on drugs. Finally, some mentioned that other family members used drugs, committed crimes, or both, and they just joined them, that drugs made them "feel better," or that they were rebellious and could not be controlled.

Obviously, asking offenders why they commit crime results in information that sheds light on their self-perception and nothing more. Also, many of these categories are overlapping. Those who cited a desire for excitement may have also mentioned peer pressure. One of the themes that stood out in all of these responses was the importance of relationships. Criminal involvement often came through relationships with friends, family members, boyfriends, or husbands. Those who discussed drug use as self-medication, discussed relationships as the cause of their pain. Abusive families and battering relationships also stood out as a strong theme in their lives. What this means is that correctional counseling for women must come to terms with how these relationships affect women's current and future behavior.

Counseling a woman in prison can never simply concentrate on her criminal behavior; rather, issues such as her "life script," who she thinks she is and where she's going, what her expectations are in a relationship, how to deal with unresolved anger and hurt from abusive or neglectful parents, suppressed incest victimization, feelings of guilt, and other personal issues must be included in any answers to the question of why she stole checks from her employer or was involved in selling drugs. It is difficult to deal with some of these issues in any counseling relationship, but the difficulties are even more pronounced in the prison setting, which discourages self-disclosure and breeds distrust.

Criminology and Corrections

Dominant theories and assumptions of why women commit crime are reflected in the treatment received by women offenders. Before the late 1800s, women were placed, first, in the same cells as male offenders, subject to sexual exploitation and rape. Later, although they were separated into their own living quarters, they were still guarded by men, some of whom used their position to exploit and abuse them. This neglect can be understood if one considers that the belief system of the time assumed women offenders were "beyond redemption" and evil. Because their criminality was attributed to genetic and biological causes, there were no attempts to reform or rehabilitate, and even basic elements of humanity were overlooked (Rafter, 1985).

Women were often housed in one ill-equipped and poorly maintained room. They were not allowed to go outside for recreation and typically all movement was restricted. Women served out their sentences in the one room allotted to them unless they were brought out to do cleaning or perform sexual services. Harsh discipline was used on women inmates. Feinman (1976, p. 47) reported that "strapping, cold douches, handcuffing to stationary objects, and overnight solitary confinement" were common. The general approach at the time indicated that those few women who were sent to prison were irredeemable, worse than male criminals, and not worthy of sympathy, care, or protection.

In the 1800s women reformers began the campaign to institute femininity into women's corrections. Elizabeth Fry, in England, promoted such principles as "useful labor" and religious instruction for women inmates. In 1825 she published *Observations on the Sitting, Superintendence and Government of Female Prisoners*. In it, she chronicled the unsanitary and shocking conditions in which women were housed in Britain's prisons and jails and advocated work, training, religion, routine, manners, and better supervision for female prisoners. By the middle of the 1800s Britain had separated women from men and used women warders—this was several decades before separate institutions for women were created in the United States (Dobash et al., 1986).

The idea of the female inmate as misguided rather than evil eventually gained ascendancy in American corrections as well. Reformers, such as Dorothea Dix, Mary Wister, Sarah Doremus, and Abby Hopper Gibbons advocated separation and supervision by females. Doremus and Gibbons founded the "Women's Prison Association of New York," a group that advocated these reforms. The same organization opened the Hopper House, a halfway house for prostitutes and other female criminals (Rafter, 1985).

In the late 1800s separate institutions for women offenders were built. Indiana and Massachusetts were the first two states to have completely separate institutions for women in the 1870s, and New York followed with Bedford Hills in 1900 (Freedman, 1974). Some of these institutions were built and run as "reformatories." The reformatories had a "softer" approach to corrections, for instance, the women inside were more often housed in cottages mimicking homelike environments, with separate kitchens and "living rooms." Female matrons were role models of femininity. The institution pursued a goal of reforming the woman to exemplify a model of chastity, cleanliness, and morality. Nevertheless, many women, especially minority women, were still sent to custodial institutions, which were usually wings of male facilities where no programs of any kind existed (Rafter, 1985).

One of the unique features of women's corrections was the vague line between criminality and sexual deviance. Reformatory staff were much more concerned about a woman's morality than her criminality; thus, committing a crime was not necessarily a requirement for her to "benefit" from the regime. Women who were committed to women's reformatories in the early 1900s were primarily young, more likely to be misdemeanants, and often victims of circumstance. Most were under 25, white, and native born. Most had no prior convictions and more than half were incarcerated for prostitution or drunkenness (Freedman, 1981). Rafter (1985) wrote that some of the women were committed by parents or husbands solely because of promiscuity. Thus, the focus of "treatment" was the woman's sexuality and her acceptance of the "natural role" of women.

In the 1930s a Dutch lawyer reported on women's reformatories in the United States (Lekkerkerker, 1931). She described them as "bucolic," where women were exposed to healthy lifestyles, honest labor (many were set up as farms), and more ladylike endeavors, such as needlework and music. Her descriptions were devoid of what the women themselves thought of such institutions. Obviously, to outsiders they were considered vast improvements over the lives the women had led before their confinement. A common pattern at the time was to parole women to domestic service with "good families." Not much is known about women's prisons—either the reformatories or the more custodial institutions—for the next several decades.

In the 1960s and 1970s women's prisons were typically devoid of any legitimate vocational programs, with a staff who often treated the women like children (Burkhart, 1973). Goals of treatment had not changed much from the first part of the century. In the 1980s litigation and advocacy demanding better programs and services for women increased. Although women never have been as litigious as male prisoners, some important court cases brought attention to the lack of programming and services provided in prisons for women, such as *Glover v. Johnson* (1979), which held that prisons could not discriminate by sex in their offering of vocational programs. As stated earlier, most early prisons for women had programs that were designed to teach women such "wifely" skills as cooking, sewing, and cleaning. Later, some programs, such as cosmetology, typing, clerical, and keypunch were added, which provided training in limited fields designated as appropriate for women. Basic education used to be the only program that one could be fairly sure to find in any prison. In recent years, many states have added nontraditional programs to the inventory, such as auto mechanics, heavy machinery operation, electronics, and others.

Crawford (1988) found that 90.2% of the prisons responding to her survey in the late 1980s had some type of vocational program. The activism of the late 1970s and 1980s led to more and better programs for women in prison, all of which basically followed an opportunity theory of criminality that lack of skills, education, and employment were the "causes" of crime. Other programs that were offered, such as parenting classes, drug treatment, and group therapy or therapeutic communities, addressed such individual issues as self-esteem, victim scripts, and drug addiction. Since the 1980s, however, these rehabilitative efforts were criticized and discounted, and consequently there are probably fewer program slots available in any given prison today than there were in the 1980s. Thus, today's prisons have programs, but many offenders continue to be simply "warehoused," with no real opportunity to change.

Women traditionally have been controlled by social norms to maintain high standards of chastity and morality. They have been perceived as the guardians of society's morality. Thus, the criminal woman, whose deviance was explained by genetic and biological theories, was feared and hated. It was no surprise that corrections treated her as little more than chattel to male wardens. Later, when the image of women changed to that of one led astray by evil men, women reformers took over and created homelike environments to teach their charges "how to be women." The principles behind the reformatory continue to influence the programming, architecture, and discipline of women's prisons, even though massive social change has occurred, necessitating a different definition of what a woman needs to be in this society.

The women's movement in the 1960s and 1970s led to improved programming for women in prison and theories of new, violent female criminals. Although statistics did not support the rise of the violent female criminal, there has been an increase in women's involvement in property crime. Greater change has taken place in our willingness to incarcerate women and in changing women's prisons to become more like those for men, although there continues to be remnants of differential supervision. Today, women's prisons may have many programs on the record but only have slots available for a small percentage of the total number of incarcerated women.

Assessment Issues

In the remainder of this chapter we will look at classification, the specific needs of women offenders, and other assessment issues. Most states have classification models they use to determine housing, job placement, and treatment options for offenders. What particular options are available to women are largely determined by what is available. Some prisons have very few programs and women take whatever is available regardless of their own particular needs. It is important, however, for the process of assessment to occur. Knowing an offender's background, health history, and skill level can help to understand her motivations and behavior inside the prison and aid in predicting success on release. Assessment, obviously, is vital to any counseling process.

Classification

Classification in prison has two major purposes: security or management and treatment or service. Over the last decade, the first has ascended in importance and the second has faded in emphasis. The history of classification efforts began with the simple classification schemes of 100 years ago that used such factors as sex and age. Later, criminal history and "amenability to treatment" were added, and then classification progressed to the quite sophisticated and multifactored classification schemes of the 1980s. Classification schemes use either objective or subjective measures (or a combination of the two). Subjective classification ordinarily begins with a classification counselor or psychologist interviewing the offender. Objective measures include everything from computer-derived risk factor score indexes to such psychological tests as the MMPI. There has been a steady move toward the use of objective measurements, probably due to legal challenges and the desire and need to treat inmates consistently and fairly. The disillusionment with the "medical model" of diagnosis and treatment probably has also affected the move toward "paper-and-pencil" classification schemes (Spencer, 1997).

Security and management classification is concerned with such things as to which prison the offender is sent (if there is more than one prison for women in the system), which custody level she should have, and what job assignments would be appropriate. If there is evidence of escape risk, she will be assigned a higher custody level and will not be eligible for trustee status or outside work assignments. If she is a suicide risk, that is a custody concern as well as a treatment concern. If she has shown assaultive behavior in the past, that will be taken into account in job assignment, living unit, and prison.

Treatment classification is concerned with an offender's needs. Health and dental needs are noted and a schedule of medical services undertaken. Medications are checked and noted for the record. The woman's educational level is assessed and, if appropriate, basic literacy, GED (General Equivalency Diploma), or college classes may be recommended. Mental health is evaluated through a mental status examination, noting any previous stays in mental hospitals, diagnoses from jail staff or probation officials, or self-reported problems. Much information can come from a presentence report if one is available.

A recent study of classification for women offenders found that, for the most part, states used identical classification systems for male and female offenders. In fact, states may be sued under equal protection if they use different classification systems and it disadvantages one or the other group (Spencer, 1997). Even with no intent to discriminate, if there is a "disparate impact" there may be a finding against the particular system. For instance, if the classification system more often categorizes women as lacking the skills necessary to benefit from vocational programs, thus reinforcing the idea that vocational programs in women's prisons are not cost-effective, this creates a disparate impact. This also means that there could likely be a legal challenge to security classifications that routinely classify women into higher security levels, because the standard instruments used for men do not adapt well to women (Burke & Adams, 1991). Security concerns predominate in classification systems developed for male offenders owing to the greater number (although not necessarily percentage) of males incarcerated for violent crimes and for their increased potential for aggressive behavior in prison and escape risk (Burke & Adams, 1991). Although security may be the dominant concern for male offenders, these authors propose that habilitation could be the dominant concern of a classification system for women offenders (Burke & Adams, 1991).

> Typically, statewide classification systems are geared toward security and safety concerns. At the same time, the profile of women offenders is often a low-security one with a significantly lesser incidence of violence and predatory behavior than among men. With greater emphasis on habilitation concerns, women's institutions may not find statewide security classification systems very helpful in organizing resources within their institutions. (p. 37)

There is the tendency for systems developed for male offenders to overclassify women offenders into higher security grades. For instance, the commission of a violent offense increases the risk score for an offender and places him or her in a higher security classification, but women and men may present different profiles of violent crime, especially homicide. For instance, women are more likely to kill intimates with some elements of victim precipitation present but pose less risk in an institutional setting.

About 40 of the states responding to a recent survey reported using the same classification system for men and women (Burke & Adams, 1991). The four models that are commonly used are objective; they are the National Institute of Corrections model, The Federal Prison System model, the Correctional Classification Profile, and the Florida model. These may be adapted to the individual state's needs. Objective classification systems use the following factors: severity of current offense, degree of violence in current offense, use of weapon, nature of sexual offense, current offense, type of sentence, length of sentence, expected length of incarceration, type of detainer, severity of prior commitments, number of prior commitments, number of prior convictions, number of prior felony convictions, number of convictions against a person, number of convictions for burglary or theft, history of violence, history of institutional violence, history of escape, history of prior supervision, institutional adjustment, behavior characteristics during incarceration, demonstrated skills in escape or assault, precommitment status, psychotic symptomatology, substance abuse, age, education, history of employment, and program or service needs.

Classification Measures

Psychological classification systems are ordinarily used to supplement objective systems and are concerned with such things as suicide risk, personality traits, and reasoning abilities (Spencer, 1997). Such tests as the MMPI or MMPI2 (Minnesota Multiphasic Personality Inventory), the CPI (California Psychological Inventory), Cattell 16PF (16 Personality Profile), Edwards Personal Preference Schedule, Beck Depression Inventory, and others have all been used in corrections, with the MMPI and the CPI probably being the most common.

The Mental Status Examination. Every classification includes a face-to-face interview with the offender. During this interview, the professional may have any number of objective psychological test scores, intelligence test scores, and other information at his or her disposal. As mentioned before, one tool for prison assessment is the presentence report if one is available. These reports are written by probation officers on order from the court and are designed to help the judge determine the appropriate sentence. Background information, such as criminal history, educational history, family history, marital history, and employment history is reported in a narrative form. Present family circumstances, children, and other dependents are noted. The current offense is described, codefendants noted, victim's injuries described, and an "offender's version" is reported. Trial information, detainers or pending charges, are included with the recommendation of the probation officer and final disposition. Not all jurisdictions require presentence reports, but those that do provide the prison counselor with a great deal of information.

On the other hand, the counselor in prison may choose to conduct a diagnostic procedure, including a mental health examination first, before reviewing the presentence report. One study indicated that presentence reports were biased against women who committed property crimes and tended to ascribe sympathetic explanations for nonminority women who committed domestic violent crimes (Wilkie, 1993). The point is, presentence reports are not simply objective recitations of facts but, rather, attempts to explain human behavior, and the authors will be somewhat biased by their own perceptions and views of the offender, sex differences, and general assumptions of criminal causation.

. The mental status examination often includes a diagnosis using the DSM-IV (Diagnostic and Statistical Manual of Mental disorders, 4th ed.). This process would cover the following evaluative categories (Enos & Southern, 1996):

> Axis I. Clinical syndromes and V Codes. A diagnosis of any clinical syndromes such as depression, schizophrenia, or delusional disorders.
>
> Axis II. Developmental disorders. Attention Deficit Disorder, conduct disorder, or antisocial personality disorder are examples of diagnoses in this category, all of which are fairly common in delinquent and adult offender populations. Antisocial personality disorder, for instance, would be diagnosed if there were three or more of the following characteristics since the age of 15: fails to conform to social norms or engages in unlawful activities, uses deceitfulness or lying to obtain pleasure or profit, is impulsive and lacks self-control, starts fights and becomes involved in physical assaults, places the safety of self and others in jeopardy, is irresponsible and disregards liability for actions.
>
> Axis III. Physical disorders and conditions. A full medical evaluation would uncover such conditions as heart disease, epilepsy, thyroid conditions, and so on. Many physical disorders create behavioral and psychological symptomatology that can be mistaken for psychiatric disorders. Endocrine system dysfunctions (thyroid, adrenal, pituitary, and parathyroid disorders), seizure disorders (especially temporal lobe epilepsy), multiple sclerosis, hypoglycemia, Wilson's Disease, and others have all been noted to have symptomatology that creates behavioral or psychological disturbances. If a diagnosis overlooks the medical source of such problems, purely psychiatric or psychological intervention will not be successful (Klonoff & Landrine, 1997).
>
> Axis IV. Severity of psychosocial stressors. All relevant current life events would be noted and rated on a scale of stressors. Stressors include marital, family, financial, occupational, or other relationship problems. Obviously, beginning a prison sentence is a significant stressor as well.
>
> Axis V. Global functioning. Evaluates the individual's overall psychological, social, and occupational functioning.

The mental status examination can be used to make treatment recommendations, prescribe appropriate medication, and assign job, program, or both placements.

The MMPI. The MMPI has long been associated with correctional classification. Several scales of the 10 found in the MMPI are particularly applicable to criminal populations. Scale 4 (Psychopathic Deviate), for instance, is highly correlated with career criminals and represents a person who is outgoing, adventurous, impulsive, and hostile (Enos & Southern, 1996).

Several classification systems specific to correctional populations have employed the MMPI. For instance, Megargee and Bohn (1979) identified 10 criminal types and their system has been used by the Federal Bureau of Prisons to assign housing and treatment programs. The classification types are described below.

Group Item: lacks significant psychopathology. They are the most well-adjusted on standardized studies and could benefit from alcohol education and chemical dependency treatment.

Group Easy: are the best adjusted and controlled but are underachievers and generally undependable. They could benefit from academic programs or insight-based psychotherapy.

Group Baker: has intrapsychic and interpersonal problems, but their problems are less severe than those of the following groups. These offenders are passive-aggressive and alcoholic.

Group Able: includes socialized delinquents and sensation-seeking extroverts. They are sociable, active, and manipulative; often white middle class who ended up in prison owing to a hedonistic lifestyle supported by crime. They benefit from group therapy and often need chemical dependency treatment as well.

Group George: are similar to Group Able but are more depressed and less well-adjusted. They are more solitary and isolated. They benefit from groups emphasizing task achievement.

Group Delta: have more serious psychological and criminal deviancy. This group is hedonistic, amoral, and impulsive with entrenched hostility and alienation. They have dysfunctional family backgrounds and chaotic lifestyles. They are highly recidivistic and prognosis is poor, but they do show some signs of maturing out of repetitive criminal behaviors.

Group Jupiter: can be described as multiproblem offenders. Composed primarily of African American males with poor social histories, they can react to stress with hostility and aggressiveness but often do well when provided with occupational opportunities.

Group Foxtrot: present extensive histories of criminality and deviance and pervasive psychopathology. They are impulsive, disorganized, antisocial, and they have deficiencies in every area of functioning. Behavior modification may be helpful. They require a high degree of structure.

Group Charlie: are hostile loners. They have experienced severe family problems and life trauma. They are antisocial, paranoid, and aggressive. They have difficulty relating to "straight" people. This group presents a poor prognosis but might benefit from cognitive behavioral interventions.

Group How: are unstable, anxious, disorganized, and typically require psychiatric treatment. They present a danger to themselves and others in a correctional setting. They may have been deinstitutionalized from the mental health setting.

It has more recently been used in community corrections to predict success in halfway houses and special treatment programs (Enos & Southern, 1996). Most of the applications of the MMPI to correctional populations have involved male offenders. The system above, for instance, was developed and is used for male offenders. There is a need to more closely analyze the applicability of such classification systems to female offenders, especially considering that the MMPI itself recognizes differences in male and female populations and employs different scales for each sex.

Developmental Level Classification Systems. One attempt to match counseling efforts with individual offenders took place in California over 20 years ago. The California Treatment Project evaluated juvenile delinquents and classified them on a developmental scale measuring social maturity. Although the classification scale proved to be equally applicable to male and female delinquents, the staff discovered that the female delinquents tended to cluster at higher maturity levels. Four percent of the males, but only 1% of females were classified at the lowest maturity level, 32% of the males and 21% of the females were placed in the second maturity level, and 64% of the males and 79% of the females were classified into the third or highest level (Warren, 1986, p. 458). The classification system also provided subtypes within each maturity level. Almost no girls were classified into the subtypes that were peer or gang-oriented ("Cultural Conformist" or "Cultural Identifier"), whereas girls were more likely than boys to be placed in a subtype called "Conflicted/ Neurotic." Three fourths of all girls tested were placed into this subtype. The description of the subtype by Warren (1986) is as follows:

> They have reached a stage of social maturity where they operate from an internalized value system which they use to judge themselves and others, to model themselves after persons they respect, to understand cause and effect relationships, to perceive needs and motives in others, to accept the concept of accountability for one's own behavior, and so on . . . [but they also] have a good deal of internal wear-and-tear involving anxiety, guilt, a "bad me" self-image, "negative life script," distorted perceptions, and dysfunctional behavior. (p. 460)

Under this general category, two subgroups were identified. The "anxious" subtype showed a number of symptoms of emotional disturbance (depression, anxiety, psychosomatic complaints). They had overriding feelings of failure, inadequacy or guilt. The "acting out" subgroup denied their own anxiety through attacking others, game playing, and distractions (Warren, 1986).

Counselors were matched to subtype profiles. Counselors for the conflicted girls needed to see through the defensive process, have a degree of openness about self to act as a role model and use introspective rather than action techniques. Counseling focused on discussion of feelings of anxiety, guilt, anger, aggression, sex, fantasies, and so on. Counselors for the "acting out" subgroup needed to do counseling "on the run." That is, the females in this subgroup had little tolerance for introspection or a direct inquiry into their private fears, so the counselor had to allow the girl to maintain a stance that there was "nothing wrong with her" and not allow the girl the opportunity to reject attempts to control through the counseling process (Warren, 1986).

The other subtypes found to be most common among female delinquents were the "power-oriented" delinquent and the "passive-conformist." Those classified as "power oriented" responded aggressively to attempts to control them. They did not have close or trusting relationships with anyone and appeared angry and threatening. Typically their backgrounds included a cold, brutal, or rejecting father and a weak, helpless, superficial mother. Counselor characteristics included the qualities of firmness and fairness and the counselor showed the girls that they were worth something by caring to control them. Rewards were given for honest communication and manipulation was resisted. The last subtype was the "passive-conformist." These girls saw themselves as weak. They would typically be submissive to whomever around them appeared to be strong. Parental love and control was weak or nonexistent. Treatment consisted of a high structure relationship that was nonthreatening. Rewards for achievement were generous to enable the girls to improve their self-image and develop a stronger sense of internal direction.

The uniqueness of the California Treatment Program was the attempt to classify offenders *and* treatment personnel, then match them to facilitate the counseling process. Just as offenders are different so too are treatment professionals. Male delinquents who fell into subtypes characterized by manipulation and a power orientation were matched with counselors who were more action oriented, maintained a formalistic relationship, and responded strongly to challenges from the boy (in other words, the counselors had to earn the respect of the boy by being "tough"). It seems obvious that counseling efforts cannot be a one-size-fits-all proposition, but unfortunately the practice of carefully classifying offenders and then matching them to counselors and counseling programs is seldom accomplished. The California Treatment Program obtained significantly more positive results with delinquents when compared with the regular probation or detention system. Whereas 91% of the experimental female delinquents had received a favorable discharge, only

78% of the control group had been favorably discharged by 60 months after entry (Warren, 1986, p. 459).

Behavioral Classification Systems. Typologies that use observations and ratings of an offender's behavior patterns are also used in correctional settings. The Adult Internal Management System (AIMS) is one such system. In this classification typology, staff members use life histories and observations of the offender's behavior in a correctional setting to place them in one of five personality types: aggressive psychopath, manipulative, situational, inadequate dependent, and neurotic anxious (Quay & Parsons, 1971). These titles have since been discarded to avoid negative labeling (Quay, 1984). This classification system is used to assign housing, education, work, and counseling treatments.

An "Omnibus Classification System." Enos and Southern (1996, p. 100) presented a classification system that included many of the types employed in other classification systems. They presented the following types:

1. Low conceptual level. Offenders who have low intellectual development; they have not learned moral reasoning skills and need high structure.
2. Mentally disordered. Offenders who present clinical syndromes of psychosis.
3. Neurotic. Offenders who present a variety of different manifestations of anxiety—they may be compulsive, passive-aggressive, histrionic, or avoidant.
4. Immature dependent. Offenders who experience social anxiety at times. They lack social skills and fall under the influence of an older, more criminal offender.
5. Situational. Offenders who commit crime owing to extraordinary psychosocial stress. They do not perceive themselves as deviant and do not have criminal associates.
6. Subcultural. Offenders who are influenced by prevailing norms in their community. Often they are gang members.
7. Character disordered. Offenders who are the classic stereotype of the antisocial individual. They are impulsive, self-centered, and aggressive. They have failed to learn empathy, altruism or prosocial values.
8. Power oriented. Offenders who are a special subgroup of Character Disordered. They commit crime to feel a sense of control; they look for opportunities to coerce and dominate others.
9. Manipulative. Offenders (also a subgroup of Character Disordered) who present above average communication skills and are extroverted. Their motivation is to "con" people and mask their true identity and personality.
10. Neurologically impaired. Offenders, such as those who suffer from Attention Deficit/Hyperactivity Disorder, who have difficulty controlling their behavior. Some are sensation seeking and some are unable to cope with ordinary stress.

11. Chemically dependent. Offenders who commit crime because of chemical dependency.
12. Violent. Offenders who will respond violently even when there are other alternatives available. Violent criminal behavior may be present in other types, but for this particular group, violence is used more frequently, with less hesitation. Violence is still primarily instrumental.
13. Sadistic. Offenders who use violence for personal and sexual gratification.

Unfortunately, these authors did not discuss the applicability of the classification system to female offenders. Because most offenders are male, most classification systems are developed with male populations and are used with male offenders. The creators of such systems either do not use the system with female offenders or apply it without much thought to the possibility that females may present different types not present in a male population.

There is evidence that women typically show higher evidence of psychopathy, psychosomatic illness, depression, and anxiety than male prisoners on objective measures (Warren, 1986). Differences between male and female offenders with regard to signs of mental distress and dysfunctional backgrounds have been chronicled by many researchers over the years (Pollock-Byrne, 1990). There has been little work on evaluating the classification measures typically used with male offenders to see if they are equally useful with female offenders. It seems clear that women offenders in prison may have fairly serious problems that may affect their adjustment to prison, and standard classification devices may not be very helpful in identifying the extent or source of their problems.

Needs Analysis

Women prisoners are individuals—their particular life histories, problems, and personalities are obviously unique. Nevertheless, there are patterns that can be discerned in the lives of women prisoners. In the following paragraphs, information is presented from several needs assessment surveys that were done with prisoners in Texas, California, and other states.

Education

As stated before, women in prison are slightly more educated than their male counterparts. In the Fletcher et al. (1993) study of Oklahoma inmates, she found that 64% of the sample had obtained a high school diploma or GED (General Equivalency Diploma). This compared with a national sample of which only 28% of women prisoners and 38% of male prisoners possessed a high school diploma or GED. Sixty-six percent of the Fletcher et al. sample went to a vocational or technical school (50% reported in the national sample). A surprisingly high number of women in the Fletcher et al. sample reported some college (39%) compared with 15% of women and 11% of men in a national sample.

In the California study, nearly 40% reported that they did not finish high school (Bloom et al., 1994, p. 3). In the Texas sample, 26.9% reported that they did not finish high school, nor did they acquire a GED, but 37.6% did obtain the GED (either in prison or on the street). Only 11.3% reported any college (Pollock et al., 1996). In most samples, a high number of women reported dropping out of high school because of pregnancy. In the most recent national figures available, about 43% of female inmates had either a high school diploma or a GED (Snell, 1994).

Women need to have access to an education program that can prepare them for work on the outside. General education programs meet the needs of most women in prison, but there is also the need for specialized education for those women who are ready to start college or acquire special certification in vocational and technical areas.

Physical and Sexual Abuse

A U.S. Department of Justice study (1991) on women in prison reported that 41% of the women in prison reported sexual or physical abuse. Women incarcerated for a violent offense were most likely to report such abuse. Although statistics vary, all studies indicate that at least a third and often a much higher percentage of incarcerated women report physical, sexual, or both abuses. Gilfus (1988), for instance, found that 88% of her sample reported childhood physical or sexual abuse or adult rape or battering.

In the Fletcher et al. (1993) study of Oklahoma inmates, they compared the abuse histories of their sample of female inmates to statistics reported for a national sample. Whereas 74% of the women in the Oklahoma sample reported abuse, only 53% of the national sample did. About the same number of women in both studies were physically abused as children (37%), but more than three times as many women (69%) in the Oklahoma sample as reported in the national sample (23%) reported abuse as adults. In addition to the physical abuse reported above, the Oklahoma sample of women prisoners reported being sexually abused, raped, or molested (39.7%), and emotionally or mentally abused (69.5%). More Oklahoma women also reported sexual assaults (55% compared with 36%).

In the California study, about 80% of the women reported either physical abuse or neglect or sexual abuse. About one third reported physical abuse as a child (similar to the Oklahoma sample), and 60% reported abuse as an adult (similar to the Oklahoma study). Sexual abuse as a child was reported by 31% of the sample, and sexual abuse as an adult was reported by 23%. Forty percent of the California sample reported emotional abuse or neglect as a child (Bloom et al., 1994, p. 3).

In Texas, about one third (31.2%) of the women reported physical abuse as a child, but roughly 60% reported abuse as an adult (these statistics are very similar to both the Oklahoma and California samples). Again, about one third (30.6%) reported sexual abuse as a child, and 11.3% also reported sexual assault (with violence) as a child, with an additional 34.4% of women reporting sexual assault as an adult. More than one third (36.6%) reported emotional abuse or neglect as a child, and 46.8% reported emotional abuse as an adult (Pollock et al., 1996).

> I was raped at the age of 12 . . . by three men . . . I was on my way walking to school . . . and when I was 15 I been beat up so badly by men. I don't know from 15 to 25 I was beat up by two men and the only time they beat me up was in front of my friends.

Women are about three times more likely to report prior physical or sexual abuse as men in prison (Snell, 1994). Blount, Kuhns, and Silverman (1993), after exploring the pattern and extent of abuse among female prisoners, had the following to say:

> To conclude that incarcerated women suffer physical abuse to a greater extent than other women would seem the grandest of understatements. This rate is many times that of women in the general population—conservatively 6 to 10 times as great. (p. 425)

Effects of the abuse may include a different pattern of offending. In an Oregon study, for instance, half of the women who had been both sexually and physically abused had been arrested at least once before the age of 15, compared with only 11% of those who reported no abuse (Oregon Department of Corrections, 1993). Almost 60% of those who had been both physically and sexually abused ran away from home four times or more, compared with only 15% of those who had not been abused. Abuse was not found to be correlated with adult convictions or convictions for assaultive crimes or drug crimes in this study (Oregon Department of Corrections, 1993). The study's authors pointed to other elements in an abusive family that interact to influence criminal behavior, such as use of violence, poor interpersonal relationships, and lack of parental interest in the child. Other studies have identified a link between childhood or adult physical, sexual, or both abuses and violent crime (Sultan & Long, 1988). This finding has yet to have much impact on programming. In one national study, for instance, it was found that of the 43 states and territories responding, 21 states had not collected any information on the numbers of women in their system who had been physically or sexually abused (Clement, 1993, p. 98).

The effects of physical and sexual abuse can be severe. Children who suffer such abuse can exhibit a range of effects, including committing sexual abuse of others, phobias, sleep disturbances, public masturbation, seductive behavior, urinary tract infections, and compulsive behavior. As they mature, they may experience difficulty with intimacy and trust, sexual problems, poor body image, amnesia about their childhood, phobias, and low self-esteem (Fletcher et al., 1993, p. 56). Other effects of such abuse include disassociation, attempted suicide, and other psychopathologies. Counselors and helping professionals in prison are perhaps the first persons ever to discuss these painful memories with female offenders. There is no doubt that this is one of the most important treatment issues counselors must deal with in working with female offenders.

A conservative estimate is that about one third of female prisoners have experienced physical, sexual, or both abuses. Many more have experienced such abuse as adult women. Women need to share their stories and understand how their childhood experiences have affected their lifestyle choices. Counseling efforts that address such issues are sorely needed.

Drug Abuse

This topic is taken up more fully in a later chapter. At this point, it is sufficient to note that women in prison use drugs and abuse drugs to the same degree as, if not more than, any male prisoner sample. Further, women are increasingly being sent to prison because of their drug use, through determinate and mandatory sentencing laws that do not distinguish between male and female drug users. Thus, women in prison are likely to be addicts or at least have a history of abusing drugs. Their motivation for drug use may be for self-medication, may be subcultural, or may even have genetic origins. Their drug use may be directly or indirectly related to their criminality. Almost every prison has at least an Alcoholics Anonymous group, even if no other treatment programs exist. There is a high correlation between drug and alcohol use and criminality.

There is no doubt that drug treatment programs help a great deal to address the problem of crime in this society. Although drug treatment programs exist in all prisons, there is a need for more slots so that more prisoners can take advantage of such programs, and there is also a need to examine the programs available to determine if they meet the unique needs of women.

Self-Esteem

In the Oklahoma study, self-esteem was found to be associated with health, locus of control, and the level of education. Nevertheless, the direction of this latter relationship was different from what one might expect inasmuch as higher levels of education were associated with lower self-esteem. These researchers did not find that family factors were related to self-esteem, although a larger number of friends and social contacts was related to positive self-esteem. As might be expected, victimization as a child or adult was related to low self-esteem, as was the use of drugs or alcohol (Fletcher et al., 1993).

> I was told I was stupid. I was told I was fat. I was told I was ugly. Just a lot of things. My dad—I think that's his favorite word—we're all stupid. We were never physically abused. I guess the mental and emotional abuse is worse. I can't compare it so I don't know. My mother never allowed him to severely reprimand us in any way . . . he was real mentally and emotionally abusive toward [my mom]. I don't think it was till I hit the age of 13 that I did see a physical abuse, and till this day I still don't want to admit that. I want to paint this perfect family. This pretty house with a white picket fence. Those will always be my dreams. . . . I wouldn't admit it. I wouldn't speak about it. And anytime anybody tried to tell me, I would tell them to leave my family out of it. That my family had nothing to do with it. It was me, I made the decision. I refused to let my family share in my humiliation. After all thinking about it, my family did play a part. There's no communication within my family. There's none. None. I couldn't go to my mother and talk to her about girl things. The things I found out, I found out on my own. The menstrual cycle, all that. I had to find out all that on my own. . . . I just got so addicted to cocaine. So my dad approached me and he propositioned me like a prostitute, just like a common street walker. And I accepted. That's how low I had sunk. (Pollock et al., 1995)

For some women, it is in a prison program that they first come to terms with their own identity. On the street they are consumed with living the "fast life" or burdened with the problems of making a living. Drug use, relationships with men, and "hanging with" others who are also involved in a life of partying, eliminate the opportunity for introspection and blunt the memories of pain.

> When I first came here I didn't care, I didn't know myself. I always thought I was nothing because I used to do any and everything to get dope or anything. . . . I mean there was no limit for me. And when I came here it really changed me a lot because it made me find my inner self. Made me know who I am, that I am somebody. (Pollock et al., 1996)

If there is no opportunity to confront one's past in a structured way with skilled and caring staff, the sobriety and emptiness of prison life may lead to brooding, depression, and sometimes attempted suicide.

Children

Issues of children will be covered more fully in a later chapter. Women in prison are overwhelmingly mothers and often mothers of small children. Immarigeon (1994) reported that the latest U.S. Department of Justice statistics indicate that two thirds of women in prison are mothers of children under 18 and only 9% of these women have visits with their children. Only about 11% were in foster care (Immarigeon, 1994, p. 5). Another national study reports that three quarters of women in prison are mothers. Only about one quarter of these women's children were living with the father (compared with 90% of the children of men in prison who were living with their mother) (Snell, 1994). Grandparents were the most common placement for the children for all races—57% of African American women, 55% of Hispanic women and 41% of white women had children living with grandparents (Snell, 1994).

Staff mention the fact that a women's prison is much different from a prison for men, and handling a caseload of women is more difficult than handling a caseload of men, primarily because of the issue of children. Women in prison are still very much concerned with their children's lives and this means that caseworkers must handle and coordinate calls from caretakers, protective service agencies, and the woman herself. Some women's demeanor and mood depend entirely on whether or not they've received their letter or been able to make their telephone call to their children during the week. Unfortunately, as we shall see in a later chapter, prison seldom makes the relationship between mother and child easy and, too often, a prison term means being sentenced to losing one's children.

Implications for Counselors

The majority of women in prison have had lives marked by abuse and other forms of victimization. They have a multitude of problems, which do not excuse their criminal behavior but certainly help to explain it. As Warren (1986, p. 460) explained, "Delinquency has some private meaning and does not represent simply a material gain or a response to cultural pressure. It may involve the acting out of a family problem, an identity crisis, or a long-standing internal conflict." Any treatment plan must start with an assessment of where the women has been and what her needs are. File information and any classification measures the prison undertakes are helpful. These would also be supplemented by an initial interview by the helping professional engaged in a specific treatment program or a more general helping relationship.

According to Enos and Southern (1996, p. 68), a correctional "diagnosis" should include the following elements:

1. A hypothesis concerning the nature of the offender's personality and particularly his or her psychological functioning
2. A hypothesis about the genesis of the offender's problems in biopsychosocial functioning as a consequence of his or her developmental history
3. A hypothesis concerning the importance of the problems in biopsychosocial function for the offender
4. A type of category, classification, or specific clinical diagnosis about the problem in biopsychosocial functioning, for example, "antisocial personality disorder;" "cocaine-induced disorders;" "cocaine dependence"

An important goal of assessment is to match program offerings with the individual's needs. This may be difficult, because there may not be many available program slots; vocational programs might be full, with waiting lists; the female prisoner may be ineligible for some vocational programs owing to a very low reading level; and, life skills courses or parenting groups may not be available or offered only sporadically. An important effect of proper classification and assessment is that better use is made of scarce resources. If a woman does not have a drug or drinking problem, there is no need to assign her to a drug program; if she has a high school diploma, she may desire and benefit from college classes, rather than a mechanics class. If she shows no vocational aptitude nor desire for a certain type of vocational program, it is a waste of time and money to put her in one. If she expresses no interest in a treatment group, that slot should be reserved for someone else who truly wants to participate.

All the issues discussed thus far are interrelated and related to (typically) a dysfunctional family. It is painfully obvious when listening to women's experiences that their problems originated in childhood; thus, any counseling with a goal of reducing criminality cannot ignore the social and personal history of these women. Their life choices are a result of their background, their current familial and friendship influences, as well as the social and economic opportunities, or lack of opportunities available to them.

4

Drug Abuse, Criminality, and Treatment

I've been on dope for most of my life. Dope killed my momma, killed my two brothers, and it's gonna kill my little sister 'cause she out here in a crew that's out cold . . . we all gonna die, just wait and see. . . . Crack is what makes us crazy, but it's the best high I know. This ain't the way I wanted things to work, but that's the way it is. We know, but what's gonna change? Nothing but that pipe makes things seem different. Crack is gonna get ya.

Taylor (1993, p. 194)

As reported in a previous chapter, drugs account for the largest increase in imprisoned women. Whereas not all women who are incarcerated for drug offenses are addicts, a number of them either are addicted or have experienced drugs as a problem in their life. Addiction has been described as having the following signs: heavy use of a substance, continued use even with life problems caused by the substance, tolerance, and withdrawal symptoms (Beck, Wright, Newman, & Liese, 1993, p. viii). This description fits many women's experience with drugs, alcohol, or both. In this chapter, we will explore some of the issues around drug and alcohol use and abuse and the treatment modalities designed for drug addicts and alcoholics.

Drugs and Crime

Drugs and criminality are linked. Although it is estimated that 2.3% of the U.S. population has a drug problem sufficient to warrant treatment, that figure rises to 33% of the incarcerated population and 25% of those on probation and parole (both men and women). Further, 25% of all property crimes and 15% of all violent crimes are related to illicit drug use (Beck et al., 1993, p. 5).

Specific drug crimes (possession or sale) account for 7% of the arrests of women and 12% of the crimes of conviction of women in prison (Wellisch, Prendergast, & Anglin, 1994, p. 1). And of those offenders who are arrested for other crimes, the majority of women interviewed at arrest, regardless of the charge, test positive for at least one illicit drug (Wellisch et al., 1994, p. 1). Addicts are involved in approximately three to five times as many crimes as nonaddicts (Fletcher et al., 1993, p. 49). "From 1982 to 1991, the number of women arrested for drug offenses, including possession, manufacturing, and sale, increased by 89 percent" (Wellisch et al., 1994, p. 1). About one out of three women in U.S. prisons were there for drug crimes in 1991; this is an increase from the 1 out of 10 women arrested for such crimes in 1979. About one third (35.9%) of these drug crimes were simple possession (Bloom et al., 1994, p. 1).

Patterns of Use

In a national sample, female prisoners used slightly more drugs and used them slightly more frequently than male prisoners. About 54% had used drugs in the month before prison (compared with 50% of men). They also reported regular use more often than men (65% compared with 62%). Nearly one out of four females reported committing their crime to get money for drugs, compared with one out of six males (Snell, 1994). Anglin and Hser (1987) found that, although addicted women in their study may have committed property crimes before their heavy drug use, the frequency and extent of offending increased after the addiction. After treatment, women showed significant reductions in their criminality.

> I would prostitute, I don't know how many times to get it. I mean . . . there was no limit to that. There was no limit. . . . I would steal from my grandmother. I would steal from the men who would call and tell me that they love me. I didn't really love them—all I wanted was their money. (p. 362)

There also seems to be a link between the type of drug used and type of crime committed, with heroin and narcotics related to prostitution and property crimes, whereas cocaine, especially crack cocaine, seems to be linked to violent crime, drug dealing, and "sex-trading" (a type of barter prostitution in which women will exchange sex for drugs in crack houses) (Inciardi, Lockwood, & Pottieger, 1993).

In various studies it has been found that of the approximately one third of female inmates who reported serious problems with drugs, their drug use started early and it was a daily habit. Most inmates reported that they had tried alcohol and marijuana. Fewer, but still substantial numbers, reported using cocaine and crack. Fewer reported heroin use or use PCP, LSD, or other drugs. Snell (1994) reported that about twice as many women in 1991 as in 1986 reported using cocaine at the time of their offense (23% compared with 12%). Nationally, about 46% of Hispanic women, 42% of white women, and 24% of black women had used a needle to inject drugs (Snell, 1994).

Interestingly, although women in prison reported using drugs more frequently than male inmates, the reverse pattern is true for alcohol. Fewer women than men reported being under the influence of alcohol at the time of their offense (22% compared with 32%) (Snell, 1994). They were also less likely to use alcohol—58% of women reported any alcohol use in the year before prison compared with 73% of men (Snell, 1994).

The U.S. Department of Justice (1991) reported that about one third of all female inmates claimed that they were under the influence of a drug at the time of their offense and 39% reported daily use. In the California study, more than one third of the women sampled indicated a drug-related motivation for crime, and an additional 15% reported "economic pressures" that may have been related to drug use (Bloom et al., 1994, p. 2).

Brochu and Levesque (1990) pointed out that it is important to analyze the connection between criminality and drug or alcohol use before starting treatment. They identified criteria like the following to answer such questions as whether addiction led to criminality or whether it is a separate and distinct issue: sequence of alcohol or drug use and first criminal activity, family background of alcohol or drug use, reasons for alcohol or drug use, reasons for criminal activity, and previous attempts to curtail alcohol or drug use.

In the study of Oklahoma inmates, the drug use histories of women were compared to a national sample with fairly similar results (Fletcher et al., 1993). Most women in both the Oklahoma and the national samples reported using alcohol (74% in Oklahoma, compared with 70%), but more Oklahoma women reported ever using drugs (72% compared with 66%). About the same number of women in both samples reported use of crack cocaine (44% to 42%). More Oklahoma women reported using marijuana (76%) than the national sample of women (46%) and men (56%). About the same number of Oklahoma women reported participating in a drug treatment program (26%) as did the national sample of women (33%) and men (29%).

Findings from California are similar to those described above. About 85% of the women surveyed reported that they had used alcohol, with 28% admitting it had been a problem for them. About 77% had reported using marijuana, with only 11% reporting it was a problem for them. Sixty-three

	Used Substance (%)	Problem in Life (%)
Alcohol	81.20	24.20
Marijuana	73.10	12.40
Heroin	34.90	18.80
Cocaine	60.80	34.90
Crack	41.90	31.70
Speed	29.00	17.20
Inhalants	11.80	3.20
Quaaludes	14.00	2.20
Speedballs	26.30	14.50
LSD	17.70	1.00
PCP	7.00	71.50
Prescription drug	16.70	8.60

Figure 4.1. Drug Use: "Ever Used" and "Perceived Problem"

percent had used cocaine, with 41% indicating it had been a problem. About 50% reported using crack, with one third reporting them as a problem. Just under half had used heroin, with 27% reporting it as a problem. About one third reported using amphetamines, with 19% reporting them as a problem. About 40% reported abusing prescription drugs, with about half reporting them as a problem. More than half (59%) reported trying drugs before the age of 18. About half reported using a needle (Bloom et al., 1994, p. 5).

In the Texas sample, most of the women had used alcohol, marijuana, and cocaine. Interestingly, relatively few reported drugs "as a problem in their life" even though large numbers reported daily use. This perception was related to the type of drug used. In Figure 4.1 it is clear that some drugs were perceived to be problematic whereas other drugs were not.

In the Texas sample, 70.8% of the women used only specific substances and 6.2% reported using anything available to them. About half (52.7%) had used a needle to inject drugs. When the women were questioned about whether they had ever participated in any programs for drugs or alcohol, 73.7% said that they had. About the same percentage (72.6%) responded that they would be interested in participating in a drug or alcohol program in prison and 76.3%

were interested in participating in such a program once they left prison (Pollock et al., 1996).

A study of female homicide offenders found that drugs played a large role in their crime as well. About 90% of the sample had used alcohol, 76% had used marijuana, and 54% had used powdered cocaine. About one third had used alcohol, marijuana, or both regularly, and about one out of four had used cocaine regularly. Overall, 7 out of 10 respondents had used some drug on a regular basis. About three quarters of the crack users, two thirds of the heroin users, and about half of the cocaine users believed they had been addicted to or dependent on the drug. More than half of the crack users reported at least one violent incident associated with the drug (Spunt et al., 1994).

Effects of Drug Abuse

Most female drug offenders have a plethora of health, social, and psychosocial problems in addition to the addiction itself (Wellisch et al., 1994, p. 1). Health problems range from weight loss, dehydration, skin problems, dental problems, gynecological and venereal disease, tuberculosis, hepatitis, to AIDS. One national sample reported that women inmates were more likely than male inmates to test positive for HIV (3.3% compared with 2.1%) (Snell, 1994). Women who used needles to inject drugs were more likely to have HIV than males who used needles (6.7% of women who used a needle were HIV positive compared with 4.7% of men) (Snell, 1994). Many lack the skills or education to support themselves.

Female drug abusers tend to come from families with high levels of mental illness, suicide, alcohol or drug dependency, and violence. They are very likely to have been victims of sexual abuse, rape, or physical abuse. Many are single mothers who receive little or no help from their children's fathers, lack supportive family networks, and have limited financial resources to care for their children. Their children are often under partial or total control of the state protective agency. Most women started using drugs at an early age. Most have been in at least one treatment program, but it has been fairly limited in time and scope (Wellisch et al., 1994, p. 2).

Theories of Addiction

"Self-medication" is one explanation for drug abuse and addiction. In other words, those who abuse drugs do so to blunt or cover the pain, boredom, or frustration of their lives (Fletcher et al., 1993). For women who have experienced physical and sexual abuse as children, drugs or alcohol act to cover their pain and screen their memories.

> It started with alcohol. When you find something that kills pain, you just keep going. Heroin was the one thing. It killed everything. You could be anything and you could be anybody for awhile. (Pollock et al., 1995)

Another explanation is that women are more likely than males to enter into the drug culture through relationships, primarily with boyfriends or husbands.

> I got involved with a man where I was working. . . . I started dating him and he was clean at the time but he had a relapse and I was so busy trying to take care of him, I just . . . what do you say—"if you can't beat 'em, join 'em,"— and I'm curious about it. And I'm thinking that I could control it. So I think that's what really got me started. (Pollock et al., 1995)

Many issues seem to be associated with abuse of alcohol or drugs, including codependency, repressed anger, problems of intimacy, and feelings of powerlessness. If a program merely detoxifies, but does not address these other issues, there is little hope for success. Alcohol and drug dependency may be linked to childhood neglect or abuse. Although this may not be true for all individuals, there certainly is evidence that women in prison fit this profile. A recent National Institute of Justice study found a significant correlation between adult arrests for alcohol and drug-related offenses and childhood victimization (Widom, 1995).

Although most women are not indiscriminate drug users, they often report a progression from alcohol to more serious drugs. Alcohol use typically started early—usually in elementary school and often with the blessing of parents.

> It began with alcohol. My alcohol led to my using marijuana to hallucinogens; from hallucinogens to speed; [from] speed to cocaine, from cocaine to heroin, and all the little things in-between. But the alcoholism also. I know that's what a lot of the guys used with me, to try to get me to experiment sexually, was always alcohol and they made me do things that I wouldn't remember the next day. (Pollock et al., 1995)

Many women in the Texas sample described how their drug use began because they felt disconnected and lonely at school and participated in these activities to "fit in" or be part of the gang. Many women reported that they never felt like they belonged at school and were unhappy as children.

> I went through all the problems of being jumped on after school, and being called a nigger. I became a fighter, though. My sister didn't. She became real withdrawn. . . . I can see where indulging my curiosity and experimenting with alcohol and all those other drugs, marijuana, and LSD, came from wanting to be accepted. Even though I ran track and was pretty good at it, I played first year clarinet, I bowled, I have several trophies in bowling—I never really felt a part of [anything], when I got around drug use, I felt a part of . . . I can't explain it to you. That's the only time I felt accepted. (Pollock et al., 1995)

Beck et al. (1993, p. 52) described the internal motivators of drug use as follows: There is an underlying belief system that "I am unlovable," then life stressors create feelings of anger or anxiety, which lead to drug cravings. Drug and alcohol use is related to pleasure but also to the individual's need to cope with internal and external stress and anxiety. Individuals use such substances to weather stress and combat feelings of loneliness and low self-esteem. Addicts seem to have a lower tolerance for frustration and are more affected when things do not go smoothly and when they are blocked in goal achievement. They are also more likely to have an external locus of control, blaming others or events for failures and misfortune (Beck et al., 1993). According to Inciardi et al. (1993), because drug use is more incompatible with the female's social identity, even infrequent patterns of use may create a deviant label.

> For females, the same kind of drug use [as males] not only violates gender role expectations in and of itself, but it is often interpreted as implying the existence of still other violations—particularly those of sexual misbehavior and emotional instability. Consequently, even a limited number of problematic drug use episodes can spoil a woman's entire social identity, stigmatizing her as wild, promiscuous, unstable. (p. 23)

This, in turn, may make it very difficult for her to develop a healthy self-esteem and prosocial lifestyle, especially after a prison sentence. The woman fulfills a prophecy by continually failing at sobriety and everything else.

Relapse

Alcoholism and drug addiction are very difficult to overcome. The relapse rates for treatment programs illustrate the difficulty of successful recovery. Many of the women in prison have made several attempts to eliminate drugs from their lives. Others admit that during a prison sentence, all they would think about would be getting out and getting that "first hit."

> I had just gotten out of prison the same day I was arrested, and I hadn't even made it home yet. My friend came to pick me up . . . by the time I got back to Houston, I was drunk. I talked him into stopping somewhere so I could buy some drugs, and when I got out, I went in and bought the drugs, and when I came back out to get in the car, the police were there and they were arresting me for P.I. [Public Intoxification]. . . . The cops said I looked like I was drunk. So they took me to the police station, and when they searched me, I had cocaine on me. (Pollock et al., 1995)

Even those who have been through a treatment program in prison may immediately return to drug use. This is especially true for those women who go back to families and neighborhoods where drug use is endemic.

> [I would] make up an excuse, well I'm just going to go see who is down on the corner now. I'm just going to go see the new faces. And 10 minutes after I go down there, 30 minutes later I'm sitting in a hotel room with a needle in my arm. (Pollock et al., 1995)

Offenders often live a vicious cycle in which drug use has created such problems as loss of job, alienation from family, homelessness, deprivation of parental rights, and health problems, all of which then lead the individual to continued use of drugs as a coping mechanism to avoid the serious problems in their lives.

"Hitting Bottom"

For some women, the motivation to change comes from "hitting bottom." As is true with alcohol treatment, many times the individual must experience the truly negative results of his or her behavior before being able to find the will to change. "Enablers" may retard recovery by helping the individual and taking care of the problems that result from alcoholism (or addiction). Enablers for men are wives and family members. Enablers for women are sometimes family members and the succession of men in their lives that give them money and bail them out when they get arrested. When these enablers give up or disappear, the woman is left to her own destruction, which sometimes provides a motivation to change.

> I hit bottom when I left my grandmother's house, see I was staying with my grandmother at first. And my grandmother put me out because I was stealing from her, and I started sleeping on tires that go on cars. At this time I wouldn't even take baths or nothing. That's what I call hitting bottom. I just didn't care. . . . I wasn't thinkin,' period. Because it just made me not think. The only thing it made me think of was just getting some more dope. That's the only thing I was thinking.

> I woke up in this abandoned house, and shooting gallery, where addicts go and shoot drugs. I hadn't taken a bath in about 3 days. My body hygiene was bad. I had destroyed my face from using cocaine. It was just the whole environment, the whole surroundings. I had abscesses on my body from using cocaine also. And I just got tired and. . . . I knew I needed help. I didn't want to live that way anymore.

> The pattern was just the same—day in, day out. It never changed. I would get up, I would be sick. I would have to beg somebody to give me some dope. I would go to the store or I would steal and it would start all over again. I would sell the stuff and I would shoot up all the money I just got and I would go back to the store and I would steal some more. And I would do it again. Late at night when I couldn't go to the store anymore, I would go to the dealer's house, or whoever had the drugs at the time and I would offer myself to them for the coke and heroin. Nine times out of ten it was coke. Finally I got tired. And I called my brother to come and get me. And they picked me up in this little fleabag motel . . . and it's a good thing they did cause according to them I looked like death walking. I was wearing I guess size ones and they were big. I was small, really small. (Pollock et al., 1995)

The prison sentence may constitute bottom for some women, especially if a prison sentence is an aberration from the experiences of their family and friends. For other women, a prison sentence is so common that it may not be perceived as anything more than a temporary rest from their lifestyle. Other women have served several prison sentences and finally reach bottom when they realize how old they are, or how little they have accomplished, or how they have affected their children.

Children: The Motivation to Change

One of the running themes in female prisoners' lives is their guilt over what they have done to their children. In fact, for those who discuss the future and their intent to stay drug free, children form a large part of the motivation. Some women in prison have had children while addicted to drugs (typically crack), causing birth problems for the babies. Many women have lost custody because of their drug use, or their family members have taken the children away from them; many dropped off their children at some family member's house and disappeared for months or years.

It has been reported that 11% of all babies have been exposed to drugs *in utero* (reported in Bagley & Merlo, 1994). The exposure rate may be even higher inasmuch as most studies were done in public hospitals and private hospitals are unwilling to share such statistics with researchers. The effects of drugs are hard to distinguish from other factors, such as poor prenatal care, poor nutrition, smoking, and drinking (Pollock-Byrne & Merlo, 1991). Even so, in the early 1990s there was a move to criminalize drug use during pregnancy. Some prosecutors attempted to use possession or distribution charges. Some states changed the definition of "child" to bring the fetus under the protection of the children's protection service to control the behavior of the woman, and many states passed informant laws that required hospital or medical personnel to report positive toxicology tests. The criminalization approach was rejected by appellate courts as unconstitutional, because the fetus could not be defined as a person; and medical personnel were typically against mandatory reporting if it led to sanctions that would scare pregnant women away from seeking prenatal care.

The other effect of the "crack baby" scare was in sentencing. In several reported cases, judges said on the record that they were incarcerating a woman *because* of her pregnancy so that she would not continue to use drugs and harm the fetus. Women's rights advocates strongly resisted these attempts to "criminalize" a health problem and subject women to unequal treatment under the law. Many pointed out that the harm created by a lack of prenatal care in this country far exceeded the harm created by drug use, yet most nations of Western Europe have more affordable, accessible prenatal care than the United States (Pollock-Byrne & Merlo, 1991). In more recent years, the social problem of "crack babies" has receded from the public's attention and, evidently, policy makers and prosecutors are less interested in the campaign to incarcerate pregnant drug users. The problems of addiction, however, and how they affect children, have not gone away.

Once in prison, sober and able to look back with some introspection over their lives, women suffer great guilt and despair for what their children had to go through and what might be in store for them in the future. Tragically, many women are putting their children through the same type of childhood that they went through with their addict or alcoholic parents.

> Here I am saying I'm not going to grow up and do the same things to my little girl and here I am going the same footsteps. She's going through the same thing I was. . . . There was an incident when she was with me. My mom and dad had custody of her and she'd come to spend some time with me during the Fourth of July. And it got late and my roommate had told me, "Why don't you just let her come spend the night with us." Before I even got anything out, my little girl said, "No, because mommy does needles.". . . . That really got to me, I was like, I could've just died that day. But she loves me. She knows what I'm here for. (Pollock et al., 1995)

Community treatment programs rarely allow children to stay with their mothers and, thus, are not unlike a prison sentence in that they separate the mother and child(ren). No current studies have investigated whether children are beneficial to the success of the treatment or not, and such a study may not be possible, given the very small number of slots available in any given state for mothers with children. It may be that a strong motivator to change is being ignored by not making it easier for women with children to seek treatment. Because many women cannot arrange adequate care for their children while they are in treatment, instead of being a motivator to change, children (and the lack of good alternative placement) are a major deterrent to enter and continue treatment in the community (Wellisch et al., 1994, p. 5).

Treatment Programs in Prison

More than one third of the women in the Oklahoma study had been in at least one treatment program before (Fletcher et al., 1993, p. 49). Nationally, 64% of female inmates who reported abusing drugs had been in at least one treatment program (Snell, 1994). Only about 38% of women in the national sample reported being involved in a drug program at the time of the survey (Snell, 1994). Most inmates indicate that they would like to be in a treatment program, even those who have completed a program in the past (Pollock et al., 1995). Yet despite the numbers of inmates with drug-related crimes, treatment programs do not meet existing needs—either in prison or in the community. In 1991, women made up only 27.5% of all clients in drug and alcohol treatment programs (reported in Bagley & Merlo, 1994, p. 135). In California, with 7,700 female inmates, there were only 120 slots for drug treatment in 1994 (Bloom et al., 1994).

> I basically begged him [judge] to send me somewhere that I could get some help, because I had a problem, and I knew I had a drug problem. And I didn't feel like the pen was rehabilitating. Of course he said that with my record and my priors he couldn't do that. (p. 7)

Reed (1987) points out that in research studies on drug addiction, data on women are typically either ignored, combined with those of men for data analysis, assumed to be the opposite of men, or findings regarding women are not consistent with those for men and so are discarded. Consequently, most descriptions of patterns of addiction are from research on white males. "Street" black males are also targeted for study, but neither description may explain very well the pattern and development of addiction for women. For instance, women with alcohol problems, compared with men with alcohol problems, have been reported as older, having experienced more changes in their family of origin (parental divorce, separation and remarriage, death), with higher levels of conflict with their fathers, more likely to have an alcoholic parent, and more likely to have been sexually abused as children (reported in Bagley & Merlo, 1994).

Early research indicated that female addicts were "sicker, less motivated and more sexually deviant" than male counterparts (Reed, 1987). This, of course, is only true if white males are taken as the "norm." Reed describes female addiction in the following quote:

> They are more likely to acknowledge that they are in trouble, and often report extreme levels of depression and anxiety as well as low self-esteem. They may not recognize that drug dependence is their problem (fueled by the stigma associated with that admission). They may be engaged in behavior that looks very self-destructive, and some may share men's patterns of blaming others and/or circumstances for their situation. More often, however, women drug abusers feel very badly about their lives, and may even be blaming themselves for things they are unable to change. (p. 155)

Treatment programs include residential halfway houses, outpatient hospital or private provider programs, inpatient hospital programs, prison or jail programs, and a combination of the above. Therapeutic interventions typically involve some type of group work or therapeutic community, along with individual counseling, and possibly chemical (Antabuse, Methadone) or nutritional support. Social learning models and cognitive therapy models are also used.

There are many barriers to successful treatment. Those programs that deal with criminal justice clients may have unwilling participants who are only there because of their prison sentence or, if it is a community program, because of a court order. Drug abusers typically do not openly disclose their feelings and tend to hide drug use, even if there are no court or sentencing consequences. The individual may even continue criminal activities during the course of treatment, such as selling drugs or being involved in a criminal lifestyle. Therapists are typically viewed as part of the "system" and distrusted. Denial is extremely difficult to overcome. There may be social, ethnic, racial, and cultural differences between the therapist and the client. Finally, therapists may harbor negative stereotypes of clients, in terms of their criminal lifestyle and their drug use (Beck et al., 1993, p. 54).

Prison programs suffer from bureaucratic snafus that may disrupt treatment. For instance, groups may be delayed because of lockdowns due to clearing "counts." What this means is that if a therapy group is supposed to start at 2:00 p.m., it is not at all unusual that the count that is taken after lunch cannot be reconciled and inmates are held in place until "count clears." This may take 20 minutes or 2 hours. Inmates are transferred or are sent to punitive segregation, preventing their attendance. Because any confessions in treatment regarding continued drug use constitute institutional infractions, it is difficult for the female prisoner to be truthful in a group or even in an individual counseling relationship. Kochis (1994) discusses therapists' frustration when the institution does not seem to place a priority on therapy, instead pulling women out of groups for routine medical exams, medication distribution, or other administrative reasons. Further, if there are no controls on participants, female prisoners may simply choose not to come to programs, instead staying in bed or watching television.

Twelve-Step Programs

Twelve-step programs, such as Alcoholics Anonymous (AA) and Narcotics Anonymous (NA), are probably the most well-known and common in prison. Sometimes they are the only treatment programs available. Founded in 1935, Alcoholics Anonymous has been the model for a multitude of self-help programs to combat forms of addiction, including drugs, sex, overeating, and gambling. The programs offer a social support network for recovery and guidance for working through such issues as denial and self-esteem (Zweben, 1995). These programs rely on the following principles:

- admission of powerlessness over addiction
- reliance on a higher power
- conducting a moral inventory
- admission to a higher power and others of wrongs
- asking for forgiveness and making amends
- conducting a personal inventory
- prompt admission of wrongs
- prayer and meditation
- spiritual awakening (Kratcoski, 1994).

The worth of such programs depends on the extent of supervision by staff and the commitment of the particular group of inmates involved. Some AA and NA group meetings are little more than social hours; others are powerful influences on the women's ability to conquer addiction. Informal opinions of some therapists indicate that women may be less helped by AA groups than men (at least in those groups outside of prison), because public admission is more threatening to women, who also tend to allow males to control the meetings and take on a fairly subservient role. In a women's prison, however, the groups are single sex and might be more effective for that reason. One advantage of AA and NA is that they are treatment modalities that can be continued outside the prison. Practically every town and city now has an established AA group that the inmate can attend on release.

On the other hand, Twelve-Step programs do not include trained therapists; and they do not offer the individual guidance and direction that individual counseling does. No "cross talk" means that members are not supposed to challenge, confront, or inquire when another member is sharing his or her experiences. Whereas this may provide a comfortable setting in which no one feels afraid to share, it also means that members must conduct their own analysis of the experience with little guidance (Zweben, 1995).

Cognitive Therapy

Cognitive approaches have been described as collaborative, active, based on open-ended questioning, and highly structured and focused. Basically, the treatment approach is to undermine underlying dysfunctional beliefs (for instance, "I can't control my drug use") through specific techniques. A "case formulation" is the composite of information that helps the therapist understand the underlying belief systems that are instrumental in how the individual perceives the world, makes decisions, and behaves. This case formulation includes the following: relevant childhood data, current life problems, core beliefs or schemata, conditional assumptions or beliefs or rules, compensatory strategies, vulnerable situations, automatic thoughts and beliefs, emotions and behaviors, and the integration of the above data to form explanations of how the individual's belief systems are preventing him or her from accomplishing behavioral goals (Beck et al., 1993).

The strengths of cognitive therapy include the following:

1. aids in modifying beliefs that exacerbate cravings;
2. ameliorates negative affective states (anger, anxiety, hopelessness);
3. teaches patients to apply a battery of cognitive and behavioral skills and techniques;
4. helps patients go beyond abstinence to make fundamental changes in the way they view themselves, their life, and helps create new lifestyles (Beck et al., 1993).

During therapy, techniques such as Socratic questioning (of beliefs or conclusions based on faulty perceptions) are used along with "homework" such as making lists of advantages or disadvantages of a particular decision, recording daily thoughts, and clarifying the client's formulation of the problem. For instance, the following questions help to develop objective responses to automatic thoughts (such as "I can't control my drug use."):

1. What concrete factual evidence supports or refutes my automatic thoughts? Beliefs?
2. Are there other ways I could view this situation and is there a blessing in disguise?
3. What is the worst thing that could happen? What is the best thing? What is most likely to realistically happen?
4. What constructive action can I take to deal with the situation?
5. What are the pros and cons of my changing the way I view this situation?
6. What helpful advice would I give my best friend if he or she were in this situation? (Beck et al., 1993, p. 144)

The goal of therapy is to help the individual improve problem-solving capabilities instead of responding to the emotions engendered by automatic thoughts. Relaxation techniques are also used, as drug use (especially relapse) can be a response to outside stress. Various forms of other coping mechanisms can be used to resist urges to use drugs, including

1. Distraction—During an urge to use drugs, the individual could engage in a pleasurable activity that would take his or her mind off drugs, such as play with his or her child, go shopping, or some other nondrug-related activity.

2. Flashcards—These could be index cards with statements written on them, such as "I will lose my child if I take drugs again." These are then carried with the individual to be a visual reminder and help keep him or her on track.

3. Imagery—The client uses either negative image replacement (imagining the negative consequences of drug use) or positive image replacement (imagining the positive consequences of resisting the craving).

4. Learning how to rationally respond to urge-related automatic thoughts—Techniques include using the questions above to analyze a decision to use drugs.

5. Activity scheduling—Organizing one's day to provide a balance of work and pleasure will prevent boredom and increase good feelings about oneself.

6. Relaxation training—As mentioned before, many of those who relapse do so because of anxiety created by life's problems. If the individual can learn alternative coping mechanisms, there will be less reason to return to drug use (Beck et al., 1993).

In the narrative below, the stressors that are all too common in female prisoners' lives are described. If the female prisoner has not learned to cope with such situations she will inevitably return to drug use (Beck et al., 1993).

> I am at my mother's house with my daughter and my mother is ragging on me for not having a job. She is calling me all kinds of names: "lazy," "worthless"; you know the list. Anyway, I feel this urge to run, but I know there's no where to go. I want to hit her but of course I don't. I want to cry, but I wouldn't give her the satisfaction of seeing that she has hurt me. And finally I start thinking about going to Michelle's house. She always knows where to find some shit. I think: "That's the one thing that will get me feeling better." I know that I can leave my daughter with my mother while I go out to get high. (p. 184)

Successful drug intervention must help the individual learn to control such thoughts, rebut them with rational analysis, and conquer the urges that lead to relapse.

Eclectic Programs

Most programs combine elements taken from several treatment approaches.

One such program was described by Kochis (1994). The Treatment Alternative to Prison Program (TAP) was a 52 session, 4-month program for women in a county jail. Several types of offenders were involved, including court referred, those serving a sentence, and those awaiting trial. The first phase of the program dealt with educating the participants on the disease concept of addiction; how to use positive confrontation and the importance of recognizing and combating denial. Phases Two and Three used the group process and dealt with personal issues of addiction, and the last phase covered relapse prevention.

Obviously, addiction is not an isolated problem and, therefore, treatment programs are multidimensional, dealing with a range of pragmatic and interpersonal issues. One of the elements of all programs is getting the individual to recognize and come to terms with emotions. Addicts are often suppressors and refuse to confront the realities of fear, anger, or frustration.

> Because when you are involved in an addiction, there are so many feelings that you suppress. That is why a lot of these women have been drugging and they haven't come to terms with a lot of issues of neglect, abandonment, not receiving enough love. That's why we talk about it. That's what this problem is about—addressing emotions and the feelings, as well as our addiction.

> There's a process here that's called the burying process. We actually have a funeral for your addiction, your pain, your fears. You'd be surprised at actually seeing nothing on the table physically, but after awhile you start to see your pain, you see your fears, you see your drug of choice. Bury it. And there's a grieving process. You go through that. It's just like when you lose a loved one. You grieve awhile, but you go on. (Pollock et al., 1995)

Specific elements of programs may include classes or discussions in personal empowerment, HIV and AIDS education, sexual abuse, battering, parenting, family planning, and legal services (Wellisch et al., 1994, p. 4). In Table 4.1, essential elements of a good drug treatment program are identified.

Because addiction may be symptomatic of other problems, detoxification and treating the drug use through rational educational means is not enough. In the following quote, a woman eloquently explains the complexity of addiction.

> I don't need anyone telling me how not to do drugs. I know how not to do drugs. I needed to be able to learn how to live life on life's terms. How to cope with life. Bam! My mother passes away. Bam! Say my daughter gets pregnant. Bam! The car broke down. I got fired from my job. I couldn't deal with it. I did not know how to cope. So I knew how to medicate myself. I knew how to just hide

Table 4.1   Services for Alcohol and Drug Dependent Women

---

1. Medical/Health
Diagnosis and treatment of problems
Gynecological services
Psychiatric assessment—coexisting disorders; agoraphobia, severe depression, eating
    disorders
Health promotion—taking control of the body, assertiveness with health care providers
Prescription drug dependency
Body image issues related to health
Pregnancy-related services

2. Child Related
Child care
Services to children—assessment, referral, education, treatment
Parenting education

3. Family Services
Wellness education
Relationship counseling
Work and education on CD family dynamics; Alanon

4. Vocational
Job readiness skills
Skills training
Job seeking support and training

5. Skill Training to Develop Self-Esteem and Coping
Assertiveness training
Financial management
Personal goal setting
Stress and crisis management
Communication skills, interpersonal skills, relationships
Gender and socialization skills
Other survival skills, for example, transportation

6. Chemical Dependency Education
Physical, social, and family consequences of the disease/disorder
Preparation for self-help programs

7. Legal Assistance
Criminal issues—prostitution
Drunk driving
Civil Matters—child custody, marital/domestic violence, financial, landlord, harassment

8. Sexuality and Intimacy
Sexuality and drugs
Counseling about fear of intimacy
Incest, rape survivor issues
Support groups
"Loving too much" issues

Adapted from "Developing Women-Sensitive Drug Dependence Treatment Services: Why So Difficult," by
B. G. Reed, 1987, *Journal of Psychoactive Drugs, 19*(2), p. 164.

all those little feelings. This program not only teaches you how to cope with being an addict, but they work with me on my self-esteem. I am somebody today. I am a very special person. Inside and out. And it doesn't matter I used to go around people-pleasing, it doesn't matter what people think of me today as long as I know that I'm a good person and that I've got a lot of self-worth. (Pollock et al., 1995)

One element of drug treatment programs that is often missing is some type of response to the purely pragmatic needs of addicts. Issues of jobs, income, housing, and transportation often form insurmountable barriers that lead to relapse. In a National Institute of Justice study of treatment programs for female addicts, fewer than 50% of the programs provided any transitional services, that is, housing, financial, employment, or legal assistance (Wellisch et al., 1994, p. 5). This is especially problematic for those who leave a prison treatment program. Going from a situation in which all aspects of life are controlled and taken care of and there are no financial worries, to release when rent is due, jobs are hard to find, and children need new school clothes, is tremendously stressful.

In their study of drug treatment programs for women offenders Wellisch et al. (1994) concluded that

- More treatment programs are available than in the past, but the numbers have not kept pace with the need.
- Many programs do not address the multiple problems of drug offenders.
- Treatment is usually limited in duration and intensity.
- Most treatment programs are single sex.
- There is a need for more transitional programs to help in adjustment to the community.
- There is a need for more family services few programs have accommodations for infants and children.

Success seems to be positively related to time spent in treatment, with the longer treatment programs having greater success rates (Wellisch et al., 1994, p. 5). Hirschel and Keny (1990) reported that the factor with the strongest association with program success seems to be length. The longer programs and the longer an addict stays in a program are correlated with more successful results than shorter treatment periods. It was also found that a continuum of treatment with segments occurring after release from prison were more effective than shorter programs.

In one such program that involved treatment continuing in halfway houses after prison release, 71% of program participants were arrest free and 76%

were drug free after 18 months. This compares to 30% of a control group being arrest free and 19% of them drug free. In a sample who had received prison treatment, but no follow-up after release, the respective percentages were 48% and 30% (National Institute of Justice, 1996a). Thus, there is information available on what works in drug treatment and evidence that some programs are successful in helping addicts change their lives. What is needed is public willingness to fund and support such programs. Unfortunately, the current governmental response seems to be punishment rather than treatment. Harsher drug laws, more prisons, and longer sentences are routinely provided as "answers" to the drug or crime problem. Because a prison bed costs $91,991 compared with $11,004 for a drug treatment bed, it seems to be a very poor way to solve the problem of drug addiction in this country (reported in Bagley & Merlo, 1994).

No woman enjoys the degradation, dependence, and despair of addiction; no addict chooses that lifestyle freely.

> I never wanted to be an addict. It's not like I wake up every day and say, "OK here's another day I am gonna go out and be a good addict." It was never like that. Every day that I was out there, doing things I was doing, I never wanted to do it. I couldn't understand how come I couldn't change it. What's wrong? Why can't I do what I want to do? (Pollock et al., 1995)

Implications for Counselors

Drugs are a real problem in today's world. There is a strong link between drug use or addiction and criminal behavior. A large number of men and women in this country's prisons and jails are there because of their drug use. Women may present a different profile of addiction in that several studies seem to indicate they are more likely to come from abusive backgrounds and have situational motivations for drug use. They also seem to be more amenable to treatment, admitting guilt and experiencing blame and shame in relation to their addiction, especially as it affects their children. Treatment programs for women are inadequate, in number and in intensity and length. Prison programs are usually full and with waiting lists to get in. Despite political rhetoric that we have "mollycoddled" criminal addicts, the facts indicate that there has never been a comprehensive, sincere attempt to provide treatment programs as the state response to criminal lawbreaking. Although the public may decide that broken laws deserve punishment, they should not be surprised if the individuals go back to the addictive patterns and criminal lifestyle engaged in before prison, if prison involves merely paying lip service to the need for drug or alcohol treatment.

Drug abusers and alcoholics are difficult people to treat in a counseling relationship. All of the problems of treating drug users are exacerbated in a prison setting with offenders as clients. Addicts are generally described as distrustful, but in prison distrust approaches paranoia. Addicts are described as dishonest. Prisoners, one might argue, have even more to lose by telling the truth. Group work is extremely difficult because of the prisoner subculture and the number of offenders who are only participating because of some external pressure. The counselor in a prison setting will initially be distrusted and seen as the "enemy." Only by carefully and consistently developing a trusting relationship will this initial presumption be overcome, and one can only develop trust by acting trustworthy. This means that one's behavior must be fair, consistent, and have integrity. Returning phone calls, being on time, not making promises about confidentiality, and not promising favors that cannot be granted are some of the ways counselors can gain trust. Further, by focusing on the goals of treatment, one avoids the possibility of manipulation or being distracted by other issues unless clearly relevant. The counselor who uses humility and empathy, who confronts but doesn't accuse, and who does not use his or her position or power to avoid clients will eventually be seen as trustworthy by many prisoners.

It is important for the correctional professional to understand the linkage between the offender's drug or alcohol use and her criminality. Criminality may have preceded drug use or, alternatively, drug use may be the only form of criminality an individual engaged in. Continued exposure to the drug subculture predisposes an individual to an antisocial outlook, but some women in prison are more or less conventional in their values and opinions; it is only drug use that has placed them in a criminal justice setting. On the other hand, some women have criminalistic values and drug use is only one element of a lifestyle that does not conform to societal norms. As pointed out before, although drug use seems to be endemic to criminal populations, it should not be assumed that criminality is caused by the drug use. Regardless of the relationship with criminality, problems in this area should be addressed throughout treatment.

Although female prisoners are imprisoned, there are still opportunities for obtaining illicit drugs. Women's prisons have been reported to have less contraband (including drugs) than men's prisons, but a certain amount is always present (Pollock-Byrne, 1990). The presence of drugs ensures that the woman in a drug program is exposed to the risk of temptation. Because drugs are available in prison, there is some opportunity to practice control over one's urges and evaluate the success of treatment or counseling. Nevertheless, there are obviously major differences between the temptations presented by a prison environment and those presented by the outside world. The true test of a woman's commitment to a drug-free lifestyle will always have to wait until release.

Issues of HIV and AIDS are intertwined with drug use. Many women contract the disease either by sharing needles or indiscriminate sexual activity in pursuit of drugs. While in prison, they are diagnosed and so are dealing with the newfound knowledge of carrying the disease, as well as dealing with issues of drug dependency (Wallace, 1995). The counselor will need to help some women come to terms with a diagnosis of AIDS and the consequent issues that emerge from such a diagnosis. Although such information is held confidential in prisons, counselors generally have access to such information for treatment purposes.

All evidence indicates that the counselor involved in drug counseling female offenders will also need to be sensitive to and deal with issues of incest, childhood sexual abuse and neglect, and other forms of personal victimization. If these underlying problems are not resolved, drug addiction may simply be replaced by food addictions, change in drug of choice, or other forms of dysfunctional behavior. "Compulsive and destructive behaviors may represent elaborate defensive strategies relied on by women to block painful affects and memories. The potential, spontaneous emergence of affects, impulses, and images represents a legacy of past trauma" (Wallace, 1995, p. 480).

In the next chapter, we will explore problems of incest and childhood abuse in more detail, as well as other issues dealing with offenders' families.

5

Family Issues and Treatment Approaches

My father was an alcoholic and my mother was divorced from him when I was 6 years old so I don't really remember him, I only remember he stayed drunk all the time and he would beat my mother. And she got a divorce from him and was remarried when I was seven. My stepfather seemed to be a real caring person. But it led to where it seem[ed] like he cared too much, and he ended up raping me when I was 9 years old. . . . I told [my mother] but she didn't believe me . . . she said I was lying, and I was trying to get her to make him leave because I didn't like him. So this went on for 2 years. And by the time I was 11, I kept running away from home. But the police would come find me, and take me back home. And she would start crying, and asking, "Why are you running away? You are driving me crazy, having to worry about you." And I told her I would keep running away forever as long as he lived there, because I didn't want to put up with the sexual abuse that was happening.

Pollock et al. (1995)

Dysfunctional families are self-perpetuating. The women who experience the type of childhood described in the previous quote have great difficulty emerging as well-adjusted adults who can be loving mothers to their own children or have healthy and positive relationships with partners. It should be stated at the outset that the majority of individuals who experience sexual and physical abuse as children do not end up in prison, and many people in prison have not had a childhood marked by abuse or neglect. One can overcome such a childhood and become a positive contributing member of society with a healthy parenting style. Nevertheless, physical abuse, sexual abuse, and neglect are all too often the precursors to a criminal lifestyle.

Childhood Abuse

Rosenbaum (1989) reviewed research that identified a link between family dysfunction and delinquency and added to such research with her study of a sample of female delinquents in the California Youth Authority. The correlation between abuse, neglect, or both, and delinquency has been identified by the earliest research in criminology. Further, many studies support the notion that female delinquents are more likely than male delinquents to have grown up in dysfunctional families. In effect, it is believed that females are more likely to have been influenced by family problems than males (Seydlitz, 1993).

In an ongoing study funded by the National Institute of Justice, the National Institute of Alcohol Abuse and Alcoholism, and the National Institute of Mental Health, a sample of 1,575 victims of abuse or neglect have been monitored since 1986 along with a control group matched on gender, age, race, and family socioeconomic status. To date, 48% of those who were identified as abused or neglected have been arrested, 18% for a violent crime, compared with 38% of the control group, with 14% arrested for a violent crime. There seems to be little difference whether the child is abused or neglected in this pattern of consequent delinquency (National Institute of Justice, 1996b).

Widom (1989, 1991, 1995) also reported on a longitudinal study of the relationship between abuse or neglect and later delinquency. She found that abuse is correlated with offending, at a statistically significant level. Whereas 26% of the sample were arrested as juveniles, only 16% of the control group were arrested. Nevertheless, there was less of a difference for adult arrests—28.6% versus 21% respectively (Widom, 1995, p. 5). It was found that those who were sexually abused were no more likely than those who were physically abused or neglected to commit sex crimes, except for the crime of prostitution, which was significantly correlated to childhood sexual abuse (Widom, 1995, p. 5).

Smith and Thornberry (1995) also reviewed the research on childhood abuse and delinquency and contributed their own findings to the body of literature. Using a sample drawn from the Rochester Youth Development Study (a massive, longitudinal study of delinquency), they identified those individuals who had official records indicating they had been victimized either by abuse or neglect. They then compared this abused sample with those who had not been abused and discovered that 45% of the abused group had committed delinquent acts (measured by official acts of delinquency) whereas only 31.7% of the nonabused group had been officially identified as delinquent.

The California study of female prisoners referred to in earlier chapters also explored the relationship between childhood abuse and adult criminality. Using their sample of California female inmates, researchers identified a correlation between childhood abuse (physical, sexual, and emotional) and violent crime. Those female prisoners who were abused as children were nearly twice as likely to be serving a sentence for a violent crime than those who reported no abuse (Bloom, Lee, & Owen, 1995).

The studies that explore the relationship between childhood abuse and adult criminality must overcome a number of methodological problems. Obviously one cannot assume that because large numbers of prisoners have been victims, the victimization led to criminality, because we must also consider how many people who have not committed crimes have also been victimized by childhood abuse. Most studies rely on official reports of abuse and also official reports of delinquency—this reliance on official records may underestimate the amount of abuse and delinquency. Also, families in which abuse takes place also may have other correlates of crime, for instance, criminal parents or siblings, alcoholism, addiction, separation, and so on. Thus, it is hard to separate the effects of the abuse from the other elements of that particular upbringing. Some studies have attempted to deal with this issue by studying siblings (when one has been identified as a victim of abuse or neglect), however, it seems obvious that the family dynamics that lead to one sibling being abused must also affect the other siblings, even if they are not reported to official agencies as victims.

> I have five brothers. Three of them was in the penitentiary. . . . One was on robbery, two was on drugs and my baby brother still going to school. He's 17. And I have a baby sister and she has two husbands that have been killed in the last 2 months since I've been locked up. . . . They took her children, she's an addict also. (Pollock et al., 1995)

As the quote above indicates, many women in prison have lived lives marked by imprisonment, addiction, alcoholism, and death. The individual who grows up in such an environment learns dysfunctional coping skills and deviant value systems from parents and other family members. If they are victims of neglect and abuse, they learn to deal with such abuse by disassociation, self-medication with drugs or alcohol, hypersexuality in a search for affection, or other dysfunctional behavior patterns.

As discussed earlier, studies show that anywhere from one third to three fourths of a female prison population report prior sexual, physical, or both abuses (see Chapter 1). Often these women have never sought assistance to help them with the personal trauma that this victimization may induce. There is a link between childhood sexual abuse and various kinds of addictive behavior (drugs, alcohol, and eating disorders). Effects of childhood sexual abuse include low self-esteem, depression, troubled relationships, abusive relationships, sexual dysfunctions, and dependence on drugs and alcohol (Young, 1995, p. 456). Victims may seek out relationships with abusive men; and they may have great difficulty developing any intimate relationships at all.

Incest survivors may suppress memories and never make a link between what happened to them during childhood and the negative choices they make in their adult life. It may be while in some form of prison counseling, in fact, when they are free from the influence of drugs and are inclined to be more introspective, that they first acknowledge such abuse. Counselors should be sensitive to the possibility of childhood victimization, even if the woman does not bring out such information. Some women paint a perfect picture of their childhood, and it is only when they become comfortable and discuss specific incidents that the reality begins to emerge. Although such victimization must be admitted before one can heal, the woman herself must choose when to bring out such information. The prison counselor must help incest survivors understand how early victimization has affected their self-concept and life choices. Programs are beginning to become available to deal with these issues.

Programs for Survivors of Incest and Physical Abuse

One solution-based therapy model proposed for victims of abuse focuses on (a) a thorough assessment and identification of maladaptive coping strategies, (b) developing the therapist-client relationship as quickly as possible using neurolinguistic programming (NLP), (c) empowering the client throughout the assessment and treatment process, (d) teaching the client to express feelings appropriately, (e) integration of various aspects of the traumatic experience and of the self, and (f) cognitive restructuring aimed at success in the present and sorting out or letting go of past trauma (Solomon & Heide, 1994).

The authors used an assessment tool they developed that identifies the presence of any of the following coping strategies: disassociation, running away, alcohol, drugs, food, compulsive behavior, traumatic reenactment that may involve self-mutilation or taking risks so that someone else will inflict the injury, and suicidal gestures. The severity of the trauma is assessed (looking at such variables as age of onset, duration, frequency, predictability, number and intimacy of perpetrators, intrusiveness of abuse and sadism, among other factors). Symptoms of severe trauma include high tolerance for pain, numbing or otherwise suppressing feelings, fear of emotional intimacy, intense self-hate, self-defeating behavior, self-mutilating behavior, and suicidal gestures. There also may be psychosomatic illnesses and symptoms of post-traumatic stress disorder (i.e., exaggerated startle response and flashbacks).

Survivors of abuse tend to have dysfunctional cognitive patterns, that is, black and white thinking (someone is either good or bad), to react catastrophically (if something negative occurs, it is blown out of proportion in degree of seriousness), to personalize ("why does this always happen to me"), to engage in magical thinking and trance logic (i.e., hurting oneself will avoid pain from others). The survivor may not remember the abuse or remember it as happening to someone else with herself as an observer. Flashbacks or nightmares may be the only memory when she may feel the pain and terror of the experience. In dysfunctional families, children learn to hide feelings, especially their rage. Impulsive or compulsive behavior is also common with survivors of abuse.

These behaviors are maladaptive and are addressed in the intervention model in the following way: First, the types of maladaptive coping strategies are identified, then goals are established (that are specific and measurable). The client, through setting goals and working through homework, is empowered to be in control of her own treatment. Various techniques are used to move the client to a more developed stage of competence. For instance, she may be asked to imagine when she felt most competent or in control (guided visual imagery) and use the experience to recover those feelings. She may be asked to exaggerate her feelings or put them in a box to control them. Through the interaction with the therapist, the client learns to take control over her memories and her coping strategies (Solomon & Heide, 1994).

Another study of a treatment program for survivors of incest and abuse reported on a 16-week program using a didactic support model administered by two clinicians in a prison for women. It was found that self-esteem and trust in people significantly increased, alienation significantly decreased, and a measure of internal-external locus of control showed that there was a move toward internal locus of control, although it did not reach the significance level (Sulton & Long, 1988, p. 140).

Most prisoners report that there is a need for programs to help them deal with issues of prior abuse. One issue, however, is the difficulty of trust in a prison environment. Because many women in prison have spent a lifetime denying the events of their childhood, it is very difficult for them to share these experiences. In a prison environment, trusting other women with such information, as is necessary in a group therapy program, is extremely problematic.

This is not to say that group therapy is not a powerful tool in helping women with such backgrounds. Very often they experience great relief from knowing that other women have led similar lives and suffered similar pains. Nevertheless, the prison subculture of nondisclosure and lack of trust works against group therapy and it takes a skilled and sensitive group leader to create an environment that would discourage breaches of confidence and encourage openness. It would probably be best to let such a group form naturally, not require attendance, and carefully select the women through individual case-work relationships.

Prisoners as Partners and Parents

There is no question that incarceration is extremely detrimental to family ties. There also seems to be little question that family ties are important for the prevention of recidivism (van Voorhis, Braswell, & Morrow, 1992). Research indicates that the loss of family and relationships is an extreme deprivation of prison life. This comes out clearly in studies of female inmates, but it is true for male inmates as well (Hairston, 1991). It is interesting, then, that there is so little effort on the part of correctional administrators to make family visitation more conducive to maintaining family connections. The thousands upon thousands of family members of prisoners are ignored, for the most part, and their needs are of little concern to the public at large or correctional officials.

Divorce is common for prisoners with spouses on the outside. Although no good statistics exist for how many divorces occur during the period of imprisonment, one study reported that 75% of male prisoners who were married at the time of arrest became divorced sometime during their imprisonment (Hairston, 1991). No similar statistics seem to be available for women, but fewer women are in relationships with partners on entry into prison, and fewer plan to return to a relationship on release. For instance, in the California study, the majority of inmates sampled were single, with about 42% never having been married (Bloom et al., 1994, p. 5). In the Texas sample, only 17% were currently married (Pollock et al., 1996).

One indication of the deterioration of a marriage relationship is the frequency of visitation. Hairston (1991) reports on several studies that found that visitation decreased over time for long termers. Other studies that analyzed marital communication found that the relationship deteriorated in intimacy over time. In the Texas sample, 38.7% said they had someone on the outside they considered their partner and with whom they maintained contact.

Of those women who said they were in such a relationship, only 14% said they had ever had a telephone conversation with that person, only 20% said they had received a visit from the person, and only 22% received a letter at least once a week (Pollock et al., 1996).

Communication with other family members was not much better. Of the women surveyed, 16.1% called their families every 3 months, 11% called them every month and the rest of the women never or randomly called their families. Seventy percent of the women were never visited by a family member and only 10% had sporadic visits. About half (45.3%) received letters from family members at least once a week, 11% received letters at least once every 2 weeks, and about 10% (9.9%) received letters at least once a month. The rest received letters less than once a month or sporadically (Pollock et al., 1996).

One of the most consistent patterns one observes in the relationships of women in prison with intimate partners is their tendency to pick men who abuse and exploit them. Even some women themselves explain that if they had a relationship with a man who seemed supportive, hardworking, and did not abuse them, they left these men for others who would then treat them badly.

> We met in a club in North Montreal and because he was big and maybe because he was crude, I don't know, I was attracted to him. I fell in love with him and when I'm in love with somebody, I'll do anything. If you tell me to go slap the person across the street, if I'm really in love I'll go and do it. And that was the problem, I had no judgment at all. So even though I knew it was wrong, I started helping him with his crimes. I thought I was being brave and gutsy. . . . I certainly wasn't getting a future, or stability or security. But I was always hoping that one day he would change or love me enough that he would go straight. (Adelberg & Currie, 1987, p. 76)

Women are sometimes introduced to the drug subculture through a relationship with a male partner. They may eventually take an active role in selling drugs, and some women continue such activities even if the relationship breaks up. Others, however, are arrested for crimes that they committed arguably because (and only because) of such a relationship. Although society cannot excuse such women from legal culpability, these issues are extremely important for counselors to know and incorporate into a treatment approach. Such women tend to find other similar men on release if they have not learned what motivates them to seek out such partners.

> I was scared. I stayed with him because I was scared of him killing me or doing something bad to me or my family. At the end I was in a love affair that had

turned into a scary nightmare. He used to beat me up and that was another
reason I liked to take drugs—it made me feel like everything was okay. Even
when I was black and blue, if I was on drugs, I felt like it didn't matter.
(Adelberg & Currie, 1987, p. 77)

Once the woman is in prison, the relationship with the partner disinte-
grates; nevertheless, many women repeat this pattern over and over again.
Examining "lifescripts" in groups or individual therapy is very helpful to
illustrate the similarities and repetitiveness of her relationships. There does
not seem to be the same pattern of exploitation and abuse in homosexual
relationships, and some women will describe a relationship started in a prison
with another female prisoner as the only relationship in her life when she felt
loved instead of used.

Several studies have been conducted on the number of women who are in
prison for killing abusive spouses (Browne, 1987; Ewing, 1987). There have
even been moves in certain states to reevaluate prison sentences if there is
evidence that the homicide was related to domestic abuse and a few women
have had their sentences commuted (Pollock-Byrne, 1990). The "battered
woman" syndrome has become fairly well accepted in the courts as a defense
for a charge of murder (Hale & Menniti, 1994). Nevertheless, women continue
to be sent to prison for voluntary manslaughter or homicide, even when there
is evidence of abuse and self-defense.

Women serving prison sentences for killing abusive partners may have
loved their partners, even though they felt they had to kill them, and so they
are suffering from guilt as well as the trauma of a prison sentence. They may
have children and have difficulty explaining to their children what happened.
Very often they do not have a criminal outlook or background and find the
prison experience traumatic. Counseling for such women can include education on the battering cycle and a treatment approach that will help them deal
with guilt and repair self-esteem. Counseling can address these issues and reduce the possibility that these women will seek out other abusive men on release.

Children

About three quarters of women in prison are mothers. There is no doubt
that the biggest difference in the "pains of imprisonment" between men and
women is the impact of incarceration on their relationship with their children.
Women consistently report that the people most important to them are their
children (Crawford, 1988).

Women experience and relate overwhelming feelings of despair, frustration, and depression related to their imprisonment and subsequent inability to care for their children. These feelings occur even though many women were not good mothers before their incarceration. Drugs, lifestyle, or both, often resulted in the mother offender abdicating her parental role to her mother or other caregivers. She may have abandoned her children to pursue a life in the drug culture or her children may have been placed with foster parents. She may have exposed her children to drugs either during pregnancy or after birth. Once in prison, however, women have the time and clarity of mind to think about their children and their failings regarding them. Unfortunately, the incarceration experience sometimes is a fatal blow to parent-child relationships. The concern of prisoners that the state will take their children away is a very real one, although imprisonment in and of itself is not grounds for the deprivation of parental rights (McGowan & Blumenthal, 1976; Stanton, 1980). Most prisoners (both males and females) are parents. Most plan to reunite with their children on release, although statistics vary widely in this regard, all the way from 34% to 88%, as reported by Hairston (1991, p. 92).

Historically, the responsibility of children was taken into account when sentencing. Women, arguably, were sentenced less severely if they had been responsible parents before their sentencing. More recently, courts have seemed to ignore this issue in a "gender blind" approach to sentencing. Mandatory sentences, determinate sentence systems, and guidelines, as in the federal system, ignore these essential differences between men and women. Family responsibilities, for instance, are not *ordinarily* relevant when sentencing under federal guideline rules (only when the situation is "extraordinary" can the court consider these circumstances). Because it is not "extraordinary" for a female offender to be a single parent, evidently her responsibilities cannot be taken into account. The opposing argument, of course, is that it is statistically extraordinary for a criminal offender to be the single parent with responsibility when considering all offenders—male as well as female. Because 91% of male offenders, but only 33% of female offenders, report that their children currently live with the other parent, it should be important to take this issue into consideration when sentencing females (Raeder, 1993).

Raeder (1993) reported that case law is not consistent on this issue, but it appears that hostility from appellate courts toward decisions when judges did take family responsibilities into account has reduced the number of sentences adjusted downward for single mothers. This, despite legislative intent for such an exception. Thus, sex "neutral" sentencing actually has more of a negative effect on women and their children.

When women are incarcerated, visitation is extremely problematic and, again, there is evidence that they are in a worse position than men in their ability to maintain ties with their children while in prison. Most states have only one prison for women, so they are usually farther away from families. In a 1980 study, it was found that only 37% of responding women's institutions made special allowances for those relatives or visitors who could not make the regular visiting time periods (Neto & Ranier, 1983). Weisheit (1985) reported that 25 out of 36 responding institutions allowed weekend visits with children. Twenty of these provided transportation to and from the prison. Thus, it may be that the opportunities are expanding.

Only about one third of mothers in prison see their children at least once a month (Hairston, 1991). In one national study it was reported that about 46% of women had telephone contact with their children at least once a week, but only about 9% had visits with their children once a week. More than half (52%) reported *never* receiving a visit from their children during their prison term (Snell, 1994).

The most frequent reason cited for the absence of visitation is distance and difficulty (Hairston, 1991). Fathers in prison see their children even less often than mothers in prison (Hairston, 1991). Nevertheless, it is also true that the children of fathers in prison are usually being taken care of by their mothers in a stable environment that was not torn apart by the imprisonment. Many children of fathers were estranged from them before the imprisonment and this is less often the case for women in prison. Even if the child was not living with the mother, typically a relationship was disrupted by the mother's imprisonment. Koban (1983) compared inmate mothers and fathers and reached the following conclusions:

1. Female offenders have closer relationships with their children prior to incarceration than do male offenders.
2. Women's relationships with their children are more affected by incarceration.
3. Women prisoners experienced a "significant disadvantage" compared with male prisoners in attempting to maintain contact and had reunification problems because of this.
4. More mothers than fathers received at least one visit, but the visits to mothers decreased over time, whereas the visits to father remained stable.

Visitation is extremely important to maintain bonds, encourage the mother to continue in some parental capacity, help the children alleviate anxiety about their mother's safety, and aid in reintegration. Koban (1983) reports that the frequency of visits was an important factor in predicting whether an inmate planned to reunite with his or her children. Except in very few instances, prison staff should take active steps to encourage or facilitate visitation and incorporate visitation and communication with children and their caregivers into a planned treatment approach.

Impact of Imprisonment on Children

> My youngest son, he's 14, we had a lot of problems right before I got here because he . . . said, "well, you're not doing what you're supposed to be doing so why do have to do what I have to do?" And we had a lot of hard times over that. But he finally came around and he realized that I was trying to help myself. (Pollock et al., 1995)

Research results on the impact of imprisonment on the children of prisoners are mixed. Many studies report elevated levels of misbehavior, poor school performance, withdrawal, and running away. Baunach (1982) reported that the effects may include physical, emotional or psychological, and academic problems, including hypertension, aggressive behavior, withdrawal, and academic difficulties. Researchers have documented anxiety disorders, a decline in school performance, and a range of acting out behaviors among the children of incarcerated women (see review in Pollock-Byrne, 1990). Nevertheless, it is unclear what problems exist specifically because of the women's separation from the children and what problems existed prior to the incarceration that were exacerbated by the separation.

It should be noted that children are dealing not only with separation but also with the stigma of having a parent in prison. Thus, they receive less support from those around them than children who lose parents through divorce or death.

> The children suffer a great deal. Just like my child is going through a lot . . . through school, he can't even tell his friends where his mom's at. He usually tells them she's away in school, she's at work or something making something up because it is seen as . . . "oh, your mother's in prison walls . . . we can't have anything to do with you." (Pollock et al., 1995)

Gaudin (1984) found that children separated from mothers exhibited whining, crying, or aggressive behavior, reflecting their anxiety and distress. Older children may become withdrawn, have problems in school, run away, or become involved in delinquent behavior. The child is dealing with abandonment fears, anger that his or her mother left, fear of the future, and shame.

There seems to be some relationship between the amount of time the parent spent with the child before incarceration and the severity of the effects of deprivation, with the most severe effects occurring in those cases in which the parent spent a great deal of time with the child (Hairston, 1991). The most damage may be done if there was a relationship between mother and child and if the separation occurred before the age of two because of the developmental stage of attachment.

Attachment is defined as the relationship that an infant develops with one or two primary caregivers (usually a mother) during the first 2 years of life (Ainsworth, 1978). Attachment is the first relationship the child forms and sets the model for the capacity to give and receive love and trust. It is characterized by strong interdependence—attachment operates in two directions; the caregiver and the infant are involved. This need is so strong that infants deprived of it will show various degrees of malfunctioning, such as high dependency, noncompliance, hostility, impulsivity, and poor social skills. Conversely, research shows that children who were securely attached as infants possess higher levels of competence in all aspects of their development, that is, cognitive, social, and emotional functioning, than children evaluated as insecurely attached. Attachment is the mechanism that spurs other developmental behaviors, such as signaling behavior (crying, smiling, vocalizing), following the movements of a caregiver, embracing, or clinging (Ainsworth, 1978).

Children who are deprived of a primary caregiver, or who are separated from a person with whom they have formed an attachment suffer. The risk is greatest before the age of two (Ainsworth, 1978; Bowlby, 1969). Effects may include crying, loss of appetite, sleep disturbances, and a longer-term effects may be difficulty in forming trusting relationships. Although it is not necessary for the attachment figure to be a mother, it is important that caregiving is consistent and one or two people are a stable presence in the infant's world. Whereas a relationship formed with another primary caregiver before separation is helpful, in that it mitigates the anxiety of maternal separation, it is detrimental to the child to have too many caregivers. Thus, one might conclude that the practice of moving children around from family member to family member during the period of incarceration creates anxiety and makes it difficult to form an attachment to one primary caregiver.

During the period of the mother's imprisonment, the most common living arrangement for the child is with a maternal grandmother over the age of 50 (Boudouris, 1996). This arrangement can be troublesome, given the possibility that the grandmother is incapable, owing to age, infirmity, or inclination, of being a stable, responsive caregiver who can develop a quality relationship with the child. It is also important that the relationship with a caregiver be one in which the caregiver is nurturing and responds to the needs of the infant, spending a great deal of time holding and caring for the baby and, in general, making it possible for the child to test its environment and gain mastery over it—by receiving food in response to crying, for instance. It is possible that many grandmothers are incapable of such giving. One might hypothesize that many inmate mothers were insecurely attached to their own mothers and have not formed secure attachments to their own children born outside of prison. From personal history accounts, it seems apparent that dysfunctional families are prevalent and that female prisoners' children are only the latest generation experiencing lack of attachment and subsequent behavioral problems.

Although visits would seem to be important to maintain the parent-child contact, it also should be noted that visitation can be disruptive to children. Foster parents and caregivers have reported that children may misbehave and act aggressively after a prison visit (Hairston, 1991). What this illustrates, however, is that the visit occasions stress—stress can be used constructively or dealt with destructively, depending on the nature of support and skill of the individuals experiencing it. Visitation is also made either more or less difficult depending on the prison staffs' recognition that it is a fearful and intimidating experience for children. Lack of physical contact in some instances, noise, hard surfaces and sterile surroundings, smells, and such procedures as patting down children, all combine to make the visitation experience an ordeal rather than a joyful occasion.

According to Hairston (1991), family contact during imprisonment serves three important functions: First, contact contributes to the maintenance and continuation of the family unit; second, it enhances the well-being of the prisoner; and, third, it facilitates the prisoner's success after release. Visitation also normalizes the environment, and it aids in management as an incentive for good behavior. There seems to be good evidence that the level of visitation is positively related to success on parole (Hairston, 1991). Interestingly, this seems to be the case despite the less than ideal family relationships that individuals in prison may experience, that is, families may be dysfunctional and characterized by alcoholism, drug addiction, and criminal background.

Intergenerational Criminality

One of the sad facts of incarceration is that it sometimes becomes a family pattern. In most prisons in this country, administrators can describe mother-daughter pairs or father-son pairs in the same prison. Even three generations have been represented at times.

[discussing having her daughter in the same prison] . . . when they come up to me now when they say "my daughter . . . " the first thing happens is my heart falls. You know, because I know how it goes in prison. . . . I know that every day is not a good day in prison. You might wake up this morning, you might say, "good morning," and you might wake up tomorrow morning and you don't want to say nothing. I just don't want nobody going off on her, you know. And by me being in another dorm and she in another dorm, you know, I just always feel threatened by my time, because I know any minute I'm probably gonna explode. (Pollock et al., 1995)

All too often crime is an intergenerational affair. Factors such as inconsistent discipline, poor relationships with parents, physical or sexual abuse, and neglect are passed down from generation to generation, as well as criminality.

I myself have a son who is 19 years old and he's sitting in a county jail . . . that's all he saw . . . motorcycles, drugs, guns, and his mom in and out of prison. His dad was never around. He left when he was a child. (Pollock et al., 1995)

As stated earlier, the most common placement of children is with the maternal grandmother. Thus, the incarcerated woman's children are experiencing the same upbringing that possibly contributed to her criminality. If the mother was sexually or physically abused, it is possible that the same family member perpetrators of her abuse are still present. Foster homes or state care are not necessarily a better answer, because separation from all family may not be advisable. The woman in prison may be the best hope her children have for changing the generational predictions of criminality. For this reason, it is vitally important that there are programs in prison that will help female offenders learn about themselves, how to improve relationships and avoid destructive partners, how to be better parents to their own children, and, perhaps, even solve long-standing communication problems with their parents, siblings, and/or other family members.

Family Programs

Given the evidence that a strong family seems to insulate against further recidivism (Boudouris, 1996), one would assume that programs to improve the health of the prisoners' families would be prevalent. This is not the case. Distance, lack of resources, and disinterest work against the prevalence of such programs.

Family Therapy

Family therapy treats the family as a unit rather than the individuals in the family. The family is implicated in many psychological problems, schizophrenia, autism, suicide, alcoholism, and so on. Role playing, communication patterns, and intimacy are issues that are central to all models of family therapy. According to the principles of family therapy, each family strives for homeostasis (balance). Changes in one individual will result in changes in the family as a unit as it tries to adjust back to a balance. The classic example of this is when an alcoholic or addict changes, counselors have observed that another family member may take on the "sick" role. Dysfunctional family units have some or all of the following characteristics: secrets (incest, abuse, alcoholism), poor communication patterns, boundary problems (lack of autonomy among members), enmeshments (involved in each other's lives to an extreme), stifled feeling, lack of honesty, lack of freedom and power, system rules (i.e., ignoring one's behavior, never discussing a particular problem), and unmet needs (Masters, 1994). Family therapy may concentrate on the following problems: role playing, communication patterns, issues of abandonment, anger, humiliation, life scripts, practical economic issues, child rearing, and faithfulness (Kaslow, 1987).

Family therapy is an approach that responds to a number of focal concerns, including the following: internal dynamics that create physical abuse; marital discord; aggressive sibling interactions and violence; alcohol and drug-related factors; child sexual abuse, including incest; poor self-image of the parents; stress. Family stressors are identified as an excessive number of children, employment and economic problems, poor home and financial management skills, age of the mother, emotional loss resulting from death or separation, chronic illness, rapid life changes, and social isolation (van Voorhis et al., 1992, p. 169).

Clearly, family therapy is particularly appropriate for the offender who will return to the family, especially for women who will return to children. As mentioned previously, women offenders may come from dysfunctional families and may be perpetuating the dysfunctional communication patterns, abuse and neglect with which they were raised. It is obvious that without some change in parenting patterns, their children are bound to develop similar problems. It has been reported, for instance, that families with delinquents exhibit the following characteristics: members talk less with each other, are more defensive and less supportive, and are less active than families without delinquents. These families also appear to have more rules but with inconsistent discipline, a lack of ability to negotiate resolutions to conflict, and a tendency to reinforce deviant behaviors (van Voorhis et al., 1992, p. 166).

The problems with family therapy in prison are distance and disinterest. Visits are rare, because travel to the prison is often too expensive or inconvenient. Few prisoners have relatives who live close enough to make family therapy feasible. Even if distance were not a problem, many family members are entrenched in a criminal lifestyle and/or would not see the need to attend counseling sessions. Female offenders may be estranged from their family owing to the woman's drug use and many years of disappointing the family through continued drug addiction. For these reasons, as well as the general setting of the prison, it is difficult to conceive of a family therapy program working well in prison, although the presence of such a program in a halfway house after a prison sentence seems more feasible. Programs do exist that target the woman herself and her role as a mother.

Parenting Programs

It teaches me a lot because my other two kids I didn't raise. My mother did. And this is like all new to me. I will know what to do. Whatever I missed out on my other two children I already seen it through her so and I know what my mother went through and it's not easy raising kids. There's too many kids in the world being neglected so I'm not going to neglect my kids anymore like I had been in the past.

Franklin is like my first child . . . [his] needs and wants come first, whereas the kids, I just had—I have seven children. I have six boys and one girl. I see now that I deprived five of my kids of a lot of love. Because I didn't know love because my love was to drugs. And I know this now, that it wasn't love I was giving them. . . . I sent my kids through a lot and I didn't know I was doing it. I really didn't know I was hurting them. I thought it was all right, because they were always clean. They always went to school. They were fed. I thought it was all right. Never once, until I got incarcerated . . . that I thought—love. (Pollock et al., 1995)

In a national study with 43 states and territories responding, it was found that many states did not have parenting programs, and a surprising number did not even keep records on the number of female offenders that had children or planned to reunite with their children. Clement (1993) reported from this national study that 32 out of 43 states had no knowledge of how many children would be living with mothers after incarceration. Fifteen states had no information on the number of women in the prison system who had dependent children. Thirty-six states reported some type of parenting program, although the programs ranged from 4 weeks to 20 weeks. Most programs met only one or two hours weekly, and most had slots available for only 25 women or less. The programs included communication skills, development of self-esteem, parenting skills, knowledge of child development stages, recognition of feelings, parent education, and mothers' support groups. Fifteen were modeled after STEP (Systematic Training for Effective Parenting) or PET (Parent Effectiveness Training). Most classes were taught by volunteers. Only 23 programs offered separate or additional visitation with children outside of the regular visitation privileges (Clement, 1993).

Women in prison show great enthusiasm for parenting programs. They routinely report the need for such programs on needs assessments and every program or class available is always full. This is especially true if the program incorporates some form of visitation. Interestingly, one observes that most women in prison do not resent others "telling them" how to be better mothers. They show great interest in factual lectures (e.g., on ear infections) as well as open discussions on how to deal with such things as discipline. Addiction and criminality are extremely incongruent with good parenting. Thus, a drug treatment program may turn into a parenting class, or a parenting class may deal with issues of addiction.

> [Discussing a parenting program that addressed addiction issues] [It teaches us] how to do parenting. How to get up at 6:00 a.m. in the morning and be on time for a job and eat three normal meals and go to bed at a regular time. How to go to a social function and be social instead of intoxicating yourself to the point of not remembering what happened. Becoming involved in what's going on in the community around you. (Pollock et al., 1995)

One program described in more detail by Clement (1993) was the Virginia program MILK (Mothers Inside Loving Kids). This program, administered by Parents Anonymous—an outside volunteer group concerned with the elimination of child abuse and support to parents—included a program orientation; child development classes; parent education classes; independent living skills classes; all day physical contact visitations with children, in a setting with age-graded play equipment; ongoing support and education programs, which met weekly and were modeled after the Parents Anonymous self-help philosophy; special programs for the guardians raising the inmate's children; housing and transportation, when necessary, for the children to the correctional facility; and connections to Parents Anonymous chapters or other support groups outside (Clement, 1993, p. 97).

The MATCH (Mothers and Their Children) program in Bexar County Jail (San Antonio) provides jailed mothers the opportunity to have extended, protected visits with their children every weekend on a special floor of the jail facility, as long as they participate in the program of training and education in parenting during the week. This program was modeled after the MATCH program at the Federal Correctional Institution at Pleasanton, California. Program staff use professional volunteers to teach classes in health issues, parenting, child development, drug abuse prevention, domestic violence, and GED. Group support is also part of the program. The program also uses ongoing services after the woman is released and has satellite offices where the woman can obtain counseling, networking and advocacy in housing, employment, and parenting issues.

"Girl Scouts Behind Bars" is a program that has been implemented in Maryland, Florida, Ohio, and Arizona. In the Maryland program the daughters (ages 5 to 17) of women in prison join their mothers on two Saturdays each month for a Girl Scout meeting. The 2-hour meetings allow supervised time between mother and daughter in structured play and group projects. The meeting is more than just a visit—it is educational, and sessions are included on violence prevention, self-esteem, drug abuse, relationships, and teenage pregnancy prevention. On the alternate Saturdays the daughters meet as a troop in a downtown location and spend time with volunteers. Nevertheless, the program's weakness is that there is little counseling or individual support for the girls, mothers or caregivers outside of the group meetings. Also, there is little parenting education provided for the mothers involved in the program (Moses, 1995).

In the Florida Girl Scouts program, the imprisoned mothers meet regularly with a prison psychologist who provides parenting training and support. Mothers meet regularly outside of the twice monthly troop meetings. There are referral services available for release, as well as social service referrals for the daughters and their caregivers (Moses, 1995). This program allows a structured, enriched opportunity for mother-daughter contact. One criticism is that the program ignores the needs of the sons of inmate mothers. Another criticism is that the visits may be impracticable in those states in which long distances exist between the prison and city from which most women are sentenced.

Another extended visitation program is Camp Celebration at the Dwight Correctional Center in Illinois (Stumbo & Little, 1991). This program opened in 1988 and provides weekend camping outings for women and their children. The campground is located on the grounds of the facility and is outfitted with a dining pavilion, tents, and bathroom facilities. Eligible women apply to the program, which runs every weekend, through the summer months. Children are searched and brought into the prison grounds and the female inmates meet them at the campgrounds. Between Friday afternoon and Sunday afternoon, the mothers and children engage in structured games and campfires or just spend time together without becoming involved in the planned activities. There are no obvious security personnel at the campground and there is a trained social worker to facilitate activities. No problems with contraband, fighting, or misbehavior have occurred. The female inmates have expressed extreme appreciation for the program, as exemplified in the following quote (Stumbo & Little, 1991).

It has been the best thing that has happened to me in the six years I've been here at Dwight. I just thank God that I had the chance to have a dream come true to be with my daughter and lie next to her. We even talked about the day I'll return home and what it will feel like. If it feels like a little part of this campout, I know I'll feel as if I just entered heaven. (p. 143)

Although Camp Celebration was started with a federal grant, after the grant ended the program was picked up and included in the prison budget and now is a permanent feature of the prison programming. This model could work well for other programs in other prisons. Outside funding is sometimes the only way a program can get started, but to ensure stability and permanence, states will need to incorporate such programs into the general prison budget. It is hoped that as more evidence accumulates about the value of such programs, administrators and legislators will agree that spending money on programs to help the children of incarcerated women is money well spent.

Special programs are needed for those women who are in prison for abusing or killing their children. One such program is the WINAS (Women in Need of Alternate Solutions) in Massachusetts. This program teaches inmates to develop alternative strategies for managing anger, and the women are also required to participate in the Parents Anonymous group in the prison. Another program in Illinois is a therapeutic community for abusers. Other prisons use groups, so women can discuss their feelings with those who can understand and empathize with them (Boudouris, 1996). Parents Anonymous is a volunteer organization that helps parents deal with anger management, stress, and other elements of parenting. There are chapters in most large cities and the organization is involved with outreach and intervention services, both court referred and voluntary, related to such problems as physical abuse and neglect, sexual abuse, and more general problems of parenting.

Infants

Whereas parenting classes and programs respond to children of all ages, pregnancy and birth during a prison term present unique issues. Only three states allow infants of mothers in prison to stay with the women—New York, Washington, and California. The American Correctional Association (Crawford, 1988, p. 32) and the U.S. Department of Justice (1994a) studies reported that, nationally, about 6% of women are pregnant when committed to prison. Women who give birth while in prison encounter special difficulties. One survey found that less than half of women's prisons provided prenatal care, only 15% provided special diets for pregnant women, only 15% provided counseling to help mothers find placements after birth, and only 11% provided postnatal counseling (Wooldredge & Masters, 1993). This same study also reported that prisons typically did not have the medical resources to deal with false labor or premature births and miscarriages, they did not have maternity clothes for pregnant inmates, women were forced to wear belly chains when being transported to the hospital to give birth, and there were no visiting facilities available for infants away from the general visiting area. An American Civil Liberties Union report indicated that pregnant women in one state prison were pressured to abort and that they were routinely denied medical care (Leonard, 1983). More studies should be conducted to determine whether these experiences are widespread.

Most prisons have no arrangements for postnatal nurseries. This means that, ordinarily, women who give birth must give up custody to the state immediately or make arrangements for relatives to care for the infant. Often the woman is permitted only a short visit in the hospital before the baby is taken away and she is returned to prison. There are arguments on both sides on the advisability of having infants in prison. Some studies have found that other countries have a much more relaxed approach to children and allow women inmates to keep their children with them up to the age of five or six (Henriques, 1994). Many correctional administrators are opposed to the idea of babies in prison and, thus, even those states that have statutes allowing the mother and child to remain together if it is in "the best interest of the child" typically follow a policy of separation at birth. All studies report a need for more research on the effects of separation versus the baby spending the first several months in a prison (Boudouris, 1996).

A British study found that there were small differences in development between infants who spent their first months in a prison setting and those who were immediately placed in a community setting (Catan, 1992). Those babies who spent time with their mothers in prison exhibited a gradual decline over a 4-month period in the areas of locomotor and cognitive development. The reason for such a decline was believed to be the somewhat sterile surroundings of the prison nursery. The authors of this study did not conclude that prison nurseries were detrimental to infants, but they did advocate making sure such placements include ample opportunities to practice locomotive skills, allow free movement and play, provide educational toys and other stimulating activities, and employ properly trained staff.

The Mother Infant Program in California allows some female inmates to spend time with their infants. California has created seven small community-based facilities where inmate mothers may live with their children. There are specialized parenting classes and counseling. Preemployment training is also provided, as well as drug education classes. Passes allow women to attend school or visit home. The mother is responsible for a child care arrangement if she chooses to participate in a work furlough program. Only women with no history of violence or escape and no record of child abuse are admitted. The woman must have no more than 6 years to serve and she must have been the primary caretaker of her children before incarceration. Children can be 6 years of age or younger in this program. Pregnant women can enroll and attend childbirth classes during their pregnancy. These facilities are operated by private agencies under contract to the state. Some criticism has been leveled at the program for the small number of slots available, given the huge population of imprisoned women in California. Also, some argue that the requirements for entry are so stringent that few women are able to take advantage of its existence.

Other programs also allow the female offender to spend time with her baby in a community setting. In Fort Worth, Texas, the Volunteers of America run a small community facility where a few federal inmate mothers can come, after giving birth, to stay with their baby for a few months (Lenhart, 1995).

Alcohol and Drug Abuse Prenatal Treatment Program (ADAPT) is a jail program that serves pregnant substance abusers. The program is a joint effort between Multnomah County Health Division, the Department of Community Corrections, and the Alcohol and Drug Program. This program provides services to women, including prenatal care, substance-abuse education, case management, home visits, child care, and transportation. Transition housing can be arranged and there are weekly problem-solving group sessions. The program seeks to divert women from the criminal justice system and ensure that the child is born to a healthy mother in an improved living situation, compared with what she was in after her entry into the jail (Oregon Department of Corrections, 1991). One evaluation showed that those who participated in the program had a lower percentage of positive drug tests at the time of delivery; they were more likely to have had prenatal care, they gave births to babies with higher average birth weights, and participants were more likely to retain custody of their infants (ADAPT, 1993).

Immarigeon (1994) described the Hooper Home Alternative to Incarceration Program in New York City. This is a residential facility for women that also works in cooperation with the Child Welfare Administration—the goal is keeping children out of foster care or at least limiting the amount of time spent in foster care. The women are sent to the facility in lieu of a prison sentence where they obtain individual and group counseling, services in the areas of HIV, health care education, self-esteem counseling, decision-making skills, visitation and parenting workshops, and on-site recreational activities for mothers and children.

Finally, the Neil J. Houston House in Boston, Massachusetts is a community-based residential prerelease treatment facility. It is administered by Social Justice for Women, a nonprofit organization devoted to serving the needs of women offenders. Women who have been sentenced to Massachusetts Prison for Women at Framingham and who will give birth during their sentence are eligible for the Houston House program. They are allowed to keep their babies with them after birth at the House, and they receive an integrated treatment program, including prenatal and postnatal medical care and counseling, drug counseling, life skills, and self-esteem counseling. They are also eligible for continuing services after release, including housing, individual and group counseling, and educational services.

The content of parenting programs, whether for newborns or older children, must cover a multitude of issues in addition to child development. All program staff point out that the women must deal with their own problems before they can become effective parents to their children. Table 5.1 presents one program model.

After conducting a national survey of parenting programs, Boudouris (1996) concluded that

1. Parenting education programs are diverse and of varying qualities.
2. The availability of furloughs to maintain family contacts has declined since 1985.
3. Overnight visits have declined, as have children's centers or day care centers.
4. There has been an increase in community placements for incarcerated women, where they can live with their children.
5. There are a few more states that have prison nurseries (although other states have discontinued their use).

Table 5.1 Parenting Program Model

Young Children:
Parenting rights and responsibilities (legal issues)
Parenting heritage (history of the family, how our parents influence us)
Family system (how the family works as a system)
Building self-esteem (how we behave influences how a child feels)
Communication (what we communicate to our children)
Raising the responsible child (rules, choices, and consequences)
Learning the discipline of logical consequences

Adolescents:
Parenting rights and responsibilities
Expectations (of being a parent) (how we learn to be parents, what we expect)
Communication (effective communication)
Influencing your child (motivating and disciplining children)
Understanding misbehavior (peer pressure, sexual issues, suicide prevention)
Parenting under difficult circumstances (divorce, abandonment, rejection, addiction)
Self-esteem (for self and child)

Adapted from *Prisoners as Parents: Building Parenting Skills on the Inside* (Tilbur, 1993).

Implications for Counselors

Women in prison very often come from dysfunctional families. The children of inmate mothers all too often become the next generation in a cycle of abuse, neglect, and poor parenting. One of the sad facts of the increased number of women in prison is the effect such incarceration has on their children. Children are often placed in unstable, transitory living environments that are not conducive to positive growth and development. If the state takes custody, the child is placed in foster care and lives in limbo, sometimes for many years, not eligible for adoption because the mother in prison continues to have parental rights.

One can identify an approach in corrections that can be described as a premise of parenting as a privilege that must be earned. The public at large often expresses the attitude that "she should have thought of her children before she committed the crime" when presented with the idea of parenting programs with increased visitation. Another premise, just as valid, is that parenting is a responsibility that cannot (or should not) be ignored. When we deprive women of their children, it is obvious, but perhaps needs more emphasis, that we are also depriving her children of her presence. They are also being punished but have not committed a crime—yet. The responding argument is that she was probably a bad mother and they are better off without her. The fact is though, if she was a bad mother she will inevitably return and may pick up her mothering responsibilities and continue to practice poor parenting unless intervention occurs. We have the opportunity, while the female offender is in prison, to affect the future of her children by providing parenting programs and enriched visitation. Instead of taking this opportunity seriously, what sometimes occurs is the use of parenting programs or visitation as a reward for good behavior and something that is taken away as punishment. Thus, even those prisons with parenting programs sometimes may make them available only to women who meet strict criteria of behavior. Ironically, this may mean that those women who have the greatest need for help in becoming better parents do not receive it. Whereas this approach may make sense if parental rights have been terminated, that is not typically the case, and the children will be returned to her care on release. This practice of treating motherhood as a privilege is unrealistic and not conducive to the development of good parenting skills.

Many women in prison miss their children but are somewhat relieved to be exempt from the burden of caring for them. Further, they may have unrealistic expectations of release and may underestimate the difficulties associated with child care, because they see their children (if at all) for short periods of time and are not responsible for disciplining, feeding, or taking care of them when they are sick. An hour in a visiting room once a month is not a good picture of what parenting is all about, nor is talking on the telephone or receiving letters. Parenting is about being up at 3:00 a.m. with a feverish child, or cleaning up vomit, changing dirty diapers, and changing a toddler's clothes three times a day. It's arguing with them about why they can't wear a bathing suit in January, or worrying about what a teenager is doing at ll:30 p.m., or figuring out whether there is enough money at the end of the month to buy the *Power Ranger*™ doll that your son wants. Often women in prison have never experienced these aspects of parenting because of the haze of addiction and alcoholism or because they transferred their responsibilities to other family members. Many women in prison have an idealized view of parenting—they express great love and excitement about reuniting with their children, but in their descriptions one gets the impression that their children are perfect, untouched, or rising above what they have gone through. They view the mother-child relationship as a loving one, but rarely do more pragmatic or difficult issues seem to be a part of their visions of the future. If they leave prison with these ideals, they are sure to be disillusioned by the reality of parenting that is not always loving and not always perfect.

Counselors in prison often state that when they have women on their caseload, it multiplies 10 times because they also have all the children of the women on their caseload (Pollock, 1986; Pollock-Byrne, 1990). It is true that women are very involved in their children's lives and the counselors often act as troubleshooters and liaisons with school officials or the child welfare organization. Very often women in prison are extremely distraught over what they have done to their children. This may lead to depression and even suicide attempts. Counselors need to be alert to these possibilities, especially if the children are in unfavorable living situations or get into trouble during the period of imprisonment. They can also help by assisting in facilitating visitation and communication with the woman's children. If there are parenting classes at the institution, every woman who is a parent should attend. If there are no opportunities for enriched visitation, counselors should advocate for them.

A special group of inmate mothers are those who are in prison for killing their children. Another special group are those women who are in prison for failing to protect their children from an abusive partner who ultimately killed the child. These woman are vilified by the prison subculture, typically have serious psychological problems, and may need to be placed in special settings; in hospital settings or administrative segregation under a suicide watch at least during the initial entry into prison. Some prisons run group therapy for women who have killed their children. It is natural to have extremely negative feelings for such women; their actions, unless clearly the result of delusions or extreme psychosis, seem so terrible and contrary to human nature that it is impossible to understand or maintain a professional objective stance. Still, even these women may be mothers of other children and could possibly regain parental rights over them or give birth to other children after their prison sentence. To ensure the future of their children, it is vital that prison counselors and helping professionals attempt to address the causes of such a crime.

Counselors may find that children present the best motivator for change. Almost all women want their children to love them and to think well of them. Ordinarily, by the time a woman has entered prison, she has experienced many failures as a person and as a mother. One of the greatest joys in a woman's life is when she has accomplished a goal, completed a program, or otherwise has successfully accomplished something. She looks forward to sharing that goal with her children.

We must recognize that the children of women in prison may be the next generation of prisoners if there are not solid, successful intervention programs available. Arguably, the needs of children should take priority over the needs of offenders; and the needs of children are to have sober, employable, loving parents who know how to discipline and instill values in their children. Women who plan to leave prison and resume care of their children must have access to programs and counseling opportunities that help them develop such skills.

6

Prison Programs

I think I would have been dead. . . . I don't understand why with the overdoses and everything that I went through and the life-threatening situations that I would put myself in why I didn't die. In fact, when I went into the program, I didn't go in there looking for a change. I went in there looking to get off the work crew that they have in the prison system. And something was said in there. . . . I saw care in somebody's eyes who had never been through this before, and it was just real curious, and that was it. That's what turned it. I probably would have been back out there and either dead or back on the streets doing what I do best. And I like to use the terms "ripping and running" because it's a nice way to put what I did. . . . It wasn't simple. It's a lot of hard work. It was not simple at all. What this class gave me, you know, was not some magic potion that I could walk out those gates and that life was going to be okay, because it wasn't. What this class gave me was the desire and the willingness to make things okay.

Pollock et al. (1995)

Programs in prison include everything from landscape maintenance to confrontational group therapy. Medical services, religious services, recreational or leisure activities, service groups, or visitation programs have all been defined by some authors as rehabilitative programs, but in this chapter only those programs that have specific goals, are based on a clear concept or theory, have a specific structure or method, are intense, require a period of time, *may* have a history of success, and are run by trained staff will be defined as "treatment programs" (see discussion in Pollock, 1997b). It also may be the case that the treatment professional reading this may not be administering any formally defined program but, rather, is engaged in a more traditional case-work relationship with female offenders. The first part of the chapter discusses selected personality disorders that the correctional counselor will encounter in correctional populations. These individuals present special problems of treatment. The second part of the chapter discusses certain selected programs or treatment approaches.

Personality Disorders in Prison

It is estimated that as many as 10% of inmates may suffer from serious mental health problems (Smith & Faubert, 1990, p. 133). Many more may be identified as having serious enough mental health problems that they would benefit from some form of intensive counseling or psychotherapy. As described in Chapter 3, usually mental disorders are diagnosed during the classification period. The individuals who possess diagnosed personality disorders or other mental health problems pose special problems for the correctional counselor. Most standard prison programs are not designed to deal with individuals with serious mental health problems. Individuals who exhibited the personality disorders below would probably not succeed very well in conventional treatment programs in prison and should receive more intensive intervention.

Beck and Freeman (1990) presented numerous personality disorders and goals of treatment. In the box below, only a few of the personality disorders that they describe are presented. These disorders are likely to be found in any prison population. Personality disorders are more difficult to treat than depression or anxiety and are more integrated structurally in the personality make-up of the individual (Beck & Freeman, 1990).

Selected Personality Disorders		
Personality	**Characteristics**	**Goals**
Dependent	Help seeking, dependent	Self-sufficiency, mobility
Passive-Aggressive	Autonomy, resistance, passivity, sabotage	Intimacy, assertiveness, activity, cooperativeness
Paranoid	Vigilance, mistrust suspiciousness	Serenity, trust, acceptance
Narcissistic	Self-aggrandizement competitiveness	Sharing, group identification
Antisocial	Combativeness, exploitativeness, predation	Empathy, reciprocity, social sensitivity
Histrionic	Exhibitionism, expressiveness, impressionism	Reflectiveness, control systematization

Adapted from *Cognitive Therapy of Personality Disorders* (Beck & Freeman, 1990).

The personality disorder most commonly associated with criminality and criminal populations is the antisocial personality disorder (Beck & Freeman, 1990). These individuals exhibit the following characteristics: an inability to profit from experience, form meaningful relationships, experience guilt; lack of a sense of responsibility, impulse control, a moral sense; consistent antisocial behavior; resistance to punishment as a behavior change tool; emotional immaturity; and, extreme self-centeredness (Walsh, 1988, p. 14). Other authors use similar descriptions, citing characteristics that include glibness or charm, a grandiose sense of self-worth, low tolerance for boredom, manipulativeness, lack of remorse or guilt, shallow affect, callousness, lack of empathy, a parasitic lifestyle, poor behavior controls, promiscuity, early behavioral problems, an inability to do long-range planning, impulsivity, irresponsibility, failure to accept responsibility, and delinquency and criminality (Beck & Freeman, 1990, p. 150).

Individuals with antisocial personality disorders are highly resistant to most types of psychotherapy. Intervention must address basic belief systems of the antisocial individual that are egocentric. Individuals with this disorder believe that their needs come first. They make no distinction between wanting and needing; they believe that they are incapable of making bad decisions, that others are unimportant and irrelevant, especially if they are contrary to the individual achieving her goals, and that nothing bad will happen because of behavior decisions (Beck & Freeman, 1990, p. 154).

It is suggested that the counselors who deal with individuals with antisocial personality disorders should guard against manipulation and possess qualities of firmness and consistency. They need a clear sense of personal values and self-assurance to counter the persuasiveness and inherent deviousness of the antisocial personality. Cognitive therapy has been used with antisocial personality disorders. It uses a risk-benefit approach to help the individual to see the effects of her behavior. Behavior modification has been used as well. Being incarcerated in a prison is not evidence, in itself, of an antisocial personality disorder, but it is a fairly common diagnosis with correctional populations.

Another personality disorder one is likely to encounter among female inmates is the borderline personality disorder. These individuals display disproportional intensity of emotions, a variety of symptoms; have a record of unstable relationships, an identity disturbance (such as self-image or sexual orientation), chronic feelings of emptiness or boredom, excessive fears of abandonment; are erratic, inconsistent, impulsive; express recurrent suicidal threats; may self-mutilate; go through episodes of intense, uncontrolled anger;

and engage in other forms of "acting out" behavior (Beck & Freeman, 1990, p.178). These individuals may be chronic troublemakers in prison and spend a lot of time in segregation for attacking correctional officers. Treatment staff are called on to intervene in these incidents, but the correctional institution largely views such "acting out" incidents as a behavior problem.

Beck and Freeman (1990) proposed that treatment address the dichotomous thinking that is typical of those with borderline personality disorder. Establishing trust is more difficult with this group than other groups and will take longer. Control issues and power struggles also are problematic. This individual may not complete homework assignments and may resist any form of direction. Collaborative approaches are more effective, but obviously in a prison environment issues of trust, power, and control are going to be extremely exaggerated.

The histrionic personality disorder is another type that may be found in female offender populations. These individuals express extreme emotions, display nonlogical thinking, dichotomous thinking, shallow emotions, have a fear of rejection, a constant need for reassurance, and are overly concerned with physical attractiveness (Beck & Freeman, 1990, p. 231). Another common problem is the narcissistic personality disorder. This disorder includes the following characteristics: displays of grandiosity, hypersensitivity to evaluations, a lack of empathy for others, belief that one's problems are unique, a sense of entitlement (regarding resources or gifts) and envy of others (Beck & Freeman, 1990, p. 233).

These types of personality disorders must be diagnosed and met with appropriate treatment responses. Beck and Freeman (1990) proposed that the cognitive model can work with these personality disorders. If the individual suffering from one or more of these personality disorders is involved in other treatment programs, it is important that she not disrupt the treatment process for those less seriously impaired. Additional attention or more intensive forms of counseling than some of the programs described below can provide are needed.

Selected Prison Programs

Many programs one might find in a prison can be labeled as self-help programs, meaning that inmates either have been the initiators of the program or are primarily responsible for the organization and management of the program. Alcoholics Anonymous and Narcotics Anonymous can be considered self-help programs. Other programs are not specifically drug treatment programs, such as The Seventh Step or The Fortune Society. Both of these programs originated to serve the needs of male prisoners, but they help women as well in finding housing, jobs, and offering a support group on release. Lifer's groups, craft groups, and volunteer organizations (in which inmates volunteer for outside charities) also can be found in some prisons. Some of these programs do not meet the definition given above for a treatment program, although they may be very beneficial to those involved (Pollock, 1997b).

Other types of programs are "top down," that is, they are implemented by the prison staff with little input from those involved. These programs are usually "eclectic," meaning that a variety of different treatment modalities might be used to develop the approach and intervention format. The programs may be managed by a private provider. Many prisons are now contracting with private enterprise to offer drug programs, as well as more general treatment programs in prisons. The approach may be largely informative or educational (i.e., life skills classes or parenting classes), or the approach may address more intrapersonal issues through group or individual counseling. Many programs mix the two approaches.

There is no attempt here to cover all the varieties of programs that might be found across the country. The selection of those below is somewhat arbitrary, however, cognitive approaches are emphasized because of findings that they seem to have more effect on recidivism than other treatment approaches (Palmer, 1994). There is no doubt that other programs also could have been included here. Basic issues of evaluation relating to all treatment programs and counseling in general will be taken up in the last chapter.

Boot Camps

One of the results of equality in sentencing has been the development and use of boot camps for women. Arguably, the most extreme illustration of how parity for women offenders typically means applying male standards, boot camps have been created for female offenders with the same paramilitary, hypermasculine approach used for young male offenders. The idea behind boot camps is that criminal offenders need to experience discipline in their lives and what better model of discipline than the military?

However one feels about the appropriateness of the idea, it is obvious that fitting female inmates into the "in your face—push-ups as discipline" mode is inconsistent with socialization and the realities of sex differences in this society. Further, given the information provided in previous chapters regarding the need for individualized treatment, it seems obvious that the highly controlled, confrontational approach will not be effective for some groups of inmates, although it might be for others. For instance, the findings of the California Treatment Program indicate that one might hypothesize that the boot camp approach is most successful with the power-oriented subtypes (a group that requires strong controls and "tests" the counselor for strength before trust is established) and less effective or perhaps even detrimental to the anxious subtypes, who respond best to treaters who are open, supportive, and extend themselves as role models. As mentioned previously, female delinquents tended to fall more frequently into the anxious subtypes, so one might assume that adult women as well are probably less likely to benefit from the disciplinarian approach typical of the boot camp model.

The components of boot camp programs include education, training, substance abuse counseling, exercise, drilling, and strict military discipline. The benefits of boot camp are said to be facilitating the development of self-discipline and helping the inmate develop self-respect by accomplishing difficult tasks. They may leave more prepared to deal with the outside, through the accomplishment of a GED or high school diploma, or at least have more self-discipline with which to develop and meet goals. Evaluators hypothesize that these elements account for any success shown by boot camp intervention, rather than the militaristic elements (Camp & Sandhu, 1995).

Camp and Sandhu (1995) presented findings that illustrate that boot camps nationwide have shown little success in affecting recidivism. In their evaluation of a boot camp for female offenders in Oklahoma, they also found that the boot camp experience showed only marginal improvement in recidivism rates, which deteriorated over time. Their findings regarding the explanations for failure of those women who ended up back in prison are instructive. Interviews with these women revealed that jobs (or more accurately the lack of jobs) was the most frequent explanation for failure, followed by social integration problems (drug and alcohol, pressure from criminal peers and relatives, discrimination and poor self-image), and family problems. Relapse into drug use was a major reason for failure for some inmates. Close to 80% of those who went back to drug use were rearrested, compared with almost 80% of those who did not go back to drug use and were not rearrested and remained successful. One of the most influential factors in success was found to be continued participation in a drug program after release.

Thus, it appears that any success of boot camps may have more to do with the supplementary programs, such as drug treatment, job placement, or other transitional services that are provided, rather than the number of push-ups performed or the ability to keep a clean locker. The public's attraction to the "tough" approach of boot camps may bear little relevance to the successful elements incorporated within them.

Behavior Modification Programs

Behavior modification programs have been around since the 1970s and have been used in a multitude of settings, including the prison. All programs using this model operate under the assumption that all behavior is affected by environmental rewards, thus to affect behavior, one must structure the environment to reward desirable behavior and not reward discouraged behavior. Programs have used aversive conditioning and positive conditioning to achieve these goals. Taking away privileges, reassignment to a less desirable housing block, or the administration of drugs that cause extreme discomfort have all been used in aversive conditioning. Rewards include greater privileges, more freedom of movement, and "tokens" that can be exchanged for desired goods or activities. Many are concerned with the potential for abuse. Prison is already an environment of deprivation, and to use further deprivations raises the charge of cruel and unusual punishment. Another deeper problem is the criticism that behavior modification in prison is nothing more than control, not treatment. In such programs outside of prison, the client chooses the intervention, participates in the plan of treatment, and has the choice to stop treatment at any time. Courts have indicated that the latter element also must be present in prison programs using behavior modification approaches. Court holdings protect the right of inmates to withhold consent or withdraw consent for programs designated as experimental (Pollock, 1997b).

Another problem is that often behavior modification programs rely entirely on external rewards or punishments with no attempt to ready individuals to become their own "rewarder." In this case, once the individual leaves the structured environment of the program, either back to the general population or parole to the outside, the positive behavioral effects may dissipate. Behavior modification may be combined with other approaches, such as the cognitive-based programs described below.

Cognitive Approaches

Cognitive therapy assumes that underlying beliefs affect the way individuals respond to external stimuli. It contrasts with behavioral therapy by placing a greater emphasis on the client's internal experiences, such as thoughts, feelings, wishes, daydreams, and attitudes (Beck, Rush, Shaw, & Emory, 1979). Some of the principles of cognitive therapy are the following:

1. Perception and experiencing in general are active processes that involve both inspective and introspective data.
2. The patient's cognitions represent a synthesis of internal and external stimuli.
3. How a person appraises a situation is generally evident in his [or her] cognitions.
4. These cognitions constitute the person's "stream of consciousness" or phenomenal field . . . the person's configuration of himself [or herself].
5. Alterations in the content of the person's underlying cognitive structures affect his or her affective state and behavioral pattern.
6. Through psychological therapy a patient can become aware of his [or her] cognitive distortions.
7. Correction of these faulty dysfunctional constructs can lead to clinical improvement. (Beck et al., 1979, p. 9)

The goals of cognitive therapy for the client are to be able to (a) identify and monitor negative thoughts, (b) recognize the connections between cognitions and behavior, (c) examine the evidence for and against distorted thoughts, (d) substitute more reality-oriented interpretations for biased cognitions, (e) learn to identify and alter the dysfunctional beliefs that predispose one to distort experiences (Beck et al., 1979).

Cognitive strategies include guided discovery, searches for idiosyncratic meanings, labeling of inaccurate inferences or distortions, collaborative empiricism (testing the validity of one's beliefs), examining explanations for others' behavior, scaling (translating extreme interpretations into dimensional terms), reattribution (reassigning responsibility for action), deliberate exaggeration, examining advantages and disadvantages of maintaining or changing beliefs or behaviors, and decatastrophizing (enabling the client to recognize and counter the tendency to expect the worst) (Beck & Freeman, 1990, p. 80).

During cognitive therapy, the individuals may be asked to monitor their activities, schedule activities, conduct behavioral rehearsals of goal behavior and model behavior, practice relaxation techniques, and perform tasks such as role playing, reliving childhood experiences, and using imagery (Beck & Freeman, 1990, p. 90). In the box below the model is presented in summary form.

Cognitive Therapy Model

1. Conceptualization of case (Identify history and core beliefs.)

2. Collaboration and guided discovery

3. Therapeutic relationship (Provide role model, guidance, transference reaction.)

4. Identify automatic thoughts and rational responses

5. Role playing (Also other forms of skill development)

6. Imagery

7. Identify and test basic beliefs

8. Build new "schemas"

9. Set goals

10. Use homework (Keep a diary, identify automatic thoughts, label errors.)

Adapted from *Cognitive Therapy of Personality Disorders* (Beck and Freeman, 1990, p. 352).

In Canada, Ross, Fabiano, and Ewles (1988) reported on an intervention program that is based on cognitive therapy. This program operates under the assumption that offenders have deficits in cognitive skills essential for pro-social adjustment. Training is provided to increase offenders' cognitive abilities with the expectation that this will influence their criminal behavior. The intervention program was developed after an extensive study of rehabilitative programs that identified those with any level of success in affecting recidivism. All successful programs seemed to have some element of changing the offender's "thinking" patterns. According to these researchers (Ross et al., 1988), offenders were found to have cognitive deficiencies in the following areas:

> in the ability to conceptualize the consequences of their behavior and are unable to use means-end reasoning to achieve their goals. Often the offender is concretistic, action oriented, non-reflective and impulsive. Many offenders have not progressed beyond an egocentric stage of cognitive development and are unable to understand the behavior, thoughts and feelings of other people. Consequently, many juvenile and adult offenders have major deficits in social skills and in interpersonal problem-solving. (p. 30)

A program of intervention was designed that included previously tested and used techniques as well as new techniques designed after the analysis of successful programs. It also was decided that the program must be able to be delivered by line staff, not by psychologists or psychiatrists, to be cost-effective and available to larger numbers of offenders. This program has been administered in juvenile institutions, adult institutions, and to probation populations. It includes structured-learning therapy (to teach social skills), lateral thinking techniques (to teach creative problem solving), critical thinking (to teach logical, rational thinking), values education (to teach values and concern for others), assertiveness training (to teach nonaggressive, socially appropriate ways to meet needs), negotiation skills training (to teach alternatives to belligerent or violent behaviors in interpersonal conflict situations), interpersonal cognitive problem solving (to teach the thinking skills required to deal with interpersonal problems and conflicts), social-perspective training (to teach the offenders how to recognize and understand other people's views and feelings), and role playing and modeling (to demonstrate and practice socially acceptable interpersonal behavior). In the words of its authors (Ross et al., 1988), the 80-hour program was designed to

> modif[y] the impulsive, egocentric, illogical and rigid thinking of the offenders and teaching them to stop and think before acting, to consider the consequences of their behavior, to conceptualize alternative ways of responding to interpersonal problems and to consider the impact of their behavior on other people, particularly their victims. (p. 30)

Cognitive approaches are based on the early work of Albert Ellis (rational-emotive therapy). In all cognitive approaches, the thinking of the offender is believed to affect subsequent behavior. Irrational thinking patterns may prevent personal growth, that is, "I'm a failure." "Everyone dislikes me." "I must succeed at everything I attempt." In correctional environments, the irrational thinking that needs to be addressed might be along the lines of "The world owes me a living." "Everyone steals or is crooked in some way." "It's OK to take what you want." "Violence is OK," and so on. Identifying, confronting, and changing these irrational beliefs form the basis of this treatment approach.

Lombardo and Smith (1996) reported on a rational-cognitive therapy program for female offenders. Their program's goals were to understand the theory and application of rational cognitive therapy; deal rationally with their stress provocation and rejection, the stress and anger of their spouses or significant others, the stress and anger of their children; use RCT (Rational Cognitive Therapy) for decision making and problem solving; and, help others use RCT for decision making and problem solving. The program was conducted in a classroom setting and provided skills for inmates to practice improving their ability to rationally respond to life stressors. Some of the techniques taught to inmates are presented below, with an example of how an inmate might complete the exercise.

1. Write down an event exactly, as opposed to how one perceived it.
   (The C.O. told me I couldn't go to commissary.)
2. Write out one's personal response to the event.
   (She's picking on me. This institution sucks! I hate this place!)
3. Write out the emotions and actions of the event.
   (Anger! Unfairness! I yell and scream at her and get a ticket for disruptive behavior.)
4. Create rational challenges to one's responses.
   (She's picking on me: She also told two other women they couldn't go because we all had had a special commissary visit during Saturday visitation.)
   (This institution sucks!: Commissary is important, but I don't truly need anything and I can ask one of my friends to get me candy and soda.)
   (I hate this place!: I do but I don't let the hate consume me every hour of the day or get me disciplined so that it might make me stay here longer.)
5. Create new feelings for similar events in the future.
   (Find out first if I'm being picked on or if it is a rule that affects more people; then either put up with it or file a grievance.)

Cognitive therapy has been used in various settings and with various populations. It addresses fundamental belief systems that, in turn, affect perceptions of events, and behavioral choices. As discussed in previous chapters, women in prison often have been victims of physical and sexual abuse that have destroyed their self-esteem. Beliefs that "I am worthless" or "I don't deserve anything good to happen to me" are very powerful inhibitors to overcoming drug addiction or leading a lifestyle free from negative choices. This form of therapy addresses those fundamental beliefs and teaches the individual how to challenge and test their perceptions of reality.

Moral Development Approaches

Another related type of program incorporates the work of Lawrence Kohlberg (1976, 1981), specifically, his identification of moral stages and theories regarding moral development. Lawrence Kohlberg added to the contributions of Jean Piaget (1965). The basic assumption of their work was that moral development and cognitive development were positively corre-lated. As the child develops cognitive abilities that move from concrete to abstract thinking, so, too, do the moral development capabilities of the child change, increasing the child's ability to understand such abstract concepts as altruism and utilitarianism. Kohlberg (1976) developed his theory of moral development at Harvard and has been the progenitor of a host of other work in the areas of education and morality. According to Kohlberg, all people go through the following stages of moral development:

Stage 1. Obedience to authority and avoidance of punishment are the elements of moral reasoning. Associated with a young child, what is right is what parents say is right. What is wrong is what is punished. There is little independent thought regarding right and wrong; and an egoistic view of the world prevails.

Stage 2. There is still a strong egoistic element to morality. What is right is what feels good to self. There is, however, awareness of relativism, that is, what feels good may be different to different people. There is some commitment to exchange and reciprocity.

Stage 3. This is the good boy-good girl orientation. Role modeling is a major mechanism for shaping values and behavior. Actions are judged by intent as well as consequences.

Stage 4. Morality is associated with doing one's duty and showing respect for authority. Maintaining the social order is seen as the sum result of moral rules.

Stage 5. There is recognition of legalistic agreement in the social order and that the social order may be an arbitrary creation at any particular point in time. Majority rules is a rule of morality.

Stage 6. This is the conscience or principles-based orientation. Social universality and consistency are the themes that are used to determine moral decisions.

Offenders, compared with nonoffenders with similar backgrounds, tend to cluster in Stages 1 and 2, whereas most nonoffender adults tend to cluster in Stages 3 and 4. Few people reach Stages 5 and 6. Intervention has been shown to improve moral development scores. Typically, what the treatment program does is to engage the offenders in moral reasoning discussions when offenders are expected to support judgments. Those with less developed moral reasoning have more difficulty presenting logical arguments for why their rationale is superior and learn from those in the group who present higher level thinking.

One example of the use of moral development theory in corrections was Scharf and Hickey's work in Niantic, a prison in Connecticut. There, they created the elements of a therapeutic community but employed Kohlberg's

(1976) moral reasoning findings to guide the development and implementation of the group meetings. They found that participation in their "just community" raised moral development scores (Scharf & Hickey, 1981).

Another program using "sociomoral" reasoning with offenders was conducted with juvenile delinquents (both male and female). The treatment consisted of eight weekly small-group discussions of sociomoral dilemmas. There was a significant improvement in test scores of the experimental sample compared with scores of the control sample. Most delinquents tested in Stage 2 when the groups started and shifted to Stage 3 in a posttest. Only 14.3% of the control sample showed such improvement (Gibbs, Arnold, Ahlborn, & Cheesman, 1984).

Other applications with correctional populations involved adults. van Voorhis (1985) described a program that did not include an intervention to improve test scores but used Kohlberg's stages to determine offenders' attitudes toward restitution and how their attitude influenced success. She found that low-maturity offenders were more likely to pay restitution because it benefited them and offenders with high-maturity scores were more likely to appreciate restitution's value for victims. Low-maturity offenders were more likely to pay (because of strict controls and punishments) but perceived it as a benefit to themselves rather than the victim.

Arbuthnot (1984) reported on an intervention program with adult prison inmates. Again, program intervention resulted in a significant improvement in test scores measuring moral maturity. He also discussed a few other programs with adult offenders but noted that such programs are less common than programs directed toward juveniles.

Arbuthnot and Gordon (1988) reported on programs that used sociomoral reasoning skills. They discovered that the more successful community programs were those that enjoyed a high level of support, clearly matched organizational needs and intervention goals, possessed clear evidence of prior success, were cost-effective, had continuing contact with a credible and effective expert consultant, and had active participation on the part of all interventionists. They also identified important factors in success as carefully selecting staff who have the inherent skills to employ the process, frequent contact between the trainers and the staff, and a network of therapists to share information.

Fewer programs have been able to show links between stage development and behavior, although Arbuthnot and Gordon (1986) did demonstrate behavioral change with seriously behavior-disordered delinquents. There are continuing difficulties, however, in connecting moral stages with corresponding behavior differences. Another issue is the effectiveness of such program interventions in a prison environment. Arbuthnot (1984) reported on the difficulties of a moral development program in a prison, because prisons typically do not provide rewards for higher-stage behaviors. Before such programs could be expected to achieve significant success, there would have to be protection against the negative prison environment; for instance, the program might be administered in a protected living environment with rewards created for moral reasoning advances. He also proposed that it should be an educational setting that maximized the growth and practice of moral development skills; and, there should be postrelease support to facilitate the continued practice of sociomoral reasoning skills.

Applications to Female Offenders. Gilligan (1982) and others criticized Kohlberg's (1976, 1981) stage theory for being male-centered and ethnocentric. Most of Kohlberg's early work was conducted with males and with those in the United States. It is possible that other cultures do not have the same moral principles, and, therefore, the moral stage hierarchy may not apply to those socialized with other value systems. Gilligan also proposed that the stage sequence did not accurately reflect women's moral development. She found that women tended to cluster in Stage 3, which emphasized relationships, whereas males clustered in Stage 4, which emphasized rules and principles of behavior. In Kohlberg's schema, moral reasoning that was based on relationships was defined as less "mature" than that based on rules and principles. Gilligan proposed that women spoke in a "different voice" and that the hierarchical nature of Kohlberg's stage theory was questionable (Gilligan, 1982). In other words, when asked if one should steal an otherwise unattainable drug to cure one's wife of cancer, men would respond with reasoning focused on laws and rules of society, whereas women might be more likely to focus on the love one has for one's spouse. Decision making for some women, but for fewer men, seems to be based on needs and relationships and how someone else might feel about the outcome. The "more ethical" response—at least by Western philosophical thought—is to apply such universalist principles as utilitarianism.

The possibility that women and men may approach moral reasoning differently is extremely interesting and might be used in treatment approaches. Stage sequence may be less important than helping the individual practice moral reasoning skills. For women, it may be more effective to help them learn to empathize with others rather than emphasize the efficacy of universalist rules of behavior. Women, in other words, already may have an "edge" on an ability to empathize with a victim and perhaps be more likely to develop altruistic values that will prevent further lawbreaking.

Group Therapy

Group therapy is not a specific therapy, rather it is an approach that can be used with treatment modalities as diverse as psychotherapy and cognitive therapies. Groups have special powers that individual counselor-client relationships do not have. They give the individual the sense that others share their problems and there is a greater support for progress. A more comprehensive list of the advantages of the group process follows (Lester & van Voorhis, 1992, p. 175):

1. The group is able to present more information than a single counselor. Several individuals give advice, guidance, and suggest solutions, rather than just one.
2. Group members instill hope by exposing members to others who are further along in treatment.
3. Members see that others share their problems and they realize they are not alone in their troubles.
4. Members help and support one another; members can concentrate on someone else for a change and stop being self-absorbed.
5. The group provides a partial family system in which the members can transfer their feelings regarding family members to group members and resolve long-standing interpersonal problems with the counselor's guidance.
6. The group experience provides a laboratory for practicing social skills.
7. Social learning is also facilitated by role modeling. Members may use each other as role models and imitate prosocial behavior.
8. Each member grows and learns from the group process through feedback and other communication dynamics.
9. The group is a setting for emotional catharsis.
10. Members develop social cohesion and a feeling of belongingness in the group.

There are specific advantages of the group process for prisoner populations. Masters (1994, p. 146) identified the following:

1. It is more economical than individual treatment.
2. It can provide immediate peer pressure, feedback, and information.
3. Challenges from peers are harder for offenders to deny or rationalize.
4. It helps to relieve everyday tension from the prison environment and provides a better way to deal with conflicts.
5. It can help to address the prisoners' subculture.
6. It can help communication between staff and offenders.
7. It is helpful to use for problem solving.
8. It provides reinforcement for positive values.

9. Lay group leaders do not need extensive training.
10. Many different treatment modalities can be adapted to the group process.

Masters (1994) also recognized the problems that group counseling presents in a prison: It may be the site for mere game playing with no sincere effort to deal with problems. Members may discuss only superficial concerns rather than substantive issues. Quiet inmates may hide in the group without dealing with their own problems. Dominant inmates may exploit and control the group. Prison norms that explicitly reject the principles of the group process (for example, confidentiality and sharing confidences) may be more powerful than the group itself.

Two major factors contribute to the use of group counseling for offender populations. The first is economic—counselors can interact with several inmates during the same time period rather than conduct many individual sessions. The second factor that contributes to the popularity of the group approach is that offenders are notoriously manipulative and resistant to change. Other offenders are sometimes more effective than counselors in identifying game playing or confronting the individual who is attempting to delude herself or others regarding treatment. Many different techniques are used in the group approach, depending on the particular treatment modality in use. Group members may help each other by role playing significant others, they may learn communication skills to help them interact in the group process (such as paraphrasing, mirroring, etc.). Many of these skills are taken from the group and used in other interactions.

Applications to Female Offenders. As mentioned before, women tend to be more disclosing and cooperative in the group process. Although female inmates are just as prone to game playing as male inmates, they develop closer relationships more quickly than do the males. In the groups described by Scharf and Hickey (1981), for instance, they noted that women tended to develop groups that were focused on relationships, feelings, and emotional support, whereas the groups of male inmates were more formalistic, focused on rules and political power.

Therapeutic Communities

The origin of the therapeutic community was Maxwell Jones's efforts to create an alternative to institutionalized treatment of war combat veterans after World War II (Jones, 1968). The typical hospital environment was one in which the individual was made dependent and not allowed to take responsibility for his or her own recovery. In the therapeutic community developed by Jones, patients became partners in the therapeutic process instead of subjects to be acted on. Doctors were given no more authority than others in the group meetings in which rules and responsibilities for the unit were decided. Voting was conducted on all issues concerning the running of the ward and groups were conducted to deal with issues of irresponsibility and to encourage patients to take on greater and greater responsibility.

> I can bring your attitude or your inappropriate behavior to you and you're not gonna lash out at me. You're not going to cuss me out. And you're certainly not going to throw hot, scalding water on me.

> We're there for each other. We help each other. We care. There's a lot of concern between us. If we see something totally inappropriate we can point it out and be safe and secure in knowing that there's not going to be any one who gets hard feelings. (Pollock et al., 1995)

"Therapeutic communities" were developed for many types of people, from mentally retarded to prisoners. Therapeutic communities have problems in prison because of power issues. Early programs had problems when prisoners voted to give those who had violated prison rules no punishment or less punishment than what prison officials would have given them. Ordinarily, however, program staff found that prisoners were harsher in distributing punishment than officials or staff persons (Toch, 1980).

Therapeutic communities attempt to negate the overwhelming negativity of the prison environment. Programs are typically housed in such a way as to segregate the members from the general population. They tend to be successful in developing a general atmosphere of positivism and reciprocal self-worth. The members express very positive feelings toward the staff and fellow residents.

> We have a lot of love in here. We come to love each other 'cause that's the only family—ya know 9 months is a long time. I mean especially to someone that's never been locked up before, and um, we get close. (Pollock et al., 1995)

Unfortunately, when individuals leave these communities to go back home, they leave behind the strong positive support that the therapeutic community provides.

> My biggest fear is to know in 55 days that I will be going out that gate and that's a big fear to me because I've been enclosed with my sisters with no

worries and no craziness and no "doing" for 9 months. And I'm just going to go out in that crazy world again and it's scary. (Pollock et al., 1995)

A therapeutic community program is inclusive of everything and anything that happens in the living unit. Relationships, conflicts, irresponsible behavior, and letters from home may be fodder for the group sessions that occur at least once and sometimes twice a day. In addition to group sessions, participants often have jobs and school. This makes for a busy day for some women.

Lights come on at 4:00 a.m., we go to breakfast, we have early showers if you choose to go. My day starts at 6:00 a.m. as assistant expediter in the dorm. That's where we have a hierarchy board here . . . to make sure that groups start and end on time, to keep track of all the inmates coming and going, to make sure that everybody's cubicle is in compliance. Just keeping on top of the noise level and stuff like that. Everybody is responsible for using their house tools also. But anyway I would work from 6:00 a.m. to 12:00, I would go eat, then from 12:30 to 4:00 p.m. or 4:45 p.m. we go to group, and then at 5:30 I go eat dinner. Five-thirty to 10 I go to college at night. (Pollock et al., 1995)

One of the biggest hurdles in prison programs that rely on group therapy or milieu therapy techniques is getting the woman to the position in which she feels comfortable sharing her life story. This element of disclosure is essential for the success of the program and its ability to have an impact on her in any meaningful way. Some women report that there are those in the group who never "get real" and will play along without a true commitment to change or an honest attempt to discuss their problems. Others, sometimes despite themselves, get drawn into the process.

In addition to disclosure, another element of the therapeutic community, that is antithetical to the prison subculture, is the concept that each participant is responsible for the behavior of all. To "police" each other is a difficult concept to grasp for some women and goes against the "us versus them" and "snitch" mentality that is pervasive in prison.

You don't come and act one way in group and outside group act a different way. That's what I mean by people sliding . . . we bring that to each other's attention. We call each other "push-ups," that's letting them know of a positive behavior. Like we'll "push-up" for helping ___ when she was reaching out.

I say "ladies, please 'pull up' on your noise." And at the same time I always say "and someone can say 'thank you, I'll get right on top of that.' " And imagine 48 women saying "thank you, I'll get on top of that." (Pollock et al., 1995)

Arguably, therapeutic communities create the ideal family that some women never had. They learn how to care about each other, how to express their emotions, how to effectively call negative behavior to another's attention, and to accept constructive criticism themselves. There are some problems with this approach, and the primary issue seems to be that the positive elements of such a living environment are difficult to replicate in the real world. Thus, graduates feel abandoned and, for some, their stay in the T.C. (therapeutic community) is looked back on with nostalgia. This does not bode well for staying out of prison. What is needed is a transition from the T.C. to the real world. Some programs have incorporated this element into the approach. For instance, Texas has a drug treatment program that starts in prison using a therapeutic community model, but then there is a mandatory halfway-house stay after the prison term is completed. This time in the halfway house acclimates the individual to the outside and helps them prepare for final release. They are also expected to come back to group meetings at the halfway house in their community. These continued ties further strengthen the potential of success. In fact, the first evaluations of the program showed that it significantly reduced recidivism—program graduates were twice as likely to be successful on parole as a control sample who did not participate (Texas Criminal Justice Policy Council, 1994).

Elements of Intervention Programs

Carp and Schade (1992) found that women offenders needed programs that teach self-sufficiency, responsible behavior, and improve interpersonal relationships. Unfortunately, prison is a poor place to acquire these skills. The nature of prison retards self-control and responsibility; basic decisions about when to eat, where to work, whether to work, and when to get up are usurped by prison authority. Kendall (1994b) discussed this feature of prison life in an evaluation of prison programs. She found that the "rigid control" imposed on women by the prison staff was perceived by them to be the most damaging feature of prison life. This control and arbitrary enforcement of countless rules reproduced the powerlessness and unpredictability that they had experienced in their lives outside prison. Consequently counseling, which sought to help the women gain more control over their lives and take self-determined action, was thwarted by prison that eliminated all autonomy from prisoners' lives.

> [discussing another inmate] she literally did her growing up years in a prison environment, and with choices that were so limited and the way you spend your

> time and the way you spend your money and what choices you make and clothes and just everything from top to bottom, that she spent a lot of time crying before she left prison because she was so frightened. It's easier to stay in than to go out for many of these women. (Pollock et al., 1995)

It is clear from the preceding discussion as well as the earlier chapters that prison programs must be holistic in approach. A program cannot deal with drug problems without also addressing relevant issues of parenting, a history of incest, or the more concrete concerns of finding a job. Another aspect of prison programming that must be recognized is that some individuals are not ready to change. The female inmate either has accepted her life path or not yet arrived at the time in her life when she questions her choices and determines to change.

> [in response to a question whether she would have been helped by the program the first time she went to prison] because I was so young and I was . . . I liked the fast and exciting lane. I know that I could have gone either way. It might have helped me not to come back, by the same token, I might have just had to live the life I had to live in order to get where I am today. Some people are more pigheaded and stubborn than others and I'm one of those. It's taken me a whole 9 months to admit that there was a dysfunction in my family. So it just takes me a long time to understand something and to realize that it's for my benefit. (Pollock et al., 1995)

One of the criticisms leveled at prison programs has been the tendency to assume that a one-stop shop approach will work for all offenders. Female inmates (and male inmates as well) comprise a variety of personality types, with a variety of motivations for criminal activity, and some may suffer from mental health problems. It is unrealistic to expect that any one program would be equally effective for all offenders. Very few programs address the issue of individualized treatment.

There also should be the recognition of women's specific needs and foci—the cycle of abuse, self-image, relationships with men, and multiple addictions (food, men, drugs, alcohol), parenting skills and family issues. Many authors point to the need for special sensitivities when counseling female offenders, and the need for programs that address these issues.

Bloom et al. (1994) presented findings from a Commission's study of the needs of female inmates and parolees in California as follows: (a) Women inmates are significantly different from males in needs; (b) they are less violent and therefore present the opportunity to implement community alternatives and intermediate sanctions without compromising public safety; and,

(c) communities should share this responsibility by providing reintegration services, such as supervision, care, and treatment. Bloom (1992) found that the elements of a successful treatment program were a continuum-of-care design following the women out into the community, clearly stated program expectations and goals, rules and sanctions that were fairly and consistently enforced, consistent supervision, diverse and representative staffing, coordination of community resources, and access to on-going social and emotional support.

More will be said in the last chapter regarding the success of prison programs. It seems obvious at this point, however, that some programs can be more successful than others in meeting the needs of offenders. When the offenders are women, there must be an attempt to address their special needs.

Implications for Counselors

In this chapter we described certain personality disorders one might encounter with prisoner populations and selected prison programs. Some issues of intervention in a prison environment were also discussed. "Rehabilitation" is contrary to the trend of the times. The public seems to want more prisons and longer sentences for criminals. At least the vocal element and politicos would have us think so. Ironically, those who are in favor of prisons being "harder" probably do not realize that treatment is "hard." To come face-to-face with one's past is not easy; to confront one's weaknesses and recreate an identity as an adult is a painful and difficult process. A standard prison term without intervention opportunities will not facilitate a change in lifestyle for most people.

> Working on the hoe squad. That's really tough. I thought the whole time I was there, I thought, God if they ever let me out of here, I'll never come back again. And as you've seen, 12 hours later I was arrested again, so really working the hard part didn't prevent me from coming back. (Pollock et al., 1995)

Some women in prison need intensive psychotherapy or counseling to help them deal with personality disorders, issues from their past, or drug addiction. Others may need the skills and insight that can be gleaned from any number of programs, such as those described earlier. Counselors in prison should be alert for those women who do not seem to be benefiting from opportunities.

It may be that they are not in the right program, are not ready to change, or have more serious problems than the program can handle.

Women are often unable to recognize and appropriately deal with anger and other emotions. Anger is often internalized or sublimated to depression. They may meet others' needs and then not recognize their resentfulness over this sacrifice. Women in prison often deny their victimization from family members and intimates. Their anger over victimization is sublimated to depression or displaced to others. Women in prison may express anger more readily but it is often misdirected or the origin of the emotion is confused. For instance, the woman will explode with an angry reaction to noise on the tier when she is frustrated and angry that her mother cancelled a planned visit with her children. Anger issues will be discussed in more detail in a later chapter.

In prison, there is a unique opportunity, often unavailable out in the community, to deal with such issues as abusive relationships, parenting, drinking or drug use, victimization and so on, in an all-female environment. Although some female offenders refuse to participate, citing confidentiality problems, many women find comfort in the group process. Without men in the group, they have the freedom and safety to discuss relationships with men or women, feelings and behaviors that other women can understand, and not feel the need to "pose" for male attention.

Women often defer their own needs and avoid personal issues of responsibility in their need to fulfill roles of caregivers. Thus, they avoid treatment because of family concerns, identify other family members as having worse problems, or in other ways minimize the emphasis of their own problems and needs in favor of family members or loved ones, especially children. Often women will not go to a halfway house after release, even though that would probably add to the probability of successful reintegration, because most halfway houses do not allow women to have their children live with them, and they are anxious to regain custody. In prison, they have the rare opportunity of concentrating on themselves in an environment where introspection is possible.

Counselors can improve their skills by being aware of program efforts across the country and programs developed in other countries. Not all programs work. Not all programs work for all prisoners. Counselors should stay out of a "box" of rote program assignments for offenders. Sometimes a prison will run a particular program for years with no attempt at evaluation or effort to see if other approaches might better meet offenders' needs. If a particular institution does not have any programs, there is a wonderful opportunity to start one, relying on cognitive therapy, or some of the other approaches described earlier.

In the next chapter we continue the discussion of prison programs with a focus on "life skills"—a very common class or program found in prison, and a description of some of the skills every woman will need if she is to be successful on release.

7

Life Skills:
Making It on the Outside

The old person in me—I was a type that you couldn't talk to me. If you say something out of line to me, we're fighting or something. If it's not that, I'm looking at you like you're crazy, ready to fight. I didn't like myself, didn't care about nothing. It was just like, hey life wasn't nothin until I came and joined this program. I feel better about myself now, and I know how to talk to people, attitude's been changed, self-esteem went up, my pride. . . . I want to do all this for my community [discussing fire-fighting program].

Pollock et al. (1995)

In every study of prisoner needs, the issue of jobs and full employment comes to the forefront. Most inmates identify pragmatic needs of job skills, vocational training, and placement as the most important factor in success on the outside. This should not be surprising, because all statistics indicate that prisoners tend to be undereducated, unemployed, or underemployed and without the resources to earn a living wage on the outside.

Earning a living is not the only "life skill" necessary for a successful transition to the outside. Women offenders must also learn how to live independently of a prison environment, meaning developing the self-control necessary to go to work every morning, take care of daily chores, and plan for the future. Many women have never been on their own—going from one relationship to another with men who were perhaps abusive but provided financial support. Being alone is terrifying to many women. Another "life skill" is learning to deal with such emotions as depression and anger. Many women in prison suffer from depression. Others have extremely maladaptive habits in the way they express their anger, suppress it, or use anger to mask underlying emotions. Finally, another element of a positive lifestyle is learning to accept oneself, an issue that is extremely problematic for many women in prison. Self-esteem classes (even though most have other names) help the woman learn about herself and develop a positive self-image.

Women and Work

In the California study, only 37% of the women sampled had worked at a legitimate job in the year before imprisonment. Drug dealing was mentioned as a secondary income for almost half of the respondents. Approximately one third had been involved in prostitution at some point in their lives (Bloom et al., 1994, p. 5). Similarly, in the Texas sample, almost one third had engaged in prostitution. Most, as reported in a previous chapter, held low-paying, unskilled jobs if they worked at all. About 42% of the Texas sample had worked at a legitimate job in the year before incarceration. About 20% reported that they received some form of public assistance and 14% were supported by family or friends. The rest reported other, including criminal, means of support (Pollock et al., 1996).

Typically, women in prison drop out of high school and have never had any career goals. A few in the Texas sample aspired to be nurses or own their own beauty parlor, but that was the extent to which they planned or hoped for a future. What is even more disheartening is the number of women in prison who have no future goals after release from prison. In the Texas sample of female prisoners, a large number, when asked what job they would like to have, responded by saying "anything" (Pollock et al., 1996). This lack of goal setting is, to some degree, related to the lack of programming in prison; if they are not trained to do anything, they will be lucky to find any job at all on the outside. Nevertheless, if they have no strong goals or direction for their future, it is not surprising that they drift back into dysfunctional relationships, depend on family members for income, or quit dead-end jobs in favor of making "easy" money in the drug trade.

Prison Industry and Employment

The history of prisons includes a history of forced labor. The slaves who built the pyramids of Egypt, the galley slaves of the Dark Ages, and those who labored under the lessee system in the American South after the Civil War were all prisoners used for slave labor. Women, weaker and sometimes pregnant, have been considered less useful workers. For radical historians, this may be a more cogent reason for the lower incarceration rate of women, historically, than any so-called chivalry explanation.

Early prisons in England and in this country viewed labor as essential to the management of the institution. Whereas men engaged in agricultural, manufacturing, or both tasks, women often served as support labor, such as by cooking, laundering, and cleaning. Some institutions, with few women and little need for their services, left them idle. One of the innovations in the early reformatories for women was a wider array of work; women took care of livestock, they planted crops, and engaged in minor repairs around the facility. This "healthy living" was one of the touted features of women's reformatories (Pollock-Byrne, 1990). Nevertheless, domestic service was obviously the more common labor expected of women. Some prisons, especially in the South, employed women as house servants to prison administrators; female prisoners in the North were released to "good" families as their domestic servant in an early form of parole (Pollock-Byrne, 1990; Rafter, 1985).

The history of prison labor is largely silent regarding women during the 1940s through the 1980s. In the 1970s and 1980s a few unique and creative work opportunities for women in prison were developed. For instance, large companies using telephone ordering or telephone reservation systems have set up in women's prisons, paying women free-world wages. Data processing by governmental entities and private companies is conducted in some women's prisons. Still, there is a dearth of opportunities. At the beginning of this decade, it was reported that less than 1% of all prisoners had access to some meaningful work opportunities—a statistic that includes male prisoners as well (Stone, 1997).

The largest job category employing women and men is prison maintenance, specifically cleaning, landscaping, and cooking for the prison population. The largest single category of prison work is food service. In some prisons, assignment to kitchen duty is labeled culinary arts and is counted as a vocational program, but there is probably little application in the free world to the large cafeteria-style cooking done in prisons, except perhaps in other institutions. In the Texas sample, about 90% reported working at some type of job in prison. Jobs mentioned most frequently were in the kitchen, as an orderly or porter, or with an outside crew responsible for landscaping. Most of these jobs were not full-time, some were actually only a few hours a day. In one prison, a number of women reported their job was with a "special crew," which was explained as a crew of workers who did "whatever the assistant warden told us to do." In the meantime, they were idle (Pollock et al., 1996). Basically, when a prison reports close to full employment, it doesn't necessarily mean that the jobs are meaningful, pay a wage, or even are full-time.

There are two potential models for inmate industry—the partnership model and the prison industry model. The partnership model applies when private industry sets up a factory or work situation close to or inside the prison, pays the inmates, and the state provides the custody and control; for example, the telephone reservation system mentioned previously. The other model applies when the prison itself runs an industry or manufacturing company. An example of this second model is UNICOR, the federal prison system's industry program. This is a huge entity that employs thousands of inmates across the country and makes large numbers of products, from furniture to office supplies.

As Stone (1997) pointed out, the same issues considering inmate labor that were discussed 100 years ago are still current today: the potential displacement of civilian jobs, whether and how much compensation to give to inmate workers, inmate safety and security, and the cost-effectiveness of prison industry programs. Prison industry often overlaps into vocational programming, because most inmates are unskilled and require training. If the training is in an area that has free-world applicability, then the prison job may provide the opportunity to obtain the same type of job on the outside.

Whereas the opportunities for women are greater today than they have been in the past, it is still safe to say that there are not enough industry programs. Because most of the labor force in the United States is moving from agricultural or heavy manufacturing to service and skilled occupations, the old argument that women are unsuited to labor programs becomes even less viable than it ever was, to justify the exclusion of women prisoners from opportunities to make a small wage, learn a skill, and create the opportunity for them to get a job on release.

In addition to having the qualifications for a job, individuals must be able to have the self-confidence to apply and interview for a position and then to "sell" themselves. Many inmates feel helpless and uncomfortable in the "skills" of applying for a job. Some prison programs attempt to alleviate these fears by helping the inmate practice these skills.

The Crime Prevention Institute. One such program in Texas has been developed and implemented by the Crime Prevention Institute, a private nonprofit agency that contracts with the state to hold job fairs in some correctional facilities (National Institute of Justice, 1996a). In these job fairs, volunteer employers come and perform practice interviews with the inmate participants. The day is a culmination of working with counselors and CPI (Crime Prevention Institute) staff, who help them prepare a resumé and discuss interview skills. From the questions asked by inmates, it seems clear that this experience is sorely needed. Staff routinely respond to such questions as "I have never had a job other than in prison; what should I write on the application?" "How do I answer the 'felony' question?" "What do I put down for salary? I don't get paid for my prison job." Each inmate has the opportunity to interview with up to six different employers for 30-minute interviews. Twenty minutes of this time is the mock job interview, and in the last 10 minutes the interviewer provides verbal feedback to the inmate on his or her performance. The employers also provide written evaluations that are shared with the inmate the next day and used to improve their skills.

The volunteer employers range from very large companies to state agencies. In the several years of operation of this program, hundreds of person-hours have been donated by these employers who often travel long distances at their own expense to reach the prison where the job fair is located. Although they are recruited with the explanation that they are not expected to hire prisoners, just practice interviews with them, many have been so impressed with their make-believe interviewees that they have either hired them, found them a job, or in one case the personnel director managed to convince his company to change their policy prohibiting hiring of ex-offenders to hire a promising candidate. One large company has hired 18 ex-offenders, because a human resource officer in the company became involved (National Institute of Justice, 1996a). Employers participate because of a perception that helping the offender succeed will benefit everyone, as explained by a successful businessman who was one of the first volunteer interviewers with the program (National Institute of Justice, 1996a).

> You are a business person with your head in the sand if you are not concerned about crime and its impact on your business, your customers, and you as an individual. . . . While I was concerned, I didn't know of any way to plug into the problem and make a difference. (p. 9)

The program started with one correctional institution and nine employers and in 4 years has grown to include several correctional institutions and over 300 volunteer employers. Programs such as this improve the confidence level of the offender as well as dispel some myths of employers regarding offenders. Employers routinely express surprise at the skill level and general employability of prisoner interviewees. They are also given information regarding tax breaks for hiring ex-offenders that include federal-job-tax credits, as well as special Texas state-tax refunds and credits created to encourage the hiring of ex-offenders.

Educational and Vocational Programs

In early reformatories and custodial prisons, women were taught to read so that they could read the Bible and impart Christian values to their children.

It was believed that the purpose of education, for women, was to make them better mothers. Prisoners were expected to conform to an ideal of chastity and piety representing the place of women in society. Today, educational and vocational programs are offered because of the realization that women will need to support themselves and possibly their children after they are released.

Almost all prisons today offer some sort of basic education (Crawford, 1988) and many have college-level programs. Also, about 90% of all prisons have some sort of vocational programming, with some states reporting a dozen or more different programs. Texas, California, Georgia, Nevada, Oklahoma, and Pennsylvania reported the most programs in a study done in the mid 1980s (Crawford, 1988). Women enrolled in and most often preferred clerical and business education fields. Nontraditional programs, such as auto mechanics, heavy machinery driving, or floor cleaning are not as popular, and prison staff perhaps do not "sell" these programs as energetically as they could.

Although women in prison have, on average, a few more years of school than men in prison, adult basic education is still a pressing need for large numbers of women inmates. In the Texas sample, 64.5% did not graduate from high school, although a little less than 40% had obtained a GED (one third of these received it in prison) (Pollock et al., 1996). In Texas, there is a requirement that every inmate be placed in either an adult basic education class or a GED class if they do not have a high school diploma (Stone, 1997). About 10% of the women sampled had some college education, and another 10% had some vocational schooling (usually in business or secretarial courses or cosmetology).

Whereas adult basic education teaches basic literacy, GED programs prepare the student to take an equivalency exam that substitutes for a high school diploma. The largest prison GED program in the country is in Texas, which awarded 4000 GED certificates in 1993 (Stone, 1997). In fact, Texas's Wyndham School District is the only prison school district in the country and is larger than all but a few of the school districts in the entire country.

Education for adults poses special problems, especially for an offender population who may have failed at school in the past, have little motivation, or are distracted and suffer from health problems that impair concentration. Evans (1978) presented six principles necessary for successful prison education programs.

1. It must be meaningful.
2. It must be offered in short, attainable, and measurable segments.
3. There must be reinforcement.

4. There must be balance—education is only one part of an integrated delivery system.
5. The education program must be accredited.
6. There should be an interpersonal relationship established between the teacher and the student.

No correlation has been found between obtaining the GED and reducing recidivism (Stone, 1997). Nevertheless, there may be methodological problems with the few studies that explore the relationship between education and recidivism. For instance, prisoners who obtain GEDs are typically younger than the average prisoner. We also know that recidivism is correlated with youth. Thus, those in GED programs are also those with the highest recidivism rates. The age factor may eclipse the impact of the GED on subsequent success on parole.

Citizens' anger regarding providing college programs for criminals seems misguided, because relatively few prisoners are able to take advantage of such programs even if they exist. Although most states report some availability of college programs, most often these are a few classes offered by a local community college. To actually obtain a degree would take many years, and only certain subject areas are available. Only 17 states report having 4-year degrees available (Stone, 1997). Although studies do not support a correlation between GED programs and a reduction of recidivism, there does seem to be such a relationship for college programs. In one study it was found that graduates of a college program were significantly less likely to recidivate than noncollege releasees (26.4% versus 44.6%) (Clark, 1991).

The proliferation of vocational programs in women's prisons is at least partially spurred by such court cases as *Glover v. Johnson* (1979), in which the court found that Michigan had fewer programs for women inmates than men, and this differential treatment was unconstitutional. In the 1970s most vocational programs in prisons for women were in the areas of culinary arts, cleaning, "floriculture," cosmetology, and office skills. One of the problems with offering vocational programs to women is that they are typically less cost-effective than if they were offered in institutions for men because of the small numbers of women in prison. One result of the increasing numbers of women sent to prison and the larger size of newer prisons for women is that this argument is losing its vitality. Unfortunately, states often have the money to build new prisons but then run out of funds to operate any programs inside the new prisons. One survey found that at least half of the states have cut back in vocational programming owing to budget problems (Stone, 1997).

Another recent change in opportunities for federal Pell grants has eliminated the opportunity for many inmates to take advantage of vocational
programs operated by community colleges. Many states use community
colleges to provide vocational programs and tap into federal financial aid for
students in the form of Pell grants. Recently, these grants have been made
unavailable to inmates as part of the national fiscal conservatism and "get
tough" approach to offenders. The consequence is that many inmates, unable
to afford such programs on their own, are effectively barred from learning any
skill while incarcerated (Stone, 1997).

Since the 1980s, some states have experimented with nontraditional programming for women. Auto mechanics, carpentry, electrical trades, heavy
equipment operation and other programs now exist in some state prisons. One
program in California is a joint partnership between the state prison and the
state forestry service to train women to be forest firefighters. During the
course of this training, they are bused early in the morning to the foothills an
hour away to learn how to use the tools, set a fire line and gain knowledge of
the safety issues of fighting fires. During the day, this group of roughly 20
women are supervised by one correctional officer and taught by a trainer from
the forestry department. In the event of forest fires, these women will be used,
along with male prisoners receiving the same training, to work alongside
firefighters. Although the job opportunities for this training may be limited—
only a few will be hired by the forestry service—they do gain invaluable skills
of self-reliance, pride, and confidence that they can perform difficult work.

States that offer nontraditional programs for women find that many
women are not interested in auto mechanics, heavy equipment operation, or
commercial floor cleaning. In fact, they are confused about why these programs are in "their" prisons and perceive it as yet another way in which state
prison administrators treat them "like men." When it is explained that the
average wage of these occupations is sometimes double or triple the wage that
could be earned in typically "female occupations," they see the logic. It must
be accepted, however, that just as few women in society choose to go into
nontraditional areas, women in prison will most likely represent the same
small percentage of interest. For instance, if only 6% of those employed in
the construction trade outside prison are women, then it should be expected
that roughly the same small percentage of women in prison might be interested
in such an occupation. Some go through the nontraditional programs because
they believe it will help them obtain parole but explain that they plan to go
back to being a beautician or get a job working with children when they are
released. If this is true, the expensive training provided by prison is being
wasted. Another issue that cannot be ignored is that discrimination still exists

in hiring women in these nontraditional fields. If an employer were disinclined to hire a woman, even though she met the job qualifications, he could not legally refuse to hire her because of her sex; nevertheless, he could decide that her prison record made her unacceptable. Therefore, women who receive nontraditional training may face two forms of job discrimination: as women and as ex-felons.

One area that seems to be desired by both men and women is any training related to computers. This may be one nontraditional area of vocational programming that has the potential to attract larger numbers of women and provide them jobs on the outside. It also is clear that the vocational programs of the future are going to require education; thus, many women may not be eligible for such programs until they complete basic education, GED, and perhaps even some college courses.

Even in the largest states that offer the broadest range of vocational programming, relatively few inmates participate. Stone (1997) points out that in Texas, California, and New York, only about 15% to 20% of all inmates participate in some form of vocational program. This is low but twice as high as the national average, which is around 9%. If one acknowledges that a good portion of even these small percentages are in areas that have relatively little potential for outside employment, such as "culinary arts" or "agricultural science," then it is clear that an extremely small portion of offenders will leave prison with a new, marketable skill.

Whether vocational skills successfully reduce recidivism is debatable. Stone (1997) reviewed the literature and concluded that many issues influence the vocational program's ability to affect the decision to return to crime. For instance, he points out that if the program does not address work attitudes and values, then the specific vocational skills attained may not be enough to obtain and keep a job. In other words, an individual may receive a mechanic's certificate or an electrician's license, but if he or she shows up to work late and is antagonistic to the boss while at work, then that person will not hold onto a job for long.

Whether or not the vocational skills achieved in prison translate into getting a job in that vocational area, on release, is the single most important element in the success of a vocational program providing lasting change in the individual's lifestyle. Most programs do not include a placement component. If there is no commitment to place an individual in a job, then often what happens is the inmate takes the first job available to comply with parole conditions and then little or no attempt is made by the individual offender to continue to search in the field of training. It may be that partnerships with private industry are most successful because of enhanced opportunities—

companies may routinely place released offenders who achieve good work records in other divisions or outlets in the same company.

Life Skills: Personal Development

There is a correlation between unemployment and recidivism, but what is probably also true, although there have been no studies on this topic, is that there is a correlation between having a strong sense of direction with clearly defined goals and parole success. An overwhelming impression one receives after talking to many women inmates about their future is how few have any sense of where they are going or how they are going to get there.

"Life skills," as the term is used in prison, includes classes in balancing a checkbook, self-esteem, parenting, and many other practical skills or personal development components. When one thinks about what it takes to lead a "successful" life, it is clear that there are objective and subjective features of "success." A skill is useless unless there is some degree of self-confidence to go along with it. Making money is necessary but so is managing money so that there is enough to pay the bills at the end of the month. Learning healthy leisure activities can replace less healthy ones, such as drug use and drinking. Finally, learning to understand one's emotions and how to express them and control them is essential for healthy parenting, keeping a job, and having healthy, loving relationships with partners and family members.

Another aspect of life skills, and why this chapter is so necessary in a book concerned with "treatment," is that *doing* is just as important, if not more so, than *talking* about doing. Therefore, although group therapy or one-on-one counseling may help the woman understand her past, the only way she will be able to affect her future is through action. Any successful intervention must involve activity designed to learn a skill, develop self-confidence, gain an education, and/or otherwise improve the skills necessary for a positive lifestyle. Doing something productive may, in fact, be a basic human need.

In "life skills" programs, women may learn how to balance a checkbook, how to apply for food stamps, what to look for in buying a car, cautions regarding buying on credit, rights regarding equal protection in housing, lease agreements and what they mean, and so on. Classes also may cover more personal issues: value systems, decision making, recognizing emotions, how to deal with anger, communication styles of individuals, study skills, goal setting, and so on. They are taught by volunteers in some prisons, by staff in others. Tools used may be vocational interest surveys, value exercises, visiting experts in the areas of women's health issues, parenting, or drug abuse.

Practice sessions on interviewing, role playing on how to deal with difficult people, and self-studies are just some of the activities practiced in these life skills classes. The methods of teaching range from straight lecture or classroom to something that approaches group therapy. One thing is clear: Unlike most of us, many female prisoners never learned some of the relatively simple lessons of life. Communication, health education, nutrition, relaxation, identifying emotions, handling stress—all of these issues may be dealt with in a life skills course.

WICS. WICS (Women In Community Service) is a program that was formed through a coalition of The Church Women United, The National Council of Jewish Women, The American G.I. Forum Women, The National Council of Catholic Women, and The National Council of Negro Women. It was founded in 1964 and now has programs in three states. The branch in Oregon is the only one based in a correctional institution. The goal of the program is to provide training and support for women who are near their release date. The WICS program is one 7-week training session, with up to 15 women. This life skills program has four basic components: personal skills assessment, life skills empowerment workshops, community mentoring, and a volunteer internship. The personal skills assessment is done through a computer-generated analysis, to identify such traits as dexterity, motor skills, evaluative reasoning, learning style, and work temperament. The life skills empowerment workshops are designed to help the woman learn to deal with situations ranging from health issues to budget and time management. Mentoring is another part of the WICS program. Mentors are community members who commit 6 months to one year of their time. They are connected with a WICS graduate and continue the relationship, ideally for one year. The volunteer internship component places a female graduate of the program in a community service setting to complete 40 hours of service. This enables her to obtain job skills and contacts and references. Although the program is new in Oregon, initial results are encouraging. Of the 76 graduates from the program who had been paroled as of March 1994, only one had been returned to prison. (Kapsner, 1994).

Dealing With Depression

There is some evidence that, in our culture, women are more likely than men to suffer from depression (Frankel, 1992, p. 3). This may be an artifact of women's tendency to be more self-disclosing, or it may be the result of other female traits, such as suppressing anger and turning it inward. Depression may be caused by a chemical imbalance, a symptom of a bipolar disorder, or related to psychosis. It also may be the result of situational stressors (for instance, the trauma and stress of the prison sentence), or it may be long-standing and originate in the woman's early childhood experiences.

Some of the symptoms of depression include lethargy, change in appetite, weight loss or gain, loss of interest or enthusiasm about activities, feelings of hopelessness and despair, sleep disturbances, general fatigue, feelings of guilt or worthlessness, indecisiveness, inability to concentrate, and recurrent thoughts of death or suicide (Frankel, 1992, pp. 5-6).

According to a cognitive model of depression, the individual suffers from negative underlying thoughts that define herself as defective, inadequate, and worthless. These underlying thoughts then influence the individual's life experiences in a negative way and create a negative view of the future (Beck et al., 1979, p. 11). For those with such thoughts, "no good things go rewarded." In other words, any good things that happen—successes or pleasure—are reinterpreted to fit the underlying definitions of self. Therapy would consist of recognizing and disputing the underlying thoughts that define the self as bad and unworthy. Unfortunately, for women in prison this is more difficult to do because their behaviors—toward their children, their family, and themselves—have been singularly undeserving of praise. The key to this type of approach is to find some evidence of success and build on it. That is why the practical programs described earlier are complementary to more traditional psychotherapy programs—it is important for individuals to feel success, but to do so there must be opportunities to perform, whether in a vocational class, a forestry course, or as a plumber's apprentice.

Another view of depression is that women are prone to it because of a tendency, reinforced by socialization and cultural proscriptions, to suppress their anger. Early in childhood, women learn not to show when they are angry, because it is unacceptable for a woman to express such an emotion. Because emotions do not just go away, the result is a buildup of resentment, anger, and outrage—women may react with passive-aggressiveness or depression (Frankel, 1992). Observations of women in prison would lead one to believe that female prisoners do not seem to have any trouble expressing their anger but not necessarily in a healthy manner. Another common issue dealt with in life skills courses is anger management.

Anger and Aggression

"Anger management" is one specific class or program often offered to prison populations. Women in prison, as mentioned in an earlier chapter, have a greater number of disciplinary infractions than men in prison. In a study (Pollock, 1986) that tapped officers' perceptions of the differences in supervising men and women in prison, officers indicated they believed that women would "act out" more than male prisoners and that they were more "assaultive."

> When officers were asked if females "acted out" more than male inmates, an overwhelming majority said they did (85%). . . . The most frequently given descriptions of acting-out behavior by women relate to expressive emotionality. Women were described as frequently having tantrums or outbursts of anger in which they engage in verbal assaults on officers. (p. 57)

Officers also believed women were more assaultive, which is an interesting divergence from the general societal view that women are more passive and less aggressive than men by nature.

> Women are a lot more aggressive, o.k.? If a female gets mad at you, she'll scratch your eyes out, pull your hair, she'll rip your shirt off, anything that a female would do when they get emotionally mad, o.k.? If a guy gets mad at ya, he's going to cuss at ya, he might hit ya, but he'll usually walk away. (p. 80)

These perceptions extend to other countries, as shown by the following quote from a prison staff member in a British prison.

> Men build up "aggro," which bursts after a time and lasts longer than the women's aggression. On the other hand women are more emotive, have instant outbursts which however don't last very long. (Mandaraka-Sheppard, 1986, p. 137)

Obviously officers' perceptions are shaped by their stereotypes. Because they don't believe that women, in general, are violent, the violence expressed by women in prison seems more obvious and extreme. Also, the "acting-out" behavior may be an institutional reaction to different supervision styles. In an earlier chapter, evidence was presented that suggested that women were subjected to a more pervasive and petty form of supervision and discipline than male prisoners. Because women are more likely to be treated in a maternalistic fashion "like children," this, in turn, creates a probability that the reaction will be childish.

> A group of us kicked our doors because they wouldn't let us out to go to the toilet,—it just seemed pointless. Why were they so wicked? (Eaton, 1993, p. 5)

The assaultiveness of women toward each other is probably no more than that found in prisons for men but it is more open and, thus, officers see it, whereas male prisoners tend to engage in covert and planned violence. Nevertheless, there are other issues at work. Unresolved anger and depression may contribute to women's "acting-out" behavior in prison. Also, women may "act out" in prison because, quite simply, they can. That is, they are less likely to be beaten or killed in response to their anger, as might have been the case in their childhood or with their intimate partners—perhaps for the first time they feel comfortable in expressing rage, and it feels good, so they express it more frequently than they ever had on the outside. Another element may be the intense stress and frustration of the prison experience, which also leads to anger and aggression. Not having appropriate skills to channel this anger or the ability to release it through more appropriate responses, the woman strikes out or "acts out."

Obviously, one cannot be very successful in the outside world if anger becomes the immediate response to any frustration, and anger is often expressed in a loud and physically aggressive manner. Women in prison must learn to identify their anger, its source, and practice appropriate methods to handle it.

One of the elements of such a program is to become more aware of emotions. Many women in prison are not in touch with their feelings and haven't been since childhood. They may express love for parents and deny the rage and pain of abuse. They may express no anger toward boyfriends who let them take the blame for a drug deal. Their emotions sometimes seem disjointed—they blame one parent but not the other. They blame the system for their predicament but accept no personal responsibility. They feel hurt because of abandonment by family but excuse other family members' lack of responsibility. Counseling can help female prisoners learn about emotions and help them become more aware of their own emotions. Exercises can include adjective lists, emotions diaries, behavior cues, and short stories. The particular emotion of anger is sometimes the underlying cause of depression. Anger may mask fear. Especially in prison, women may choose anger over helplessness, hopelessness, or needfulness. Anger gives a feeling of power to the individual during the "acting-out" incident. The "rush" from this feeling may induce a pattern of anger outbursts.

Anger management is about learning control. For instance, anger diaries are sometimes used to help women identify what triggers their anger. By becoming their own "analysts," they can take steps to avoid these situations. Other cognitive exercises are also useful. For instance, helping the woman identify beliefs that contribute to her anger is sometimes very enlightening.

For example, such beliefs as "People always will take advantage of you," "I can't control my anger," and "Everyone is out to get me" will exacerbate a small incident to result in an anger outburst. It becomes the task of the helper to get the woman offender to see these beliefs and to counteract their power by showing their falsity. One characteristic of women in prison that has been noted by prison staff is that "little things" get them angry. It seems to be the case that there is no ability to graduate one's response to the seriousness of the frustration (Pollock, 1986). Thus, one exercise that is sometimes helpful is identifying the "levels" of anger, to learn that not everything should trigger a violent outburst. Typical behavioral responses to the graduated levels of annoyance, through irritation, anger, and rage can be discussed and practiced.

It is obviously not the intent of such interventions to deny anger or to encourage suppression. This tendency is all too common among women anyway and may have been a mechanism of survival for those women with abusive childhoods. Unfortunately suppressed anger often manifests itself in very damaging ways, such as depression, self-mutilation or homicide. Programs teaching anger management are empowering, because they help women learn about themselves and ways to control situations by controlling themselves.

> It's a program to teach you tolerance. It teaches you change or it teaches control. It shows you where your anger comes from. It teaches you where anger comes from. Where your violent points are. Like I never knew that I get angry out of fear, frustration, resentment, I never knew that. And these are the points that cause violence—scared, resentful, rejected, abandonment. All that causes violence. It shows you how to deal with situations verbally. Like you don't have to argue to get your point across. You don't have to get mad. . . . When I came to prison I was angry. Nobody liked me. I didn't get along with anybody. (Pollock et al., 1995)

To accept the proposition that one is in control of one's own emotions is a powerful realization. Women in prison generally have had lives in which they had very little control over themselves or others. They tend to be fatalistic and accept others' anger and their own as "just the way people are." To learn that they can control their anger also leads to the belief that others can control their anger, which sometimes results in a personal revelation that relationships don't have to be abusive and lives don't have to be punctuated by violence. To choose nonviolent responses is also to choose a healthier and more positive lifestyle, one that can be practiced daily, given the right resources.

Unfortunately general prison populations are not the best environments in which to learn and practice such skills. Although violence is most often associated with prisons for men, even in prisons for women inmates who are perceived as weak or unlikely to fight back will be victimized. Women learn quickly that the best response to such an environment is to feign an aggressive posture. Even correctional officers recognize that some attacks on them probably occur because the woman knows that there will be limited retaliation and the attack ensures that she will be left alone by other inmates (Pollock, 1986). Protected living environments, such as therapeutic communities, are highly sought-after program slots, because they are typically safer places to live, even though they involve a great deal more personal "work" with group meetings every day. People don't "go off" on each other and if it happens it is thoroughly explored and resolved in group meetings. Women have the chance to role model and pattern more appropriate ways of handling anger.

Anger management, it is hoped, will have long-range effects when women are released and regain custody of their children. Instead of being raised in households where physical attacks are common responses to anger, these women's children may benefit from the female prisoner learning ways to control and express anger without physical abuse.

Self-Esteem

Another component of life skills programs is self-esteem development. Program elements encourage self-discovery and learning to like oneself. Although the evidence on whether or not women in prison are more likely than the general population to suffer from low self-esteem is mixed (see Pollock-Byrne, 1990), programs seem to make a difference to the women involved in them. Often their childhood, marked by abuse, neglect, or abandonment, contributed to a self-identity of unworthiness, and their lifestyle as adults, that might include abandonment of their own children, prostitution, drug use, and an inability to keep a job, reinforced the belief that they were bad or worthless.

> I learned respect. I learned self-respect. . . . I didn't have no respect and I didn't give any respect. And I didn't have any values. And I didn't care about anybody else. (Pollock et al., 1995)

For some women, criminal acts may be something they do well; therefore, before they can give up a criminal lifestyle, they must have some other means to feel worthy.

> I didn't go back because I didn't want to be lectured about it. It was just one thing that I was clinging on to. I don't know, it's hard to explain—I was clinging

to my re-offending because it was giving me moral esteem or self-esteem—and in the end I just threw everything up. I stopped doing the course, I stopped seeing the therapist and I started to go thieving again. I made a lot of money. (Eaton, 1993, p. 8)

The female offender in the above quote continued her story, explaining how she stopped committing crimes when her "straight" boyfriend made her feel guilty. By then she was awaiting a court date for the new offenses, and he broke off their relationship. She went into a depression and couldn't find help from anyone she called, her ex-probation officer, the children's home where she was raised, social services agencies—no one could give her the help she needed to pull out of the depression she was in. Finally, after being returned to prison, she finished her prison time and received probation again, began seeing a psychologist and taking college classes. She also had a friendship with another woman she had met in prison that was positive in that she could "be herself" with this woman and not pretend. She ended her story in the following way:

I've made up my mind that I'm not going to offend any more and that's not prison that made me choose that, it was just realizing that you live a certain life and you're destined to live a certain way. . . . I just determined not to re-offend anymore. . . . But it's just the pain and everything that I can't control in me and the ghost that haunts me and my fear. (Eaton, 1993, p. 12)

Everyone needs love, respect, and self-affirmation. Some women in prison have not experienced much of any of those things all their lives. Any program or helping relationship that can genuinely reach the inmate and encourage her to find what is good in herself, to build on her successes and to develop goals for the future, has more chance of reducing recidivism than one that doesn't. Criminal lifestyles are typically chosen because they provide something that a law-abiding lifestyle does not; specifically, money, or a relationship, or a feeling of mastery over one's environment, or in the case of drug use a means of escape from one's environment. If one possesses a feeling of self-worth and a positive self-image that does not involve criminality, there is less temptation to go back to offending again on release.

Implications for Counselors

Almost everyone needs to have a job. The only exception may be those who are handicapped, elderly, or have enough personal or familial economic resources to avoid work. It's probably safe to say that the latter group are not overly represented in a prison population. Historically, there was a misperception that women were a separate category of those who did not need to work. This has never been true and is not true today. Women will leave prison most often to support themselves and perhaps their children as well. Few will go to living situations in which they will be supported by someone else. These women are overwhelmingly unskilled and, thus, unable to work at all but the most unskilled, menial jobs. They may not—in fact, statistics show they probably will not—gain a skill in prison, and that means they will go back to being nurses' aids, cutting hair, or working in fast-food outlets. Although it is possible that they will succeed under these conditions, it is also probable that the temptation to use a stolen credit card, forge a check, or shoplift will become overwhelming. If the woman has connections she may be asked to sell drugs, in which case she could earn a month's wages in one day, if she takes the chance. Of course, she also may spend it in a day if she relapses to drug use.

Women may be an easier population to create programs for, because there is less fear and antipathy on the part of the public toward female offenders. In the same way that turn-of-the-century reformers found that halfway houses for women were easier for the public to accept, it may be that job training and industry partnership programs with female offenders might be more palatable to the public if they involve early release or some form of temporary liberty. Correctional counselors can help to interest local industry and business in such programs as those described in this chapter or others.

A problematic element in the female offender's release and work plans is the issue of her children. Women may choose low-paying jobs because the hours or responsibilities are more conducive to being a single mother. Women may be forced to put off regaining custody because they cannot afford to feed their children. They may be less effective workers because of worries about childcare. All of these problems are faced by all mothers, especially single mothers, but female offenders deal with the added stress of release from a protected environment where none of those worries were present. Female parolees will explain that sometimes they sought out drugs just to feel better "for a little while," because of the overwhelming stress of work, childcare, and paying bills. Of course drug use inevitably resulted in more problems and a subsequent return to prison. Counselors can help to improve the chance of success by making sure all of these stresses have been thought through before a woman leaves the prison and helping her develop coping strategies for dealing with the problems she will face on release.

Counselors can also help women in prison by finding out what interests them, what special skills they have, and what their long-forgotten goals might be. A prison plan should not be based solely on what is available but rather on what excites the female prisoners and what she might be able to use once released. It is a waste of resources to give women vocational training that they have no intention of using on release. If the prison does not offer enough programs in a particular area in which there is a great deal of interest, it makes more sense to add more programs in that area rather than in an area that women are not interested in. One cannot dictate to another what she should do with the rest of her life. For those women who have no goals, no plans, no sense of where they want to go, the process is more difficult and may involve delving into issues of depression and self-esteem.

Ethnic and Cultural Issues

Some criticize life skills programs as imposing cultural straightjackets on the women involved in them. It might be argued that not everyone lives cookie-cutter lives of middle-class respectability. Life skills may be criticized as teaching female offenders how to be middle class. Any type of counseling must be sensitive to the client's particular social and cultural makeup. In corrections, counselors deal with a population that includes large numbers of individuals from minority groups, and ethnic and cultural differences may exist between the counselor and the client. Further, female offenders are influenced by cultural stereotypes regarding appropriate female behavior that the counselor, even if she is a female, may not have experienced. For instance, it might be argued that African American females are socialized to be more assertive and independent than Anglo women, but Hispanic women are typically socialized to a definition of femininity that emphasizes subservience, religiosity, and motherhood. Enos and Southern (1996) discussed the concept of "marianismo"—a corresponding feminine concept to the idea of machismo in the Hispanic culture. "Marianismo" describes a perfect woman as emotional, kind, instinctive, docile, compliant, vulnerable, and unassertive.

The counselor must take culture and background into account to understand actions, values, and motivations for crime. Sometimes this poses a paradox. If the Hispanic woman is in trouble with the law because she did what her husband or brother or father told her to do, and if she has been a victim of sexual abuse, and suffers from low self-esteem because she has always been told she is fat and ugly and no one will ever love her, then a feminist therapeutic approach will attempt to counteract those negative messages and build her self-esteem. If successful, she will become more assertive, sure of herself, and independent. But to what result? She will return to her family, friends, and a cultural milieu that is hostile to her newfound personality and she will go through a great deal of stress owing to her change in outlook. With her new "self," but without her cultural supports, will she be happier or more alienated? Of course, this is an exaggerated example, but these issues do face Hispanic or Latino women today and are dealt with in a body of literature by Hispanic and Latino female writers, poets, and political theorists. The point is, correctional counseling, just as all counseling, cannot ignore the cultural and social realities of clients.

Okun (1990) discussed the concept of sensitivity to ethnic and cultural differences in psychotherapy and proposes that much of traditional male-dominated psychotherapy has done women a disservice by forcing dominant stereotypes of what is normal and acceptable for women onto clients. Examples of therapeutic approaches that may be insensitive to women include family therapy, when it reinforces traditional patriarchal hierarchies of power; and cognitive therapies, if they support stereotypical notions of what is appropriate behavior for females.

Therapy of any kind may not take into account the life experiences of ethnic minorities and how these life experiences affect mental health functioning. For instance, Okun (1990) discussed the possibility that widespread societal discrimination and racism create a "learned helplessness" and external locus of control among minority group members that is symptomatic of their social experiences. Behavioral norms may differ, so that what is deviant to the middle-class counselor may be normal for the client. For example, cultural groups may differ in methods of parental discipline or the involvement of the extended family in child rearing. They differ in their definitions of appropriate sex roles and the place of the elderly in the family. According to Okun (1990, p. 393), "The important areas not acknowledged by and dealt with in . . . [the four therapy models discussed in her book] concern disease, gender, race, and culture." This is certainly true of much of correctional counseling as well.

One example of how a correctional system may respond to specific and unique ethnic needs was the proposal in Canada to build a "healing lodge" for Aboriginal female prisoners. This was proposed in response to reports from advocates and prisoner groups that Aboriginal women's needs were not being met by prison counseling and religious services that were designed for Anglo women. The Healing Lodge will meet the cultural needs of this group, provide them with a Native healer and method to help themselves by using methods appropriate to their culture and heritage (Arbour, 1996, p. 247).

It is perhaps inevitable that there will be communication chasms between the therapist and correctional client. Cultural sensitivity might help bridge this chasm if it becomes a part of every correctional counselor's training. It should be recognized that clients are the sum of their existence—that includes the world they lived in before prison and the one they will return to on release. Counseling, to be effective, must be relevant to that world.

Life Skills and Success on the Outside

The major issues regarding educational and vocational programming in prison are the costs involved and the ability of the program to affect recidivism. With respect to the cost, no vocational program in the country costs more than a subsequent prison sentence and the total cost of wasted lives and loss to victims as the result of recidivism. With respect to the program's impact on the person's ability to change his or her lifestyle, no prison program can replicate life on the outside, but there could be greater efforts at job placement, housing assistance, and financial aid to help in the transition to the free world.

Surveys indicate that women request a wide range of programs covering all manner of life skills. Inmates' needs include employment assistance, Narcotics Anonymous and Alcoholics Anonymous, self-esteem counseling, rehabilitation programs, parenting classes, family planning information, financial aid, housing assistance, transportation aid, and transition and orientation meetings to help adjust to release.

Interestingly, when asked which programs have been most useful to them, the majority of women in the Texas sample said "all of them." Women in prison report benefits from all types of programs from education to life skills to parenting classes. Most also state that there aren't enough programs. Typical responses to the question of what programs are needed were "more abuse counseling programs," "more drug and alcohol counseling," "drug counseling certification," "more education program slots," "more parenting classes," "skill development," "programs on anger control," "more relevant vocational training," "more slots for those with education already," "more victim's groups," "better screening for family violence." Some would like to go through a life skills class again just to be doing something and because it was a positive experience, but because of large numbers and limited resources, they are barred from doing so (Pollock et al., 1996).

It also may be the case that life skills classes do not necessarily result in a measurable reduction in recidivism.

> Criminal patterns are hard to break. You can take the people out of the street but you can't take the street out of the people. (Pollock et al., 1995)

Many women report receiving benefits from programs but return to prison on parole violations anyway. It must be accepted that sometimes the message must be repeated several times before the woman herself is in a position to take advantage of it. Also, other life circumstances may influence parole success even though the woman is essentially in a healthier lifestyle. For instance she might have reduced her drug use but parole is revoked for some other violation, or a woman manages to avoid an abusive relationship but gets involved with a family member who is committing crime. One thing is abundantly clear: Women in prison will go back to lives that include great temptations and present huge difficulties in staying out of trouble.

Life skills classes are about doing things better, whether it be earning a living or being in a relationship with a child, partner, or family member. Life skills attempt to break criminal patterns by showing how to have productive work, a strong self-concept and direction, drug-free leisure activities, and a healthy lifestyle.

8

Counseling in Prison: Issues and Concerns

I think the majority of people would prefer to work with men just because it's so much less stressful. . . . Staff has to be careful not to get overinvolved. Women are so much more open and sharing about what's going on inside their hearts than men are. Sometimes it's just another manipulation technique that's used to engender sympathy, pity, whatever . . . but because people are human, and anytime someone opens up to you, allowing you to experience what she's experiencing, the tendency is you start to care about that individual, which is also a lot more stressful.

Correctional officer, quoted in Pollock (1986, p. 100)

Choosing Corrections

In an earlier chapter, it was stated that if one could not put aside dislike or disgust for those who commit criminal acts, it would be best to choose other clients to work with. Not everyone is comfortable in a prison environment or working with correctional clients. Hatcher (1978) discussed some of the characteristics that are necessary for correctional workers. Although he was specifically discussing teachers, many of his ideas are appropriate to all helping professionals. Some of the characteristics include

the ability to understand and withstand provocative behavior without becoming punitive, . . . objectivity in accepting relationships with all clients in a nonjudgmental manner without either punitive or sentimental emotional involvement, . . . ability to say no with reasons when necessary, . . . a sensitivity to pathological behavior as compared with normal random behavior . . . ability to maintain discreet silence on some critical issues and "classified" information, . . . capability of exerting external controls on individuals who need contain-

ment with physical force . . . and, knowledge of the civil and constitutional
rights of prisoners, whatever their status. (p. 92)

More generally, he described the qualities of "liking for people, helpfulness,
sense of humor, honesty, maturity, intellectual effectiveness, capacity for
growth, objectivity, and a well-balanced personality" (p. 92).

The capacity to balance genuine caring with authority is essential to all
correctional-helping positions. If one emphasizes sensitivity and advocacy
and ignores accountability and responsibility to the community, the relationship with the offender becomes less effective. Evidence indicates that the
client-centered, gestalt modality is not very effective with correctional populations, because they tend to be extremely manipulative individuals, some
with antisocial values and behavior patterns. "Feel good" counseling is not
sufficient, in and of itself, to bring about change. On the other hand, if one
emphasizes authority to the exclusion of the needs of the client, then communication will break down and the "counseling relationship" will never become
established. In effect, the helping professional will fill out paperwork and be
another "cog in the wheel" of the correctional bureaucracy. What is needed is
an appropriate balance between genuine warmth and caring, the ability to hold
the offender accountable for their actions, and the wise use of authority to
support this accountability. Through this healthy relationship, the offender
may be able to learn discipline, self-motivation, and see that their behavior
does have consequences.

Working with correctional populations is difficult. This is not to say that
there aren't wonderful challenges and rewards, but there are some unique
problems related to working with correctional caseloads. Schrink (1992), for
instance, described the following as problems for correctional counselors:
lack of institutional support, maintaining confidentiality, large caseloads, a
heavy volume of paperwork, nonvolunteer clients, the fact that counselors
wear "two hats," limited opportunity for reality testing, being "conned,"
"conning" clients, and an emphasis on failure. Some of these concerns are
noted in the sections that follow. In the second section of the chapter, various
concerns more general to the counseling process will be discussed.

Personal Security in a Prison Environment

In the last chapter we discussed female prisoners' anger and aggression.
It is inevitable that at some point in time that anger will be directed toward
the helping professional. Whereas correctional officers tend to be the most
common targets of inmates' anger, counseling professionals will also, at times,

be the recipient of an angry outburst. Other clients get angry, of course, but it is important to realize that prisoners may be different in their propensity for violence. Anger may lead to a physical assault. Only juvenile delinquent populations and the seriously mentally ill present the same type of security issues for those who work with them. For this reason, it is important to always consider personal security. It would be unhealthy to work constantly under a feeling of fear. On the other hand, to be safe requires cognizance of the environmental and social cues for danger and a plan of action for those occurrences that escalate to a violent confrontation.

First, the counselor always should know where help is and how to call for assistance. In the administrative offices, counselors' doors may have windows or the telephone may have a "panic" button. If not, it would be wise to lobby for such safeguards. When one is in a living unit or other area of the prison, it is important to know the physical layout and where the exits are, where the nearest officer station is, and where telephones may be found. This may seem overcautious, but violence erupts quickly, and it is best to avoid or prevent trouble rather than to end up with bruises or worse injuries.

If one is involved in a confrontation with an angry inmate, there are several possible reactions. It is important to avoid escalating the confrontation by raising one's voice and matching the aggression level. This rarely is successful in "winning" any verbal battles and in fact may push the inmate to a physical reaction. Some women in prison have been "street fighters," they have never backed down from a "fight," and it is unlikely that a counselor or any correctional professional will accomplish anything by engaging in a yelling match.

One should quickly assess whether the heightened emotion has a chemical source. If the woman appears intoxicated from alcohol or drugs or is perhaps suffering from psychosis, it is important to get help, because it will be impossible to expect logical or rational reactions. Walking quickly away, calling for an officer, or otherwise obtaining the means to control the situation will be the best courses of action for her, as well as yourself.

If intoxication is not an issue, then there is a choice to be made. Either the counseling professional can choose to deal with the issue that is upsetting the inmate immediately, or make it clear that her reaction is inappropriate and you would be happy to talk to her as soon as she can speak rationally and calmly. Speaking quietly and making sure your offer to listen is genuine and not a "brush-off" will sometimes diffuse the incident. Nevertheless, if you say you will speak to her later when she is calm, and then avoid her or don't send a pass so she can come and see you, and especially if this has become a pattern, then this response will probably only spark greater anger.

Speaking quietly, even to the point at which the inmate has to ask you to repeat yourself, often works well to bring down the emotional level. It is important to ask her questions that make it clear that you are listening to her and interested in her problem. Asking for clarification, for instance, may help the woman focus on the particular issue instead of engaging in a general outburst. Many who work in corrections are uncomfortable with letting the power balance shift; that is, listening to complaints and demands and asking the woman offender for additional information subtly puts the professional almost in a position subservient (at least conversationally) to the inmate. This may not be an acceptable reaction for many staff members, but it can achieve a situation in which the inmate releases her anger in words instead of physical actions.

If her situation is one in which the counseling professional is powerless to help, it is important to be honest, rather than give her hope that you can do something about it. Basically, honesty and genuineness are always better and if the counseling professional develops a reputation for having these traits, the incidents of angry outbursts probably will be rare. Most offenders are fairly pleasant most of the time. They appreciate anyone who treats them with respect and cares about their problems. This section is not meant to scare or discourage anyone from correctional work, but it must be recognized that there is always the potential for violence in a prison setting.

Personal Values

Another issue when working with correctional clients is the danger of co-optation. Some offenders are extremely likable and charismatic people. They sometimes have a way of seeing the world that is seductive, even though they are asocial or antisocial. This seems to be even more true of male than female offenders. It is not uncommon for those working with certain offenders to take on the values and belief systems of the offenders—this has happened with correctional officers, as well as helping professionals and volunteers, who come into contact with offenders over an extended period of time. The offender's personality is so strong that the helper is co-opted and the correctional staff members change, rather than the other way around.

For this reason, it is important to have a clear sense of one's own values when working with correctional clients. If this element is not present in one's training, it would be useful to undertake a type of self-study, using values clarification exercises or some other means to explore and identify personal values. Okun (1997) described several sources for assisting this process. Basically, values clarification involves identifying one's beliefs and being ready to publicly affirm them. Identifying one's beliefs can be facilitated by forced-choice exercises or in other ways requiring decisions about what is more important. Of course, one's behavior must be consistent with one's beliefs, so a values clarification exercise also should examine behavior to see what consistent patterns emerge.

Although controversial, the idea that some values are "better" than others must be resolved by the individual counselor. For instance, one value is integrity. Another value is material riches. To accept all values equally means accepting that some people choose to steal because they value money over integrity. Some value personal enjoyment over caring for others. Some value the power that comes from violence. Should these values be accepted and endorsed just as readily as those values that reinforce societal solidarity and altruism?

Whereas helping professionals should avoid imposing their personal values and belief systems on clients in some areas, such as religious beliefs, there are other areas in which it may be important to be very clear about one's values and propose the notion that certain values are "better" than others, such as honesty, altruism, and personal responsibility. The moral development approach discussed in an earlier chapter specifically deals with these issues, but all helping programs should address values at some stage in the process. Therefore, helping professionals must have a clear notion of their own values before engaging in such discussions with inmates.

Counseling in a Bureaucracy

The second concern has to do with counseling in a bureaucracy. Treatment or self-help programs are inconvenient additions to the prison regime. Security staff would probably prefer that no treatment personnel or volunteers entered prison. Typically counseling staff find that the prison routine takes precedence over any priorities or agenda that the program staff may have. Faith (1993) described the difficulties of running a program in a prison. Her description of the problems of working with a prison bureaucracy while administering a volunteer program in a women's prison in the late 1970s will sound very familiar to anyone who has attempted research or run programs in a prison. She discussed incidents of being held at the gate because of missing paperwork, being searched volunteers, and "incidents" when the group was punished with banishment from the prison for such transgressions as touching a prisoner or handing a book to a prisoner. It is an irony known to many that it sometimes seems just as hard to get "into" a prison, as it is to escape from one.

Mahan and Prestwood (1993) also presented the difficulties of correctional intervention, although their discussion concerned a community facility. They discussed a community program for cocaine-abusing mothers and specifically mentioned problems of attrition, relapse, the lack of community involvement, lack of resources, and changing goals.

In community programs, day-to-day concerns will take precedence over attending classes or groups. People move, family members die, old lovers return, and staff must deal with the expectation that for any sized group starting a program, probably close to half or more will drop out for one reason or another. In prison programs, external family issues may not intervene, but custody issues do—women break rules and are punitively segregated, or they may be administratively transferred, or they may have court dates that interrupt the program's progress. Many counselors running programs in prisons have encountered situations that seemingly do not make sense—such as pulling an inmate out of a treatment program to work in an agricultural position or transferring an inmate when she is nearing completion of a program. Security concerns, such as clearing count, always take precedence over any treatment issues.

Further, in a prison environment, the counselor may encounter staff and administrators who are actively or passively hostile to the idea of treatment and who feel that inmates cannot change and deserve nothing more than punishment. If the top administration of a facility holds these views, the setting may be unpleasant for the treatment professional, and big and small barriers to effective counseling will always be present. The more typical pattern is not hostility but, rather, lethargy or inattentiveness to the program needs of the inmate population. Crisis management characterizes most prison administrators' approach to running prisons these days, with such serious problems as overcrowding, drugs, and violence overwhelming their energies and resources. Counselors who feel that their needs are not being met may need to rethink what administrators require and try to achieve a result such that everyone gets what he or she wants. For instance, counselors who need more financial resources can argue with administrators about the budget, but administrators will have to take financial resources from somewhere else in the prison to meet this need. Perhaps a more productive approach is to apply for a grant and bring in more total resources to the prison.

Risk Taking

All counseling efforts must progress to a stage at which the individual actually undertakes new behaviors, whether practicing assertiveness, practicing weight control, disengaging from a destructive relationship, or in some other way undertaking a behavioral component in the change process. In a prison setting, this stage is problematic because it is not a natural environment. If there is a problem with anger management, there are certainly opportunities for practicing skills of anger control, but the prison is very different from the outside, and anger cues and appropriate responses also may be different. The development of parenting skills is especially problematic, because typically female offenders have very little time to spend with their children, and they do so in the very artificial environment of a prison visiting room or, at best, a weekend special program, such as the camping program described in an earlier chapter. Drugs are available in prison, so temptations and the opportunity to resist do exist but not to the extent that they do outside. Issues of responsibility are especially problematic. Because so much of the woman's daily behavior is controlled by prison rules and regulations, it is almost impossible to practice any form of self-control. It is for these reasons, perhaps, that many programs in prison show so little effect on recidivism. Whatever changes have occurred may be changes the woman has tried out in prison but not in the real world, where temptations are stronger and controls are nonexistent.

Avoiding Burnout

There is a wealth of literature on the elements of, and avoiding the occurrence of, "burnout," which is an occupational hazard in the helping professions and especially in corrections. Two elements contribute to the potential for burnout in correctional counseling. The first is the nature of the institution, the second is the nature of the client. A prison is the epitome of a bureaucracy. A bureaucracy, by definition, is an organization that is run by "rules," by "paper," and by ignoring individuals in favor of procedures and precedents. Whereas this may be very effective in controlling large numbers of people and/or producing products, it is not conducive to the helping professions, and some helping professionals end up either "fighting City Hall" all the time, which is exhausting, or succumbing to bureaucratic pressures to conform, which is burnout. One may move from one to the other reaction during the course of a career.

Is there a healthy way to perform in a bureaucracy and avoid burnout? It helps to have a clear sense of the rules, a clear sense of one's goals and mission, and a consistent pattern of response that furthers the latter, so that any disagreement with the rules is taken seriously by administrators. It is important to prevent the bureaucratic process from becoming an "easy out" for why something can't be done or to avoid conflict. Some counselors will be slow in issuing "passes" to avoid seeing unpleasant inmates. Some never enter the living units, so female inmates have no way to see them other than by requesting a "pass." Other counselors go in the opposite direction and become advocates who argue every rule with officers and administrators and become less effective, because they can't be trusted to further the organization's goals. One must always remember that the goal of a prison is security, not treatment. In any conflict between the two, security must always be foremost.

The second element of burnout is the nature of the client. Correctional populations typically have a multitude of problems. Allowing oneself to care—even within the bounds of a professional relationship—becomes problematic because their lives are often so tragic. It is sometimes impossible to help them challenge injustice, and that is personally traumatic. Counselors may experience the despair of an inmate who loses her children in a parental termination proceeding or be helpless to assist a woman whose children are being moved from foster home to foster home, resulting in the deterioration of the child's personal development. Some women are in prison who should not be. Perhaps not many are legally innocent, but many seem to be more "sinned against" than sinners. The daily turmoil and tragedy that marks these women's lives is overwhelming and a self-protective response might be to "turn off."

It also hurts to be manipulated, which is inevitable with a correctional population. Officers typically go through a sequence of naiveté, then after being "burned" they become extremely cynical. Those with well-balanced personalities move through this stage also and become "mature optimists." They don't automatically assume that every inmate is lying and every inmate is out to "get them," but they also are wise to manipulation. Counselors go through a similar process of development when working with offenders, but some (like many correctional officers) never get past the cynicism stage. This is a type of burnout. Unfortunately, this may mean that the helping professionals "go through the motions," but cannot achieve an effective "helping relationship," because they are fixated on the negative characteristics of offenders, rather than being empathetic to the concerns of the individual. Offenders in prison complain that many staff members "don't care," and this may be true because of burnout due to cynicism.

To avoid burnout when working with correctional populations, it is important to have a realistic set of expectations and to prevent ego needs from interfering with counseling goals. It also helps to have a good personal-support system and a good professional-support system. Debriefing, talking through cases with other professionals, and referring clients when necessary, are all helpful ways to handle a correctional position. Learning healthy ways of dealing with stress, for instance, a judicious use of vacations, exercise, healthy habits, and so on, is always important. Finally, it helps to have a sense of humor to counteract the pervasive negativism of the environment. "Gallows humor" has a place in the coping arsenal of those who work in continuously stressful occupations. Just as only medical personnel probably appreciate the humor related to death that one might hear in hospital and nursing home settings, perhaps only law enforcement and correctional personnel appreciate the humor related to security lapses, inmates' cruelty, and other elements unique to the correctional environment.

Ethical Responsibilities of Counselors in Prison

The ethical responsibilities of psychologists and psychiatrists are provided by their respective professional associations. Other helping professionals may or may not have formal ethical codes, but all must have a developed "code of ethics" at least in their own minds for reacting to the many different issues that may arise in the correctional environment. Kitchener (1988) identified the following five fundamental ethical principles relevant to the helping professions: (a) respect autonomy, (b) do no harm, (c) benefit others, (d) be fair, and (e) be faithful.

Conflicts of Interest. All those who work in corrections have two "clients." The first is the offender, but the second is the public at large whose tax dollars pay the salary of the helper. Does the public have a right to expect the helper to protect their interests and not subject them to further risk? Many think this is true, but others feel that they are paid to be client advocates. Ideally, the interests should match. To help the offender become a better person, with more coping skills and prosocial goals, and have the skills to succeed, also helps protect the public from future lawbreaking. In more specific circumstances, however, sometimes these interests do not match. For instance, it may be in the client's best interest to be released to "test" newfound skills of resisting temptations and criminal opportunities; nevertheless, it may be in the public's interest to keep the individual incarcerated. A woman may desperately want to regain custody of her children on release, but it might also be the case that her children have been in a stable home, have loving parental figures, and have been traumatized by her in the past. Whose interest should the counseling professional advance if they are asked for a recommendation?

In prison, the conflict is usually between institutional security and inmate needs or wants. The wise and ethical counselor balances those needs everyday. Should an offender be placed in a program that requires a great deal of self-discipline, because there is freedom of movement? Should the offender be given a furlough? Should the offender be removed from close custody? All these require predictions on the counselor's part about the inmate's readiness. Counselors who place offender needs higher than institutional or community needs will perhaps always make those decisions accepting more risk than those who reverse the priorities.

There are also conflicts of interest between serving the needs of individual inmates. Should a rare slot in a coveted program be given to Inmate A or Inmate B? Should the counselor cancel one appointment with Inmate A because Inmate B refuses to come out of her cell until she talks to you? Should the counselor spend their time in group therapy because it serves more people even though several inmates have stated they will not talk in front of other inmates? The way one resolves all these problems ethically is to examine the needs of everyone, to determine the primary loyalty of the counselor role, and to act accordingly. In the case of two competing interests, both of which have legitimate demands on the counselor's allegiance, there can only be the application of a sincere attempt to be fair.

It is also important to be honest and frank in one's loyalties. If it is relevant, a counselor should always explain the extent to which the counselor's loyalties to the inmate will stretch. For instance, it may be important to explain that you will not misrepresent or "sugarcoat" a recommendation letter to a parole board regarding the inmate's behavior to increase the chance for parole or that you cannot tell a caseworker that the inmate has made progress in a parenting class if that is not the case.

Confidentiality. Most helping professionals have an ethical responsibility of confidentiality, that is, they must not divulge the confidences of their clients. For some, there is no question that the content of the interaction will become public. Psychologists who conduct diagnoses and evaluations for the court must support their recommendations with what they learned during their testing and interviewing of the defendant. Those who work in classification are creating a record for subsequent helpers; thus, what is discussed is placed in the record. These individuals do have a duty to make sure the offender understands that what she says is not private.

Other helping professionals are in somewhat different circumstances. Counselors or other helpers in a prison may have an ethical responsibility to keep most of their discussions private, such as the life histories, previous drug use, and admission of some deviance. But what if they are told about a homicide that has occurred and the offender admits guilt—is there a duty to notify the authorities? What if the offender tells the helping professional about an upcoming escape attempt or planned assault on another staff member? In the latter case, the general opinion is that the counselor has an affirmative duty to protect the security of the institution and innocents. In the first case, even attorneys don't seem to be extremely clear on the extent of their ethical responsibility of confidentiality when told of past crimes, and they are officers of the court (Pollock, 1997a). What is certain is that one should have a clear idea of the kinds of information that would not be subject to confidentiality and make sure the offender understands the limits of one's responsibility to them. It would be helpful to discuss these issues with supervisors and other helping professionals before any particular incident arises. This would be a good subject for a training session and legal representatives from the state attorney's office could provide legal advice to enlighten the discussion. Some helping professionals may find that they have a legal duty to divulge client confidences and may even be held liable if they do not come forward. Some may find that they work for a prison warden who feels that he or she should have complete access to the counselor's files, including personal notes. If this is true, it is important to know that ahead of time, before a situation occurs where the warden demands such access.

Relationships With Clients. The opportunity to engage in unhealthy relationships and unethical relationships with correctional clients is obviously present. Inmates are needy, manipulative, or both. A correctional professional may be offered sex in return for favorable decisions, or the inmate may believe that she is in love with the counselor, because he or she has expressed caring concern, perhaps the first experience of its kind for the female prisoner. Obviously, there is an ethical duty to refrain from such relationships. It is pure rationalization when a professional expresses the view that love can occur anywhere and "genuine love" excuses the fact that the helping professional has crossed over from a professional to a personal relationship with an offender client. It is also important to point out that, in addition to being an ethical violation, helping professionals may find themselves charged with a felony for engaging in such a relationship, because some states have laws that prohibit such behavior. Such a relationship would be defined as sexual harassment and/or deprivation of rights of the offender—even if the relationship was supposedly consensual.

Affirmative Duties. There may be duties of a helping professional in a prison environment that are unique to the place and setting. For instance, if one observes some abuse of an inmate, there should be some reaction to such abuse, such as stopping the abuse, informing higher authorities, testifying, and so forth. This affirmative duty also may be true for other abuse, besides physical, such as racial or sexual slurs, or more personal "baiting" or teasing.

The role of a helping professional mandates intolerance toward the mistreatment of all individuals, including offenders. Despite personal discomfort with the role of "whistle-blower," it seems clear that it comes with the responsibilities of a helping professional, and one cannot ignore such behavior if seen.

Other affirmative duties may be to advance the knowledge of other correctional staff members. Oftentimes, mental health experts who work in the field are asked to fill a training function; for instance, teach correctional officers how to handle psychotic inmates or present other types of training. One might recognize an affirmative duty to conduct such training, because it helps the correctional staff become better at their jobs and also helps the offenders. Other affirmative duties are to keep current in one's own field and develop one's professional expertise.

Limits of Competence. Attorneys have an ethical duty to reject a case if they do not have the competence to serve the client's needs. Helping professionals also should recognize such a duty. If the offender presents problems so acute or serious that the helper feels his or her expertise is not sufficient, there is an affirmative duty to refer or seek the assistance of other professionals. In corrections, some offenders are so stressed by the prison experience that they have mental health "breakdowns," resulting in psychotic episodes or other extreme forms of deterioration. There is a tendency among some correctional workers (primarily custody staff) to treat these incidents as custody or discipline problems rather than as serious medical or mental health problems. If the helping professional does not have the skills necessary to deal with these serious incidents, there is an ethical duty to ensure that there is appropriate referral and assistance received by the offender. If the custodial staff resist such a recommendation, there is a need to take on an advocate role so that further deterioration does not occur.

Other Ethical Issues. Other issues might be more similar to counseling in any setting. The approach to take in resolving most ethical dilemmas is to first look to the professional code of ethics. For many issues, there has been due consideration and a reasoned response to such dilemmas from professionals in the field that are incorporated in the code of ethics for the profession. Otherwise, asking oneself a few simple questions sometimes helps: What is the effect of my action (or each choice of actions)? Who would be hurt or helped by each course of action? How would I feel if my action were made public? How would I feel about my action, looking back on it 10 years from now? (Pollock, 1997a).

Counseling in Prison

The task of counseling offenders is not an easy one. The old saw of teachers saying "this wouldn't be a bad job except for the students" or counselors saying "this wouldn't be a bad job except for the clients" can be applied with fervor to correctional caseloads, but then one must also add the additional difficulties of working with supervision staff and bureaucrats as well.

Correctional clients might be described as irresponsible, impulsive, manipulative, with a tendency to shift blame. They have a history of poor interpersonal relationships, an inability to deal with authority, and seem unable to learn from experience. Females are described as more openly emotional than male prisoners, with a tendency to "act out" (Pollock, 1986). Women in prison are frustrated and angry. They will express these emotions in whatever way they can. Thus, like children who misbehave only with their parents, sometimes women in prison will "act out" to those who they trust will not hurt them for their outburst. A woman may test such an individual with her worst behavior, daring the person to turn his or her back and reject her, so she can justify her own lack of trust in authority figures and validate her feeling of worthlessness. All women in prison are not seeking help—some are satisfied with who they are and see no reason to change. Others are there because of personality disorders that may be immune to change. Some may suffer from mental illness to the extent that ordinary prison programs and prison staff can help only by advocating a transfer to a mental health facility.

The Counseling Relationship

The mechanism of any change effort lies in the counseling relationship. This relationship may take many forms. The counselor may interact with inmates in a continuing-group-therapy setting or with those living in a therapeutic community. He or she may be a single counselor in a program using individual therapy or be engaged in a more general caseworker relationship with correctional clients. Whatever the relationship, communication is the key to the identification and implementation of change efforts.

Most point to the stages of change as occurring through some steps, such as the following: establishing the relationship, identifying the change, undertaking change efforts and using feedback, and termination. Okun (1987) identified the following: The first stage is the relationship that includes initiation or entry, identification and clarification of problems, the structure or contract of helping, intensive exploration of problem(s), and identification of goals. Then the second stage is the "working" phase, which includes acceptance of the defined goals, planning strategies, the use of strategies, evaluation, termination, and follow-up.

In the prison, there are special problems that exist in establishing the relationship and trying to effect strategies of change. The difficulties of the relationship include agreeing on mutual goals, countertransference, resistant clients, barriers in communication, and the threat of dependency. Difficulties in implementing the second stage of change include all the problems of working in a bureaucracy and, especially, the inability to "try out" change.

Mutual Goals

Okun (1997) described the importance of agreed on and mutual goals between the helper and the one being helped. It may be the case, especially with correctional clients, that the counselor would prefer to pursue goals other than those the client expresses a desire for. For instance, it may be that the client's only desire is to perform adequately enough in prison to obtain a favorable parole outcome. Or the client may express the desire to cease most drug use but explains that she plans to continue to use marijuana on release. Another client may express the desire to work only on drug addiction even though the counselor knows that there are issues of incest and sexual abuse in the offender's background. When there are disagreements between the counselor and the client in selection of goals for treatment, the client's goals take precedence, unless they are clearly antisocial and antithetical to the treatment enterprise.

Nothing will destroy a developing helping relationship quicker than a counselor who attempts to force treatment goals on a client. Even though there may be superficial compliance, the trust that comes from acceptance is lost, and the relationship probably will be characterized by misrepresentation and passive resistance. Unfortunately, it may be the case that in correctional facilities the counselor may have clients who do not see a need for change in areas that the counselor clearly does.

Transference and Countertransference

Transference can be defined as the client's unconscious relationship to the therapist in a way that relives previous relationships, such as the parent-child relationship. It is an essential stage of the counseling relationship and may happen in any counseling relationship whether the therapist has been trained as a psychoanalyst or not. Thus it is important to understand the process.

Through the expression of emotions or reactions that seem inappropriate to the present situation, the counselor and client can shed light on unresolved issues of past relationships. For instance, if the client reacts with extreme emotion to perceived neglect by the counselor, such as if the counselor is slightly late or delayed for a planned meeting, it may be the cue that transference has occurred, and the client is responding to feelings of abandonment and neglect from her parent. Because correctional staff are in authority positions over the correctional client, transference often occurs very quickly—the staff person already is "like a mother" (or father) in terms of the power he or she has over the adult. A similar phenomenon occurs when some correctional offenders experience "flashbacks," such as when a male correctional officer touches her to conduct a patdown search and she "flashes back" to being raped or assaulted by an intimate partner. She may respond violently to such an experience and, again, the violence occurs because of the previous relationship.

In the counseling relationship, what may occur with a male helping professional is she feels "love" and constantly seeks his affection or approval. If the helping professional is a woman, this may occur as well, but it is more typical that the offender reenacts the relationship she had with her own mother, which often is one of love mixed with a lack of respect and betrayal (because her own mother did not protect her from sexual or physical abuse). Thus, she may have a very charged relationship with the helping professional, one day expressing great affection, the next day screaming "I hate you." The relationship is often manipulative—the woman is compliant and pleasant to achieve some privilege or favor, but if it is denied, she turns into an angry "child" who slams doors and threatens to cut off the relationship.

A different phenomenon is countertransference. According to Okun (1987), countertransference occurs

> when the therapist develops feelings toward or views about the client that stem from the therapist's conflicts rather than the client's. Countertransference can take the form of positive (love or excessive attachment) or negative (dislike or hostility) feelings and result in distorted interpretations. (p. 119)

Whereas countertransference may occur in any type of counseling relationship, special problems exist in the prison environment. For instance, those counselors who have strong needs for control may find that they are unconsciously meeting their own needs through correctional counseling by emphasizing the control aspects of the relationship. It is a unique feeling to know that a recommendation one makes may affect another individual's life. It is a

powerful feeling to experience an individual responding to you as an important "authority" figure. Sometimes the relationship, then, becomes rewarding
to the counseling professional but not very helpful at all to the offender.

Another possibility, of course, is that there is genuine liking and warm
feelings toward the client, because the client shows such gratitude and affection toward the counselor. If the counselor has unmet social needs and is
unaware of the processes at work, inappropriate personal relationships may
occur between the helping professional and the offender. The dependent
position of the offender creates great potential for this occurrence if the
counseling professional isn't sensitive to his or her own needs and reactions
to the offender in the context of the helping relationship.

Resistant Clients

Because prisoners are obviously unwilling residents, they also may be
unwilling participants in treatment programs or counseling relationships.
Even if they volunteer for a program, they may be doing so because of a belief
(well-founded or not) that participation will lead to release. Some participate
out of boredom or as a means to see other inmates in a setting outside of work
or school. For many reasons, then, the "clients" may not be sincerely committed to the treatment process.

The way the helping professional communicates with women may have
an influence on whether initial resistance can be overcome or whether it will
become a barrier to any meaningful change effort. In most interactions with
the criminal justice system, communication is dangerous to the offender. In
interviews with police, district attorneys, welfare workers, presentence inves-
tigators, and others, criminal justice clients have learned to say little and offer
nothing as a means of dealing with questions. In many cases, most interactions
the woman has had with prison personnel have been judgmental. That is, she
may have expressed frustration, anger, or other feelings and been told by
authority figures how she should feel, why she shouldn't feel the way she does,
or in some other way the official communication served to dismiss or not
acknowledge her existing feelings. It is no wonder, then, that the helping
professional may feel like it is "pulling teeth" to get any meaningful responses
from women in prison at the beginning of a helping relationship.

To avoid patterning the communication in the same way as an "interroga-
tion," questions should be avoided. If used, they should be open-ended and
lead to a conversation led by the woman's narrative. Strict questions will limit
communication. It is best to let her talk about what she wants to talk about,
and if she doesn't want to talk, silence is sometimes very helpful. Waiting for

several seconds (or even minutes) may sometimes prompt additional information. Some counselors have used the technique of telling the woman that she
must spend the requisite time in the counselor's office, but she doesn't have
to talk, so she can bring a book, or look out of the window or do anything else,
and the counselor would work on paperwork or be otherwise engaged. A
comfort zone may be reached in this forced relationship, when the woman
spontaneously decides that the time could be better spent. In the following
quote, Okun (1987) discussed one such relationship with a delinquent youth.

> One way [to facilitate the breakdown of resistance] . . . is to encourage the
> reluctant client to take the initiative for structuring the relationship. An example
> of this occurred in a halfway house, where the youth worker just stayed in close
> physical proximity to the reluctant client, shrugged off the verbal abuse, and
> communicated caring and genuineness more by nonverbal presence than by
> words. After four days of testing the youth worker in every conceivable fashion,
> the 14-year-old boy began to shed his bravado and share some of his real
> feelings and thoughts. (p. 184)

More commonly, there is no time to spend with resistant clients and they are
allowed to spend their prison sentence engaged in nothing more introspective
than sweeping the tier.

Another type of resistant client is the person who talks too much. This
offender is perhaps harder to deal with than the first type, because it is hard
to separate any important communication from the volume of irrelevant
chatter. This woman may be manipulating the counselor or she simply may
be trying to forestall any attempt to get her to take a good look at her life. This
is done by talking incessantly about past boyfriends, her children, prison
gossip, or whatever else seems "safe." In this case, it would be necessary to
be more forceful in controlling the conversation.

Another type of resistant client is one who appears to be sincere and
verbally cooperative in group settings or during the counseling process but,
by their actions and comments outside the presence of the counselor, make it
clear that they are manipulating the treatment process. The counselor who
discovers such game playing must confront the inmate and enforce predeter-
mined consequences if the treatment program is to have any validity with other
inmates. There is nothing that destroys the integrity of a group therapy
program, an Alcoholics Anonymous group, or other program more quickly
than inmates who make fun of it outside the presence of staff, divulge
confidences, and lie during interactions with the counselor.

It is probably not only ineffective but also unethical to force counseling
on a resistant client in a coercive setting, such as a prison. Basic human dignity

involves having the right to choose one's principles, attitudes, and values. If one's behavior falls outside the limits of the law, then one has to accept the reality of punishment, but treatment is a more personal, more pervasive, and more intrusive intervention than punishment. Resistant clients may be holding onto the only autonomy they have left in the coercive world of a prison. The counselor can express his or her willingness, concern, and readiness to help and leave the decision up to the individuals, who may drop their resistance when they discover that no one is forcing them.

Barriers in Communication

There are many elements of the prison counseling relationship that pose problems with effective communication. First, the prisoner knows that the counselor has some amount of power in determining their future. The counselor's recommendation may affect good time (early release for good behavior), parole (early release under community supervision), custody level (that affects privileges and housing), and so on. This may prevent the offender from being totally honest in her attempt to "put up a good front" to encourage good recommendations.

Another problem is simple numbers. The counselor in prison may have too many women to be responsible for, thus limiting the possibility of meaningful relationships with anyone. Group therapy is used frequently in prison not only because of the beneficial aspects of a group but also because it is "cheaper" to administer. Whereas group therapy has many advantages, as described in a previous chapter, there are some female prisoners who are not ready to discuss their lives, victimization, or drug problem in front of other inmates. These women may receive no help if they do not agree to the group process. Of course, even listening without volunteering to speak in a group may be helpful, but there should be a choice offered to female prisoners so that those who are not comfortable in a group may still have access to a helping relationship.

Another problem is that the prison environment encourages authoritarian relationships. The counselor, even with the best of intentions, may sometimes fall into the trap of "scolding," "admonishing," and "ordering" the inmate to do things. Despite training, negative communication patterns are insidious in prison, because it is a hierarchical environment in which relationships are very influenced by the power hierarchy. Some counselors, in fact, do not do much else but conduct interviews using verbal responses that are not conducive to a helping relationship, such as giving advice, blaming, asking "why" questions, directing, cajoling or preaching, and so on. Okun (1987, p. 25) described these communication patterns as dysfunctional to the counseling relationship.

The use of such communication devices as minimal verbal response (mmm, mmm), paraphrasing (so you feel . . .), probing (let's talk about that . . .), reflecting (you seem angry . . .), clarifying (do you mean by that . . .) and "checking out" (it seems as if you don't want to be here . . .) (Okun, 1987, p. 76) are more helpful, but they may also feel unnatural, especially to those who have been correctional officers before they obtained counseling positions.

It is important to have empathy and use communicative cues that indicate to the offender that even if the listener has never experienced the same lifestyle as the woman offender, there is a willingness to suspend judgment and listen. These women's lifestyles often tempt judgmental statements, especially if they involved harm to victims; nevertheless, the role of the counselor is different from that of a judge and jury. The offender is already being punished for her acts, and continued disparagement from one in a counseling position will do little to help. For this reason, it is probably necessary for the helping professional to examine his or her own feelings and attitudes toward prison clients. If there are feelings of dislike, disgust, or condemnation that the helping professional can't put aside for any client or for clients who have committed certain crimes, it is important to step away from these cases and request others to intervene.

Use of confrontation (or challenging) is especially problematic in a prison setting. When used appropriately, this is a beneficial, indeed necessary, element of a counseling relationship; nevertheless, the dynamics of a helping relationship in a prison setting may make this more difficult than for caseloads outside the prison. Some examples of challenging the correctional client include confronting the individual on some disparity between emotions and verbal responses (you say you're not angry, but you are using a very loud voice and your teeth are clenched); or some conflict in what they say compared with what would be a more usual response (you say you're not upset that your parents left you with relatives, but most people would be, I think); confronting a "game player" (you say you want to change, but I hear that you're making jokes about this program and you have been accused of stealing from others in your living unit); or questioning fantasies about what might happen on release (you talk about getting your children back, but my understanding is that your parental rights have already been terminated).

All of these are potentially explosive issues and confrontation is sometimes avoided owing to the possible effects on the relationship. Some techniques to avoid the individual client's negative reaction to confrontation are to focus on one's own perception rather than judging (I think . . . , it's my understanding . . .), avoid accusatory tones or language, don't get sidetracked on "proof" of the statement (for instance, if the issue is not taking treatment seriously, a discussion of being "framed" for stealing is not very useful). Finally, confrontation can be nonjudgmental if it is framed as an attempt to clarify or get more information.

Dependency and Furthering Personal Responsibility

Another potential problem, especially in correctional counseling, is the development of dependency. Individuals who are addicted to drugs or alcoholics often have greater dependency needs than others, and it is easy for them to fall into a dependency relationship with a counselor. Often the helping professional has been the only productive force in this individual's life. Prison itself makes her extremely vulnerable—she is typically scared, lonely, and needs affirmation in a way that most prison staff cannot give her. A warm and caring helping professional may quickly become the most important person in the woman's life. Thus, all the normal concerns and precautions against dependency are magnified in the prison setting. It is ironic that many women who have found a program that is positive and nurturing believe that it is the "best thing that ever happened to them," even though it occurs in a prison. The danger, of course, is that the program staff or helping professional may be so missed on release that the woman has no incentive to succeed outside the prison.

Correctional counseling has been criticized as a control device, as ineffective, and as "coddling." One approach that counteracts all these criticisms is to make sure the theme of the counseling relationship are empowerment, personal responsibility, and accountability. Offenders in prison are there for a reason. Even though they may have had terrible childhoods, been victimized as children and as adults, have few or no skills to advance themselves in the world, and have immense responsibilities, they still are in prison because they broke the law. Often that lawbreaking involved hurting (at least financially) an innocent victim. No intervention is effective if it does not encourage and demand personal responsibility for such actions.

Okun (1997, p.14) provided a set of assumptions for the "human relations counseling model" that seems especially appropriate to this discussion concerning counseling offenders. She proposed the following:

1. People are responsible for and capable of making their own decisions.

2. People are controlled to a certain extent by their environment, but they are able to direct their lives more than they realize. They always have some freedom to choose, even if their options are restricted by environmental variables or inherent biological or personality predispositions.

3. Behaviors are purposive and goal-oriented. People are continuously striving toward meeting their own needs, from basic physiological needs to abstract self-actualization.

4. People want to feel good about themselves and continually need positive confirmation of their own self-worth from significant others.

5. People are capable of learning new behaviors and unlearning existing behaviors, and they are subject to environmental and internal consequences of their behaviors, which in turn serve as reinforcements.

6. People's personal problems may arise from unfinished business (unresolved conflicts) stemming from the past (concerning events and relationships), and, although some exploration of causation may be beneficial in some cases, most problems can be worked through by focusing on the here and now—on what choices the person has now. Problems may also be caused by incongruencies between external and internal perception in the present—that is, discrepancies between a person's actual experience and his or her picture of that experience.

7. Many problems experienced by people today are societal or systemic rather than interpersonal or intrapersonal. Deprivation, limited access to resources, and chronic oppression due to gender, race, ethnicity, class, or sexual orientation can create psychological problems. People are capable of learning to effect choices and changes from within the system as well as from without.

This model is empowering because it assumes the individual is capable of choosing to change. It does not excuse the individual's actions due to past victimization, it does not place primary responsibility for the change effort on anyone other than the individual. If the theme of the helping relationship is personal empowerment, and the intervention is consistent with these principles, it leaves the choice up to the individual (thus meeting the critics who oppose correctional counseling as "coercive"), it holds the offender accountable (thus answering the critics who allege "coddling"), and it has the potential to facilitate change. Nevertheless, the model also recognizes that the offender is affected by systemic factors, such as racial discrimination and gender bias. There are very real and serious effects of being an African American woman in this society, or a Hispanic woman, or a Native American woman. Life experiences and system barriers have to be recognized and taken into account during the helping process. The model is complementary to many different treatment modalities; it recognizes that there is no one right way to intervene and that characteristics of the helper are more important than particular elements of the techniques or modality used.

Implications for Counselors

Unlike other chapters, the focus of the entire chapter concerned issues important to counselors; thus, this final section will merely reiterate some basic points. First, if one chooses to work in a correctional environment, it is important to understand the particular restraints, risks, and frustrations inherent in such a setting. The individual will inevitably become frustrated with the bureaucratic nature of the prison and risk burnout owing to the stress involved when working with correctional clientele. Clients may be less "likable" than other populations and they may vent their frustration and anger by attacking the counselor. The coercive nature of the prison creates a temptation for helping professionals to become authoritarian and hide behind the power of their position or engage in unhealthy and unethical relationships with clients. Counselors may be forced to defend their choice of occupations to those who believe that prisoners should be punished and nothing else.

Counselors who seek to establish helping relationships with correctional clients would do well to absorb the message of Okun's (1987) helping model as described earlier. It respects the integrity of the individual, at the same time allowing for the possibility of internal change. The helper becomes a facilitator, not a director; and the individual must take responsibility for her own destiny. The model recognizes social and economic realities and is sensitive to ethnic and cultural issues. The evidence for whether positive change and a reduction of recidivism can occur in prison will be addressed in the final chapter.

9

The "Black Box" of Prison—
Feminism and Cultural Issues

It's strange when you see the fence and everything. And they say you're in prison and everything, but . . . I've learned that it's inside. You can be free inside even if you're behind the fences or whatever—it's you. It's your attitude and everything.

Pollock et al. (1995)

The "black box" analogy refers to the prison as an entity that is not subject to scrutiny, is impenetrable, and, therefore, without controls. In other words, people go into the black box, they come out on the other side, we think that we "do" something to them while they're in there, but we can never be entirely sure what influences have affected them or what changes will occur during their stay. In this book, we have explored the history of women's prisons and what is occurring in them today. We have seen that the female offender is subject to a host of personal and social problems. Programs attempt to deal with self-esteem, drug abuse, and personal responsibility, especially parenting. Nevertheless, there are many more women than program slots, and programs do not deal adequately with the multiple problems of female prisoners. The only effect of prison that politicians and the public are interested in is whether or not the female offender recidivates. Using this measure, the evidence is mixed about whether prison programs are effective. The reader should always keep in mind the picture of the prison as a "black box" though. Female prisoners are affected only for limited amounts of time and with limited amounts of intensity when they are involved in any counseling experience in prison; the rest of the day, the rest of the week, month, and year or years, they are subject to all sorts of other influences, from racial discrimination by correctional officers and other inmates, to the dehumanizing and infantilizing elements of the prison world, to the tempting forces of the prisoner subculture, and so on. To assume that an offender's success or failure on parole is *affected solely* by the experimental program or intervention effort is to ignore the pervasive influences of whatever else is in that "black box." Counselors, too, cannot take full responsibility or credit for the inmate's performance on release, because the helping relationship may have been a positive one but not sufficient to overcome the negative environment of the prison (the black box) or the larger systemic problems of unemployment, family dysfunctions, cultural stereotypes of women, and societal discrimination.

Rehabilitation, Recidivism, and Research

The goal of prison intervention programs or individual counseling is to facilitate the adoption of law-abiding behavior. More specifically, correctional helping professionals seek to facilitate behavior change, improve positive mental health, aid in the acquisition of such skills as problem solving and responsible decision making, and improve personal effectiveness. Some correctional helpers specifically reject reducing recidivism as their goal; nevertheless, this is probably an unrealistic personal stance given current realities (Hatcher, 1978, p. 87).

What causes a person to recidivate? In Fletcher et al.'s (1993) study, both staff and inmates were asked that question. Interestingly, but not surprisingly, staff tended to use internal explanations and women prisoners offered external explanations for recidivism. For instance, staff pointed to the fact that women had no social skills, were not self-sufficient, went back to old friends and kept old habits, went back to drug use, didn't recognize the consequences of their actions, couldn't provide for themselves or their family, had no moral values, found it easier on the inside than outside, or enjoyed the thrill of the criminal lifestyle. Female inmates were more likely to give external reasons for recidivism, for instance, no money, a battering relationship, no job or skills, addiction, attorney problems, family problems, sexual abuse, association with bad people, men, being alone, or being away from family. Although no program can address all of these issues, we could certainly do a better job of at least recognizing them and providing some back-up and support.

The well-known controversy continues between the camp of researchers, starting with Martinson (1974), who found little or no success in rehabilitation programs, versus those who maintain that some rehabilitative programs show some signs of success. Wright (1995) presented one of the latest meta-analyses of treatment evaluations, and, like Martinson before him, he concluded that there is little or no reduction in recidivism gained from rehabilitative programs of any kind.

Others, especially Palmer (1992a, 1992b, 1994) and Gendreau and Ross (1987), criticized the methodology of these meta-analyses and presented their own findings that showed "pockets of success." These studies indicated that no general categories of programs are successful, only individual programs. What this means is that group therapy—generically—is not *more* successful than therapeutic communities or individual therapy. Rather, one particular group therapy program may show success and one particular therapeutic community may show success, whereas other programs using the same modality may not show any success at all. Or a particular modality may work for older property offenders but not for younger violent offenders. It has been found that generally those counseling procedures that depended on open communication and were nondirective showed negligible results with criminal populations, but those that used behavior modification programs showed either impressive successes or were dismal failures (Louis & Sparger, 1990). Palmer (1992a, 1992b) found that those programs that used multiple modalities, had intense contact, and met the individual offender's needs were most successful.

The Importance of the Counselor

Another possibility may be that the success of programs has much more to do with the personal efficacy of the counselor than the modality of the program. Research indicates that characteristics of the counselors are more important than the type of treatment in determining success. Okun's (1987) comment reflects this belief.

> An increasing amount of evidence supports the idea that helpers are only as effective as they are self-aware and able to use themselves as vehicles of change. Therefore, training in content may not be as important as training in process, skills, and self-knowledge. (p. 33)

Walsh (1988) also pointed out that "good" counselors—those who are open, warm, accepting, and empathetic—are more similar to each other, even if they operate from a very different theoretical perspective, than any of them are to poor counselors, even within the same theoretical perspective or treatment modality. The traits necessary to be an effective helper seem to be emotional maturity, flexibility, open-mindedness, intelligence, warmth, and sensitivity (Okun, 1997, p. 34). Okun specifically cited communication skills that are essential in a helping relationship: empathy, encouragement, support, honesty, caring, concern, respect, sharing, affection, protection, potency, and nonjudgmental acceptance (1997, p. 27). Although Okun was not discussing correctional counseling specifically, these comments can be applied to this discussion of correctional effectiveness.

Two of the most important characteristics of an effective helper are humility and self-awareness. Because no one is perfect, it is helpful to know how one can improve. Okun (1997) presented a helper self-assessment device that could be very helpful for those working with female prisoners. This tool is provided in the accompanying box.

Helper Self-Assessment

1. Am I aware of when I am feeling uncomfortable with a client or with a particular subject area?

2. Am I aware of my own avoidance strategies?

3. Can I really be honest with the helpee?

4. Do I always feel as though I need to be in control of situations?

5. Do I become irritated when others do not see things the way I do or when helpees do not respond the way I think they should?

6. Do I often feel as though I must be omnipotent, that I must do something to make the helpee "get better" so I can be successful?

7. Am I so problem-oriented that I'm always looking for the negative, for a problem, and never responding to the positive, to the good?

8. Am I able to be as open with clients as I want them to be with me?

Adapted from *Effective Helping: Interviewing and Counseling Techniques*, 2nd ed. (Okun, 1997, pp. 45-46).

Elements of Successful Intervention Efforts

Palmer (1992b) believes that multiple-modality programs are necessary, that increased intensity of contact is important, and that greater attention should be paid to inmate needs and characteristics. Coulson and Nutbrown (1992) have developed elements of successful programs. They include

1. Specific guidelines for the use of positive reinforcement
2. An eclectic approach, which draws from a variety of sources
3. Use of a heavily scripted program format (limiting counselor bias and guiding different counselors to present the same program)
4. Development that was based on evaluated results
5. Structured activity

6. Learning that is easily transferred to everyday life
7. Teacher monitoring
8. An outcome evaluation
9. A technique and rationale for client selection
10. A program format that is repetitive and integrated
11. A requirement of active participation from the teacher

Toch, Adams, and Grant (1989) described a program that dealt with male inmates who had engaged in a pattern of maladaptive behaviors in prison. The targeted individuals had been violent either toward others or themselves or had been extremely disruptive, most likely because of their inability to cope with the prison environment. The description of this particular program reflects elements that would be important for any intervention effort.

1. It involved the person as a "participant" rather than as a "client."
2. It was not focused on a particular "problem" (drug abuse, mental illness) to determine appropriate service.
3. It provided for gradations of environments to test developing competencies.
4. It mobilized teams of staff members.
5. It relied on the group process to support staff.
6. It accommodated individual interventions to address individual patterns of change. (Toch et al., 1989, p. 278)

There are "success stories" in prison. Many counselors in drug programs have criminal backgrounds and have chosen to obtain counseling certificates or degrees and go back to prison or halfway houses as staff. Every treatment person in every prison has a story of one of his or her successes, such as the following from a woman who has remained straight and sober for several years in the small town in which she grew up.

For a long time in the community where I came from there wasn't a day or anytime that I would walk down the street and a law enforcement officer or somebody would drive by where I wouldn't be stopped or wouldn't get searched, or at some point, something would happen. You know it was well known that chances are, I was either committing a crime or that I was carrying narcotics on me. Today, we play little jokes with each other. I would be driving down the road and one will pull up next to me and he'll go (victory sign visually) and they do things like this all the time. I have a wonderful, wonderful relationship with the community. (Pollock et al., 1995)

Recidivism may be an important measure of program success, but it is not the only measure, and counting "failures" without looking behind the numbers may be shortchanging the programs' effects. For instance, in an earlier chapter preprison drug use was discussed. In the Texas study, the number of women who had used drugs in the last year of freedom was always smaller than those who had ever used the drug (Pollock et al., 1996). Sometimes this meant that the woman had merely experimented and settled into a pattern of use with a particular drug of choice, so other drug use decreased. Sometimes, however, the woman would explain that she had been drug-free after participating in a prison (or community) drug treatment program and had come back to prison on a parole violation, or an old charge, or a detainer from another jurisdiction. Simply counting parole violations or returns to prison as failures misses important information about how prison treatment programs affect people's lives. Often the women's life histories show trouble-free periods, sometimes lasting years, before they succumb to drug use again. In a way, an 8-year drug-free period, even if it is followed by a later prison sentence, might be considered a type of success.

Sometimes the woman is in a better state mentally after participating in a program or engaging in a relationship with a helping professional, even if situations occur that lead to further crime commission. Once in prison again, she is better able to take advantage of the programs available. In the final analysis, we should be more expansive in what we mean by success and look behind simple numbers to what has occurred in the women's lives on release. It is probably no coincidence that the meta-analysis method has provided the most condemnatory evidence "against" treatment programs. Such a method loses the "trees" for the "forest." And we should be concerned with each tree (person).

For the individual helping professional, it may be important to understand the politics of recidivism to answer critics who expect to see results measured solely in terms of reduced recidivism rates. In general, budgets for helping professionals are always vulnerable. It would be helpful to develop other measures of effectiveness in addition to recidivism for any treatment efforts engaged in by the helping professional.

Feminism, Ethnocentrism, and Correctional Counseling

Okun (1997, p. 137) described a multicultural model as based on the following premises: (a) Sociocultural conditions are responsible for the problems for which people seek help, (b) each culture has meaningful ways of coping with problems, and (c) counseling as we know it is a Western cultural invention. Each of these principles will be covered in the discussions to follow.

One cannot ignore feminism and feminist discourse in any discussion of treatment of the female offender. Neither can one ignore the fact that a disproportional number of a correctional caseloads are members of minority groups and have experienced societal discrimination and systemic oppression in ways that nonminority members can only imagine. Each of these realities must be faced in the counseling relationship. The most effective response is to emphasize counseling goals that lead to personal empowerment.

Feminism

Before any particular discussion of feminism is applied to corrections, it would be wise to note that feminism is not a unitary term and encompasses a continuum of positions and paradigms. The following broad brush categories have been described:

Marxist feminists (or Socialist feminists, although some authors make distinctions between them) point to general economic conditions and women's economic role in society. Capitalism treats women as property and ensures their unequal position vis à vis men, that is, through the laws of inheritance. Powerlessness dictates the types of victimization women will experience (rape and battering as expressions of male beliefs in the woman's body as property), as well as the types of crimes they will commit (generally low level and often related to the use of her body as a commodity, i.e., prostitution or fraud.)

Radical feminists do not focus on the economic structure as do Marxist feminists, but they agree that social conditions contribute to female oppression and male domination. Patriarchy is the essential element in all social and legal relationships and determines all aspects of a female's life, from her upbringing to be "nice," to her choice of occupations, to her definition of what it means to be a woman (Belnap, 1996; Bloom et al., 1995; Simpson, 1989).

Cultural feminism has been used to describe those theorists who believe that there are differences between males and females that impact on the way the two groups view the world and the priority they place on relationships and goals. Whether these differences arise from biology or socialization seems to be less relevant to these theorists than the impact of the differences on women's lives and the lack of response legal and societal changes have made to these differences.

Postmodernist feminism, finally, has been defined as a recognition that feminist theory can never synthesize the life experiences of different groups based on class, race, sex, and cultural lines, and it is farcical to believe that there can be any shared platform of feminists, because these groupings result in different life positions, values, goals, and social realities (Smart, 1989, 1995).

The particular debate today that seems most pressing is the argument of special needs (difference) versus equality. As previously discussed, the equality argument is that women have been treated differently by the system and it is important to achieve equality in the treatment and processing of male and female offenders. Only through this equality will women avoid the paternalism and oppression that has characterized their treatment thus far. The special needs or difference argument is that women have been treated differently because they have different needs. Their treatment in the past may have elements of paternalism and maternalism and ignored the real life problems of women trying to make a living and support their children, but there were also elements, such as a greater concern for privacy, better arrangements for children's visitation and, arguably, greater hesitancy to employ imprisonment, that actually benefited women (Chesney-Lind & Pollock, 1994).

On the other hand, some also point out ironies in feminist jurisprudence and therapy professionals championing women's causes by noting how women are "different from" or have "different needs" from men (Lahey, 1985, p. 539). What often occurs is the advocacy turns into another trap for women who are then defined as in need of protection or cure. Examples include the battered woman defense, pregnancy discrimination acts, and other attempts to recognize and respond to women's unique realities.

"Women-Centered" Corrections

The new version of difference is the idea of a "woman-centered" correctional focus. This concept has many authors (see, for instance, Carlen, 1989; Daly, 1989, or for a more recent application, see McDermott, 1994). Basically, the idea is that the justice system is masculine in its emphasis on rights and retribution. A *woman-centered* justice system would be based on meeting needs. Of course, this is an oversimplification, as Daly (1989, 1994) has pointed out, because whereas the justice system itself may be offense-based, rational, and retributive, the *application* of justice, specifically, sentencing, very often takes into account other factors besides guilt, including those features more likely to be attributed to a caring or needs-based approach (family responsibilities or mitigating circumstances). McDermott (1994) distilled the woman-centered approach (although she called it "feminist") into the following principles:

1. Caring individuals are responsive to others' points of view.
2. We exist in a web of relationships.

3. Moral behavior and justice flow from caring and responsiveness. Moral judgments are contextual, although based on a universal ethic that it is wrong to hurt anyone, and it is right to sustain human relationships.
4. Responsiveness requires equality.
5. Emotions and feelings are as integral to moral judgments as intellect and reason. (p. 31)

One interesting example of a justice system that might fit this description was provided by Braithwaite and Daly (1994). In their description of the Maori response to offending in a village culture, the key emphases seem to be on the very elements identified by those who advocate a woman-centered or caring-corrections approach.

> After an offense is detected by the state, a youth justice coordinator convenes a conference. Those invited are the offender . . . the boy's family members (often extending to aunts, grandparents, cousins), other citizens who are key supports in the boy's life (perhaps a football coach he particularly respects), the police, the victim, victim supporters, and in some instances, a youth justice advocate . . . these conferences can be viewed as citizenship ceremonies of reinterpretive shaming . . . discussion of the harm and distress caused to the victim and the offender's family will communicate shame to the offender. . . .
> In a successful conference, the offender is brought to experience remorse for the effects of the crime; to understand that he or she can count on the continuing support, love, and respect of family and friends; and to agree on a plan of action to prevent further harm. (p. 193)

Interestingly, a very similar format is used in "network therapy," a type of family therapy. In this Western therapy, all individuals connected with the person in trouble (i.e., teachers, neighbors, coaches, and, of course, families) gather for a group meeting. In this group meeting, which is goal-oriented, attitudes and ideas are exchanged with a plan for the future developed. Each person may have a part in helping with whatever issues were identified as contributing to the problem (such as alcoholism, delinquency, or lack of responsibility).

Another specific application of a "woman-centered" approach was discussed by Hannah-Moffat (1994) in a Canadian correctional effort. A Canadian task force on women's corrections has concluded that, on the basis of the nature and needs of the female offender population, a special approach is important—this "woman-centered" approach will close the large federal prison currently in use for women and replace it with smaller regional correctional centers and one "healing lodge" for Aboriginal women. These facilities will supposedly promote "empowerment, meaningful and responsible choices, respect and dignity, supportive environments and shared responsibility." The woman-centered approach was characterized as "caring, empowering, supportive, respectful, and meaningful" (Hannah-Moffat, 1994, p. 9).

Nevertheless, this attempt to implement a "woman-centered" approach to corrections is not without critics. Hannah-Moffat (1994) and others pointed out that, first of all, a separate "feminine" approach to corrections is certainly not new. In the early chapters of this book I discussed the rise of the female reformatory and the attempt to make homelike environments part of the prison experience for women to learn appropriate feminine skills. This "softer" approach to corrections has characterized women's corrections for years and is probably directly responsible for the lack of vocational programs, the maternalistic relationships between staff and inmates, and the difference in rules between some women's prisons and all prisons for males in the same system. Second, critics point out that this "woman-centered" approach masks the true nature of female criminality by promoting self-esteem counseling instead of attacking the true basis for the predicament of women in prison—the unequal and male-centered power basis of society. "This emphasis on responsibility de-contextualizes feminist constructions of women's resistance and it disregards feminist analysis of the social, economic, political barriers experienced by women, and in particular by marginalized women" (Hannah-Moffat, 1994, p. 15).

A related issue is the question about whether it is appropriate or even desirable to consider women's prisons as different from men's prisons. In Hannah-Moffat's (1994) words, "The image of a woman-centered prison as benevolent, caring, therapeutic, and supportive denies the existence of similar relations in men's prisons" (p. 9). Actually, feminine corrections, in some ways, can be considered to be more coercive than corrections for men. Certainly, historically this has been so and the more recent research by McClelland (1994a, 1994b) cited in an earlier chapter indicates that even today women may be subject to more pervasive control than male inmates.

It also should be noted that the empowerment language and choices discussed in official documents bear little resemblance to the developing plans for the new women's prisons in Canada. Custodial elements in architecture and procedures are being added to the original "woman-centered" plans. Reportedly, there has been a lack of participation by inmate advocates allowed in the planning and implementation of the new prisons. Decisions were made to place the new facilities in rural areas, rather than in cities as was recommended by the task force. Finally, there may be no money left for treatment programs once they are built. What may result, then, is a system that has many more beds and no real change.

Feminist Therapy and Female Prisoners

Feminist therapy has been defined as "framing the experiences of individuals within the broader social environment" and helping "people connect their own experiences and actions and the circumstances that define their lives" (Kendall, 1994b, p. 2). Another author defined feminist therapy as when therapists "focus on understanding gender as both a cause and a consequence of women's experiences in a male-dominated culture" (Okun, 1997, p. 136). Okun went on to explain that feminist therapy differs from traditional therapy in that it is based on a relationship of equality between the helper and person to be helped, views women's problems as being inseparable from society's oppression of them, and emphasizes social, political, and economic action as a major aspect of the helping process (1997, p. 136). Feminist therapy is empowering, there is an active discouragement of the victim or patient stance. This is not substantially different from other therapies, what is different is that a broader societal view is introduced to the therapeutic process.

Kendall (1994a), in an article summarizing her evaluation of treatment programs available at one Canadian prison, expressed her concern that feminism was being co-opted by the corrections system: "I am concerned that the language of feminism is being appropriated and stripped of its subversive potential by corrections to facilitate the correctional agenda" (1994b, p. 2). She explained that the inmates themselves evaluate some of the counseling that takes place in the prison positively, but the larger issue is this: How can individual treatment address such issues as racism, sexism, and violence in the larger society? As Kendall (1994b) pointed out, a psychological therapeutic approach reduces the problems from the "political to the personal."

> The reality of poverty, violence, racism and sexism will not change, and prisons will be expanded rather than abolished. The promise of choice being offered to imprisoned women is an empty one, indeed. Yet, because the Task Force report and the resulting implementation plans are shrouded in liberal feminist scholarship and language, legitimacy is given to the scheme and resistance is weakened. (p. 2)

In her evaluation of treatment programs, Kendall was concerned that the "cult of victimhood" used in the therapeutic paradigm denies women any autonomy and focuses attention backward instead of forward. Even feminist therapy is problematic, because it must by design concentrate on personal "problems" rather than larger social realities. The reduced power imbalance common to feminist therapy is artificial in a prison setting that is rife with power and authority roles that cannot be softened (Kendall, 1994b, p. 3).

Kendall (1994b, p. 4) found that a majority of women offenders in the prison expressed support for the therapy and therapists provided by the prison. Their responses indicated that therapy was helpful in the following ways: it allowed them a space "to be themselves," it helped them gain control of their own lives, and/or it allowed an opportunity to value and be valued by others. Further, they stated that the therapists provided them with practical assistance, treated them with respect and showed support for them through advocacy on various matters (Kendall, 1994b, p. 5). Kendall pointed out that the benefits of therapy, then, resulted from the relationship, rather than any particular therapeutic mode, and that the benefits did not have to come from therapy but might also come from other sources that provided practical assistance and a positive relationship for women offenders, for instance, through hobbies, religion, exercise, friends and family, and volunteers.

Therapy has always been fundamentally more a product of a caring and supportive relationship than any particularly efficacious modality—feminist therapy is no different in this regard than any other therapy. The fact is that it may be the only positive relationship that the individual has ever had. Therapy is often learning how to value oneself because no one else ever has. This is especially true with women offenders. To say that family and friends might be able to provide the same elements as therapy is to deny the reality that family and friends have often been the victimizers of women in prison.

Ethnocentrism, Racism, and Cultural Sensitivity

The importance of such issues as racism, sexism, and economic oppression are obviously relevant to any discussion of counseling women in prison. Kendall and other theorists pointed out that therapists do a disservice by approaching the problems of women in prison as individual problems, rather than social problems. Whereas the larger social issues of poverty, racism, and sexism are real and have obvious real impact on these women's lives, to deny them individual assistance because of a fear of co-optation by the system would be tragic. There was a cartoon that made the rounds on college campuses many years ago drawn to poke fun at "radical intellectuals." The picture showed a homeless person with his hand out to a character drawn to represent a radical college student who, in response to the request for the handout, was exhorting on the capitalistic system, the oppression of the working class, and the fact that only social revolution would change the economic realities of poverty and homelessness. The last box shows the college student walking away and the homeless person looking at his empty hand with a quizzical expression. The point of the cartoon was that speeches and social agendas are all well and good but that this homeless person had to eat *today*, and he couldn't eat a speech.

Studies show that what women say they need are jobs, help with addiction, and advocacy in dealing with personal and pragmatic issues of living. Treatment can be empowering if it helps individuals become self-aware and improves their ability to achieve their goals. Anyone who has talked to women (or men for that matter, although they tend to be less disclosing) in a treatment program has heard the stories of "I would be dead if I hadn't been sent to prison," "I may be in prison now but I'm more free than I was on the outside," "These people here (meaning prisoners and counselors) are my family," and "I love myself now and I never did before." Those are paraphrases but they have to sound familiar to anyone who has worked or researched in a prison. The fact is that helpful intervention can move the woman to a position where she is able to take advantage of vocational aids, which, in turn, will enable her to make a living wage and support herself and her children in a decent lifestyle.

At the same time, to be successful counseling must understand the social realities that female prisoners come from and will return to. These social realities include cultural differences in family structure, expectations of women, and child rearing. These cultural norms may be different from those of the counselor and may be perceived as detrimental to the personal growth of the female prisoner, but the counselor must be sensitive to the power of cultural socialization and allow for the fact that the individual must choose whether or not to challenge cultural norms. Unique cultural elements that one might encounter in correctional populations include the importance of spirituality, either Christian or non-Christian, for instance Native Americans who practice their traditional religions or Latinos who practice Santeria. Whereas some cultures value autonomy as a goal in personal development, other cultures value interconnectedness and family loyalty.

Certain forms of therapeutic approaches may be less accepted by minorities. For instance, Okun (1997, p. 131) suggested the possibility that directive and confrontational treatment approaches (such as rational-emotive therapy) may be offensive to minority clients who have experienced racial or ethnic discrimination and feel that they are being blamed for their feelings of failure. Power-based therapeutic approaches should be used with care to ensure that cultural insensitivity does not occur. All of us may operate with sexist and racist preconceptions; if we are engaged in a helping relationship, these preconceptions get in the way of effective communicating and the counseling relationship. For instance, counselors in prison may unconsciously expect less from African American prisoners than Anglo prisoners. They may encourage women to accept culturally prescribed roles. They may assume that Hispanic

women are not interested in vocational programs. Wallace (1995) described
some of these biases in drug treatment—for instance, that African American
women are more violent and less likely to be successful in treatment programs.
These biases and preconceptions are sometimes subtle but have real effects
on the helping relationship.

Empowerment

One expert in the field pointed out that no one can "empower" another—
they must "empower" themselves. One thing is agreed on by most people and
that is that there is little to be gained from the old "treatment ethic" that
postulated that there was something wrong with the criminal that needed to
be treated. Life's problems—a lack of education, low self-esteem, addiction,
and an inability to stay away from dysfunctional relationships with men—are
not broken arms or influenza; therefore, no "magic pill" or "treatment" will
"fix" them. The individual herself must take control of her own will, attitudes,
values, and behavioral decisions. She must learn how to value herself and how
to take responsibility for her actions.

Women in prison demand programs, but if programs merely act as salves
for hurt and release valves for frustration, they will do nothing to "empower."
Talking and sharing is good but *doing* is better. The most successful treatment
has been shown to have active elements rather than being just a "talking cure."
Therapeutic communities in the free world often have some productive and
economically viable enterprise associated with them so that members can earn
money and contribute to the economic viability of the operation. People who
are productive and self-sufficient are happier and healthier than those who are
dependent on others—either emotionally or financially. The prison provides
little opportunity to engage in activity that can be described as productive, but
many women have managed to fill their prison life with work, school, and
volunteer activities. These women are setting a pattern for activity that they
will probably continue once they are released.

Some type of productive work is important in prison, because it gives the
individual not only a wage but a feeling of accomplishment, as does achieving
a GED or completing a college course. Ironically, we may be ignoring the
lessons of the past in what the early women's reformatories taught us about
the value of "healthy work." In the early reformatories described in the first
chapter, idealistic accounts of the activities reported matrons and inmates
working side-by-side to gather crops, feed livestock, and clean their "home."
The idea that hard work equals healthy living is simplistic—and doesn't take

into account sweat shops, exploited workers, and occupation-related deaths and illnesses,—but it does seem to be true that many successful treatment programs incorporate activity into the program, such as Outward Bound, conservation crews, restitution programs, community service, and so on. Some who participate continue their involvement even after their commitment has ended.

Conclusion

For years the numbers of women in U.S. prisons were minuscule. Women's participation in crime was only somewhat higher. More recently, their participation in crime has increased, especially in the area of drugs and property crimes, but their imprisonment rates have skyrocketed. Equality in sentencing has meant more women are being sent to prison, even though the lack of imprisonment that characterized women's treatment by the criminal justice system historically could be tied to the following: (a) continued minor participation in crime, (b) lower recidivism, (c) little violence, and (d) more intact families. Thus, any calls for improved programming are made with a mixed heart. Improvement often means building a new prison that is always bigger and always full in a very short period of time.

Chesney-Lind (1991) provided just such a cautionary tale in Hawaii, where advocates for female inmates pressured the state to provide more programs and vocational training for women inmates, and the state responded with plans for a prison that was twice the size of the current prisoner population. Although opposition prevented construction, it serves as a perfect example of what might happen in an effort to help improve the condition of women in prison. The Canadian example is not much different, because the one federal prison will be replaced by several new ones. Whether or not the number of beds will remain the same as promised remains to be seen.

There is a great need for improving vocational and counseling programs for women, especially parenting programs, but there is an even greater need to reevaluate the current national practice of increasing our incarceration of women. The public must come to realize that their "pound of flesh" is obtained at the expense of children—both current and future—of the offender mother. Most women in prison need help but it is extremely doubtful whether prison is the help they need. If we must incarcerate, then at least let's try to make sure that they exit prison at least no worse than when they went in. It is hoped that they may also have acquired some skills and self-awareness.

The helping professional can feel good about their role in corrections if they can ameliorate some of the negative influences of the prison environment.

Helping relationships that occur in prisons can facilitate female prisoners' personal growth. This can be accomplished with a recognition of the importance of the female prisoner's past and cultural influences, as well as faith in her skills, abilities, and potential for the future.

Bo Lozoff (1987) perhaps described the importance of counselors most eloquently.

> A staff person who's calm and strong and happy is worth his or her weight in gold. People who are living examples of truthfulness, good humor, patience, and courage are going to change more lives—even if they're employed as janitors—than the counselors who can't get their own lives in order. These staff persons have reached a place of discipline in their own lives. Such a sense of discipline involves one who has internalized his or her personal and professional values. These values, forged and tested through a lifetime of experiences, come from a wellspring deep within the core of the person's being. (p. 398)

References

ADAPT. (1993, November 30). *Final Report.* (Unpublished final report, Grant No. 1552). Multnomah County, OR.

Adelberg, E., & Currie, C. (1987). *Too few to count: Canadian women in conflict with the Law.* Vancouver, British Columbia: Press Gang Publishers.

Adler, F. (1975). *Sisters in crime.* New York: McGraw Hill.

Ainsworth, M. (1978). *Patterns of attachment: A psychological study of the strange situation.* Hillsdale, NJ: Lawrence Erlbaum.

Albanese, J. (1993). Women and the newest profession: Females as white-collar criminals. In C. Culliver (Ed.), *Female criminality: The state of the art* (pp. 119-131). New York: Garland.

Anglin, M. D., & Hser Y. (1987). Addicted women and crime. *Criminology, 25*(2), 359-395.

Arbour, L. (1996). *Commission inquiry into certain events at the prison for women in Kingston.* Toronto, Canada: Public Works and Government Services.

Arbuthnot, J. (1984). Moral reasoning development programs in prison: Cognitive-developmental and critical reasoning approaches. *Journal of Moral Education, 13*(2), 112-123.

Arbuthnot, J., & Gordon, D. (1986). Behavioral and cognitive effects of a moral reasoning development intervention for high risk behavior-disordered adolescents. *Journal of Consulting and Clinical Psychology, 54,* 208-216.

Arbuthnot, J., & Gordon, D. (1988). Crime and cognition: Community applications of sociomoral reasoning development. *Criminal Justice and Behavior, 15*(3), 379-393.

Bagley, K., & Merlo A. (1994). Controlling women's bodies. In A. Merlo & J. Pollock (Eds.), *Women, law and social control* (pp. 135-155). Boston: Allyn & Bacon.

Baunach, P. J. (1982). You can't be a mother and be in prison... Can you? Impacts of the mother-child separation. In B. R. Price & N. J. Sokoloff (Eds.), *The criminal justice system and women* (pp. 155-170). New York: Clark and Boardman.

Beck, A., & Freeman, A. (1990). *Cognitive therapy of personality disorders.* New York: Guilford.

Beck, A., Rush, J., Shaw, B., & Emory, G. (1979). *Cognitive therapy of depression.* New York: Guilford.

Beck, A., Wright, F., Newman, C., & Liese, B. (1993). *Cognitive therapy of substance abuse.* New York: Guilford.

Belnap, J. (1996). *The invisible woman: Gender, crime and justice.* Belmont, CA: Wadsworth.

Bloom, B. (1992). *Women offenders: Issues, concerns and strategies.* Paper presented at the meeting of the Western Society of Criminology, San Diego, CA.

Bloom, B., Chesney-Lind, M., & Owen, B. (1994). *Women in California prisons: Hidden victims of the war on drugs.* San Franciso, CA: Center on Juvenile and Criminal Justice.

Bloom, B., Lee, C., & Owen, B. (1995). *Offense patterns among women prisoners: A preliminary analysis.* Paper presented at the meeting of the American Society of Criminology Conference, Boston, MA.

Blount, W., Kuhns, J., & Silverman, I. (1993). Intimate abuse within an incarcerated female population: Rates, levels, criminality, a continuum, and some lessons about self-identification. In C. Culliver (Ed.), *Female criminality: The state of the art* (pp. 413-462). New York: Garland.

Boudouris, J. (1996). *Parents in prison: Addressing the needs of families.* Lanham, MD: American Correctional Association.

Bowlby, J. (1969). *Attachment and loss, Vol. l.* New York: Basic Books.

Braithwaite, J., & Daly, K. (1994). Masculinities, violence, and communitarian control. In T. Newburn & E. Stanko (Eds.), *Just boys doing business? Men, masculinities and crime* (pp. 189-213). London: Routledge.

Brochu, S., & Levesque, M. (1990). Treatment of prisoners for alcohol or drug abuse problems. *Alcoholism Treatment Quarterly, 7*(4), 113-121.

Browne, A. (1987). *When battered women kill.* New York: Free Press.

Burke, P., & Adams, L. (1991). *Classification of women offenders in state correctional facilities: A handbook for practitioners.* Washington, DC: National Institute of Corrections.

Burkhart, K. (1973). *Women in prison.* New York: Popular Press.

Camp, G., & Camp, C. (1993). *The corrections yearbook.* South Salem, NY: Criminal Justice Institute.

Camp, D., & Sandhu, H. (1995). *Evaluation of female offender regimented treatment program (FORT)* (Final report). Oklahoma City: Oklahoma State University, Department of Sociology.

Carlen, P. (1989). Feminist jurisprudence—Or woman-wise penology. *Probation Journal, 36*(3), 110-114.

Carp, S., & Schade, L. (1992). Tailoring facility programming to suit female offenders' needs. *Corrections Today, 54*(6), 152-159.

Catan, L. (1992). Infants with mothers in prison. In R. Shaw (Ed.), *Prisoners' children: What are the issues?* (pp. 26-42). New York: Routledge.

Chesney-Lind, M. (1991). Patriarchy, prisons and jails: A critical look at trends in women's incarceration. *The Prison Journal, LXXI*(1), 51-67.

Chesney-Lind, M., & Pollock, J. (1994). Women's prisons: Equality with a vengeance. In A. Merlo & J. Pollock (Eds.), *Women, law and social control* (pp. 155-177). Boston: Allyn & Bacon.

Chodorow, N. (1978). *Reproduction of mothering: Psychoanalysis and the sociology of gender.* Berkeley: University of California Press.

Clark, D. (1991). *Analysis of return rates of the inmate college program participants.* Unpublished manuscript, Department of Correctional Services at Albany, NY.

Clement, M. (1993). Parenting in prison: A national survey of programs for incarcerated women. *Journal of Offender Rehabilitation, 19*(1/2), 89-100.

Coulson, G., & Nutbrown, V. (1992). Properties of an ideal rehabilitative program for high need offenders. *International Journal of Offender Therapy and Comparative Criminology, 36*(3), 203-208.

Crawford, J. (1988). *Tabulation of a nationwide survey of state correctional facilities for adult and juvenile female offenders.* College Park, MD: American Correctional Association.

Daly, K. (1989). Criminal justice ideologies and practices in different voices: Some feminist questions about justice. *International Journal of the Sociology of Law, 17,* 1-18.

Daly, K. (1994). *Gender, crime and punishment.* New Haven, CT: Yale University Press.

Dawson, J. (1994). *Murder in families* (Bureau of Justice Statistics Special Report). Washington, DC: U.S. Department of Justice.

Dayton, K. (1991, March 14). Sex scandal erupts at women's prison. *Honolulu Advertiser,* A1.

Dobash, R. P., Dobash, R. E., & Gutteridge, S. (1986). *The imprisonment of women.* Totawa, NJ: Blackwell.

Eaton, M. (1993). *Women after prison.* Philadelphia, PA: Open University Press.

Eisenstein, Z. (1988). *The female body and the law.* Berkeley: University of California Press.

Enos, R., & Southern, S. (1996). *Correctional case management.* Cincinnati, OH: Anderson.

Evans, K. (1978). Reflections on education in the penitentiary. In W. Taylor & M. Braswell (Eds.), *Issues in police and criminal psychology* (pp. 251-263). Washington, DC: University Press of America.

Ewing, C. (1987). *Battered women who kill.* Lexington, MA: Lexington Books.

Faith, K. (1993). *Unruly women: The politics of confinement and resistance.* Vancouver, British Columbia: Press Gang Publishing.

Federal Bureau of Investigations. (1990). *Uniform crime reports.* Washington, DC: Government Printing Office.

Federal Bureau of Investigations. (1993). *Uniform crime reports.* Washington, DC: Government Printing Office.

Feinman, C. (1976). *Imprisoned women: A history of the treatment of women incarcerated in New York City: 1932-1975.* Unpublished doctoral dissertation, New York University, New York.

Fletcher, B. R., Shaver, L. O., & Moon, D. G. (1993). *Women prisoners: A forgotten population.* Westport, CT: Praeger.

Fox, J. (1975). Women in crisis. In H. Toch (Ed.), *Men in crisis* (pp. 181-205). Chicago: Aldin Athert.

Fox, J. (1990). Women in prison: A case study in the social reality of stress. In R. Johnson & H. Toch (Eds.), *The pains of imprisonment* (pp. 205-220). Newbury Park, CA: Sage.

Frankel, L. (1992). *Women, anger and depression.* Deerfield Beach, FL: Health Communications, Inc.

Freedman, E. (1974). Their sisters' keepers: A historical perspective of female correctional institutions in the U.S. *Feminist Studies, 2,* 77-95.

Freedman, E. (1981). *Their sisters' keepers: Women's prison reform in America, 1830-1930.* Ann Arbor: University of Michigan Press.

Gaudin, J. (1984, May). Social work roles and tasks with incarcerated mothers. *Social Casework: The Journal of Contemporary Social Work, 53,* 279-294.

Gendreau, P., & Ross, R. (1987). Revivification of rehabilitation: Evidence for the 1980s. *Justice Quarterly, 4*(3), 349-407.

Giallombardo, R. (1966). *Society of women.* New York: John Wiley.

Gibbs, J., Arnold, K., Ahlborn, H., & Cheesman, F. (1984). Facilitation of socio-moral reasoning in delinquents. *Journal of Consulting and Clinical Psychology, 52*(1), 37-45.

Gilfus, M. (1988). *Seasoned by violence/tempered by law: A qualitative study of women and crime.* Unpublished doctoral dissertation, Brandeis University, Waltham, MA.

Gilligan, C. (1982). *In a different voice.* Cambridge, MA: Harvard University Press.

Glover v. Johnson, 478 F.Supp. 1075 (E.D. Mich. 1979).

Glueck, S., & Glueck, E. (1934). *Five hundred delinquent women.* New York: Alfred Knopf.

Gottfredson, M. (1979). Treatment destruction techniques. *Journal of Research in Crime and Delinquency, 16,* 39-54.

Gottfredson, M., & Hirschi, T. (1990). *A general theory of crime.* Stanford, CA: Stanford University Press.

Gunther v. Iowa State Men's Reformatory, 612 F.2d 1079 (8th Cir.), *cert. denied,* 446 U.S. 966 (1980).

Hairston, C. (1991). Family ties during imprisonment: Important to whom and for what? *Journal of Sociology and Social Welfare, 18*(1), 87-104.

Hale, D., & Menniti, D. (1994). The battered woman syndrome as legal defense: Status in the courtroom. In A. Merlo & J. Pollock (Eds.), *Women, law and social control* (pp. 203-219). Boston: Allyn & Bacon.

Hannah-Moffat, K. (1994). *Feminine fortresses: Women-centered prisons?* Unpublished manuscript.

Hatcher, H. (1978). *Correctional casework and counseling.* Englewood Cliffs, NJ: Prentice Hall.

Heffernan, R. (1972). *The square, the cool and the life.* New York: John Wiley.

Heidensohn, F. (1986). Models of justice: Portia or Persephone? Some thoughts on equality, fairness and gender in the field of criminal justice. *International Journal of the Sociology of Law, 14,* 287-298.

Henriques, Z. W. (1994, April). *Imprisoned mothers and their children: A cross-cultural perspective.* Paper presented at "Prisons 2000 Conference," Leicester, England.

Hickey, E. (1991). *Serial murderers and their victims.* Belmont, CA: Wadsworth.

Hirschel, J. D., & Keny, J. (1990). Outpatient treatment for substance abusing offenders. In N. Pallone & S. Chaneles (Eds.), *The clinical treatment of the criminal offender in outpatient mental health settings* (pp. 111-129). New York: Haworth.

Hoffman-Bustamante, D. (1973). The nature of female criminality. *Issues in Criminology, 8,* 117-136.

Huling, T. (1991, March 4). *Breaking the silence* (Internal Report). New York: Correctional Association of New York.

Huling, T. (1995). Women drug couriers. *Criminal Justice, 9*(4), 14-20.

Immarigeon, R. (1994). When parents are sent to prison. *The National Prison Project Journal, 9*(4/5), 14-16.

Inciardi, J., Lockwood, D., & Pottieger, A. (1993). *Women and crack-cocaine.* New York: Macmillan.

Joe, K., & Chesney-Lind, M. (1993). *Just every mother's angel: An analysis of gender and ethnic variations in youth gang membership.* Paper presented at the meeting of the American Society of Criminology Conference, Phoenix, AZ.

Jones, M. (1968). *Beyond the therapeutic community.* New Haven, CT: Yale University Press.

Jordan v. Gardner, 986 F.2d 1544-1545 (9th Cir. 1993).

Kapsner, C. (1994). *Women in community service lifeskills programs.* Salem: Oregon Department of Corrections.

Kaslow, F. (1987). Couples or family therapy for prisoners and their significant others. *American Journal of Family Therapy, 15*(4), 352-360.

Keeney, B., & Heide, K. (1994). Gender differences in serial murderers. *Journal of Interpersonal Violence, 9*(3), 383-398.

Kendall, K. (1994a). Creating real choices: A program evaluation of therapeutic services at the prison for women. *Forum on Corrections Research, 6*(1), 19-21.

Kendall, K. (1994b). Therapy behind prison walls: A contradiction in terms? *Prison Service Journal, 96,* 2-11.

Kitchener, K. (1988). Dual role relationships: What makes them so problematic? *Journal of Counseling and Development, 67,* 217-221.

Klonoff, E., & Landrine, H. (1997). *Preventing misdiagnosis of women.* Thousand Oaks, CA: Sage.

Koban, L. A. (1983). Parents in prison: A comparative analysis of the effects of incarceration in the families of men and women. *Research in Law, Deviance and Social Control, 5,* 171-183.

Kochis, D. (1994). *Drugs, crime and women: A process evaluation of T.A.P.* Paper presented at the meeting of the American Society of Criminology, Boston, MA.

Kohlberg, L. (1976). Moral stages and moralization: The cognitive developmental approach. In T. Lickona (Ed.), *Moral development and behavior: Theory, research and social issues* (pp. 31-53). New York: Holt, Rinehart & Winston.

Kohlberg, L. (1981). *The philosophy of moral development.* New York: Harper and Row.

Kratcoski, P. (1994). *Correctional counseling and treatment.* Monterey, CA: Duxbury Press.

Lahey, K. (1985). Until women themselves have told all that they have to tell. *Osgoode Hall Law Journal, 23*(3), 519-540.

Lekkerkerker, E.C. (1931). *Reformatories for women in the U.S.*. Groningen, Netherlands: J.B. Wolters.

Lenhart, J. (1995, June 13). Few programs available to aid prison mothers. *Houston Chronicle,* A1, 10A.

Leonard, E. B. (1983). Judicial decisions and prison reform: The impact of litigation of women prisoners. *Social Problems, 31*(1), 45-58.

Lester, D., & van Voorhis, P. (1992). Group and milieu therapy. In D. Lester, M. Braswell, & P. van Voorhis (Eds.), *Correctional counseling* (pp. 175-191). Cincinnati, OH: Anderson.

Logan, C. H., & Gaes, G. G. (1993). Meta-analysis and the rehabilitation of punishment. *Justice Quarterly, 10,* 245-263.

Lombardo, V., & Smith, R. (1996, October). Rational emotive therapy: A model program for female offenders. *Corrections Today,* pp. 92-95.

Lombroso, C., & Ferrero, W. (1920). *The female offender.* New York: Appleton-Century-Croft. (Original work published 1894)

Louis, T., & Sparger, J. (1990). Treatment modalities within prison. In J. Murphy & J. Dison (Eds.), *Are prisons any better? Twenty years of correctional reform* (pp. 147-161). Newbury Park, CA: Sage.

Lozoff, B. (1987). *We're all doing time.* Chapel Hill, NC: Human Kindness Foundation.

Mahan, S., & Prestwood, D. (1993). A radical analysis of a treatment program for cocaine-abusing mothers. In C. Culliver (Ed.), *Female criminality: The state of the art* (pp. 503-515). New York: Garland.

Mandaraka-Sheppard, A. (1986). *The dynamics of aggression in women's prisons in England.* England: Gower.

Mann, C. R. (1993). Sister against sister: Female intrasexual homicide. In C. Culliver (Ed.), *Female criminality: The state of the art* (pp. 195-225). New York: Garland.

Martinson, R. (1974, Spring). What works? Questions and answers about prison reform. *Public Interest,* pp. 22-54.

Masters, R. (1994). *Counseling criminal justice offenders.* Thousand Oaks, CA: Sage.

McClelland, D. (1994a) Disparity in the discipline of male and female inmates in Texas prisons. *Women and Criminal Justice, 5*(2), 71-97.

McClelland, D. (1994b, November). *Women in Texas prisons: A test case for feminist and critical criminology.* Paper presented at the meeting of the American Society of Criminology Conference, Miami, FL.

McDermott, M. J. (1994). Criminology as peacemaking, feminist ethics and the victimization of women. *Women and Criminal Justice, 5*(2), 21-44.

McGowan, B., & Blumenthal, K. (1976). *Why punish the children? A study of children of women prisoners.* Hanensack, NJ: National Council on Crime and Delinquency.

McLeod, R. (1995, October 17). Number of single parent families continues to increase, report says. *Austin American Statesman,* p. A2.

Megargee, E. I., & Bohn, M. J. (1979). *Classifying criminal offenders: A new system based on the MMPI.* Beverly Hills, CA: Sage.

Morris, A. (1987). *Women, crime and criminal justice.* Oxford, UK: Basil Blackwell.

Moses, M. (1995). *Keeping incarcerated mothers and their daughters together: Girl scouts beyond bars* (National Institute of Justice: Program Focus). Washington, DC: Government Printing Office.

National Institute of Justice. (1996a). *Project reenterprise: A Texas program* (Program Focus). Washington, DC: Government Printing Office.

National Institute of Justice. (1996b). *The cycle of violence revisited* (Research Brief). Washington, DC: Government Printing Office.

Neto, V., & Ranier, L. (1983). *Mother and wife locked up: A day with the family.* San Rafael, CA: Social Action Research Center.

Okun, B. (1987). *Effective helping: Interviewing and counseling techniques.* Pacific Grove, CA: Brooks/Cole.

Okun, B. (1990). *Seeking connections in psychotherapy.* San Francisco, CA: Jossey-Bass.

Okun, B. (1997). *Effective helping: Interviewing and counseling techniques* (2nd ed.). Pacific Grove, CA: Brooks/Cole.

Oregon Department of Corrections (1991). *White paper: Oregon's women offenders.* Unpublished manuscript, Information Services Division, Research and Analysis Unit.

Oregon Department of Corrections (1993). *Childhood abuse and the female inmate.* Unpublished manuscript, Information Services Division, Research and Analysis Unit.

Owen, B. (1994, April). *In the mix: Preliminary descriptions of the culture of a women's prison.* Paper presented at the "Prisons 2000 Conference," Leicester, England.

Owen, B., & Bloom, B. (1994, February). *Profiling the needs of California's female prisoners: A study in progress.* Paper presented at the meeting of the Western Society of Criminology, city, st.

Owen, B., & Bloom, B. (1995). Profiling women prisoners: Findings from national surveys and a California sample. *The Prison Journal, 75*(2), 165-185.

Palmer, T. (1992a). Growth centered intervention: An overview of changes in recent decades. *Federal Probation, 56*(1), 62-67.

Palmer, T. (1992b). *The re-emergence of correctional intervention.* Newbury Park, CA: Sage.

Palmer, T. (1994). *A profile of correctional effectiveness and new directions for research.* Albany: SUNY Press.

Piaget, J. (1965). *The moral judgment of the child.* New York: Free Press.

Pollak, O. (1950). *The criminality of women.* New York: A.S. Barnes and Company.

Pollock, J. (1986). *Sex and supervision: Guarding male and female inmates in prison.* Westport, CT: Greenwood.

Pollock, J. (1997a). *Ethics in crime and justice: Dilemmas and decisions* (3rd ed.). Belmont, CA: Wadsworth.

Pollock, J. (Ed.). (1997b). *Prisons: Today and tomorrow.* Gaithersburg, MD: Aspen.

Pollock, J. (1997c). Rehabilitation revisited. In J. Pollock (Ed.), *Prisons: Today and tomorrow* (pp. 158-208). Gaithersburg, MD: Aspen.

Pollock, J., Chan, A., Halbert, E., Wacker, M., & Ely, G. (1995). "Moms in Prison: Again." *PBS documentary.* Quotes taken from transcribed interviews.

Pollock, J., Williams, S., & Schroeder, S. (1996). *The needs of Texas women prisoners* (Final report). Unpublished manuscript.

Pollock-Byrne, J. (1990). *Women, prison and crime.* Pacific Grove, CA: Brooks/Cole.

Pollock-Byrne, J., & Merlo, A. (1991). Against compulsory treatment: No quick fix for pregnant substance abusers. *Criminal Justice Policy Review, 5,* 79-99.

Quay, H. C. (1984). *Managing adult inmates: Classification for housing and program assignment.* College Park, MD: American Correctional Association.

Quay, H. C., & Parsons, L. B. (1971). *The differential behavioral classification of the juvenile offender.* Washington, DC: U.S. Bureau of Prisons.

Raeder, M. (1993). Gender issues in the federal sentencing guideline. *Criminal Justice, 8*(3), 20-25, 56-58, 60-63.

Rafter, N. (1985). *Partial justice: Women, prisons and social control.* New Brunswick, NJ: Transaction Books.

Rafter, N. (1990). *Partial justice: Women, prisons and social control* (2nd ed.). New Brunswick, NJ: Transaction Books.

Reed, B. G. (1987). Developing women-sensitive drug dependence treatment services: Why so difficult? *Journal of Psychoactive Drugs, 19*(2), 151-164.

Resnick, J. (1987). The limits of parity in prisons. *National Prison Project Journal, 13,* 26-28.

Rosenbaum, J. (1989). Family dysfunction and female delinquency. *Crime & Delinquency, 35*(1), 31-44.

Ross, R., Fabiano, E., & Ewles, C. (1988). Reasoning and rehabilitation. *International Journal of Offender Therapy and Comparative Criminology, 32*(1), 29-35.

Scharf, P., & Hickey, J. (1981). Ideology and correctional intervention: The creation of a just prison community. In P. Kratcoski (Ed.), *Correctional counseling and treatment* (pp. 409-422). Monterey, CA: Duxbury.

Schrink, J. (1992). Understanding the correctional counselor. In D. Lester, M. Braswell, & P. van Voorhis (Eds.), *Correctional counseling* (pp. 41-58). Cincinnati, OH: Anderson.

Senese, J., & Kalinich, D. B. (1992). Activities and rehabilitation programs for offenders. In S. Stojkovic & R. Lovell (Eds.), *Corrections: An introduction* (pp. 213-244). Cincinatti, OH: Anderson.

Seydlitz, R. (1993) Compared to what? Delinquent girls and the similarity or difference issue. In C. Culliver (Ed.), *Female criminality: The state of the art* (pp. 133-169). New York: Garland.

Simon, R. (1975). *Women and crime*. Lexington, MA: D. C. Heath.

Simon, R., & Landis, J. (1991). *The crimes women commit. The punishments they receive.* Lexington, MA: Lexington Books.

Simpson, S. (1989). Feminist theory, crime and justice. *Criminology, 27*(4), 605-631.

Smart, C. (1989). *Feminism and the power of law.* London: Routledge.

Smart, C. (1995). *Law, crime and sexuality.* London: Sage Ltd.

Smith, C., & Thornberry, T. (1995). The relationship between childhood maltreatment and adolescent involvement in delinquency. *Criminology, 33*(4), 451-481.

Smith, J., & Faubert, M. (1990). Programming and process in prisoner rehabilitation: A prison mental health center. *Journal of Offender Counseling Services and Rehabilitation, 15*(2), 131-153.

Snell, T. (1994). *Women in prison. Survey of state prison inmates, 1991* (U.S. Department of Justice, Bureau of Justice Statistics Special Report). Washington, DC: Government Printing Office.

Solomon, E., & Heide, K. (1994, November). *Intervention strategies for victims of trauma: A solution focused therapy model.* Paper presented at the meeting of the American Society of Criminology Conference, Miami, FL.

Sommers, I., & Baskin, D. R. (1991, November). *The situational context of violent female offending.* Paper presented at the meeting of the American Society of Criminology, San Francisco, CA.

Spencer, D. (1997). The classification of inmates. In J. Pollock (Ed.), *Prisons: Today and tomorrow* (pp. 84-108). Gaithersburg, MD: Aspen.

Spunt, B., Brownstein, H., Crimmins, S., & Langley, S. (1994). *Female drug relationships in murder* (Report to the National Institute on Drug Abuse). Washington, DC: Government Printing Office.

Stanton, A. M. (1980). *When mothers go to jail.* Lexington, MA: Lexington Books.

Steffensmeier, D. (1993). *National trends in female arrests, 1960-1990: Assessment and recommendations for research.* Unpublished manuscript, Pennsylvania State University.

Steffensmeier, D., Kramer, J., & Streifel, C. (1993). Gender and imprisonment decisions. *Criminology, 31*(3), 411-445.

Stone, W. (1997). Industry, agriculture and education. In J. Pollock (Ed.), *Prisons: Today and tomorrow* (pp. 116-158). Gaithersburg, MD: Aspen.

Stumbo, N. J., & Little, S. L., (1991, August). Campgrounds offer relaxed setting for children's visitation program. *Corrections Today,* pp. 136-144.

Sultan, F., & Long, G. (1988). Treatment of the sexually/physically abused female inmate: Evaluation of an intensive short-term intervention program. *Journal of Offender Counseling, Services and Rehabilitation, 12*(1), 131-143.

Taylor, C. (1993). *Girls, gangs and drugs.* East Lansing: Michigan State University Press.

Texas Criminal Justice Policy Council. (1994). *Evaluation of Texas treatment initiative* (Internal Report). Austin, TX.

Thomas, W. I. (1969). *The unadjusted girl.* Montclair, NJ: Patterson Smith. (Original work published 1923)

Tilbur, K. (1993). *Prisoners as parents: Building parenting skills on the inside* (Family and Youth Services Bureau, Administration for Children and Families). Washington, DC: U. S. Department of Health and Human Services.

Timm v. Gunter, 917 F.2d 1093 (9th Cir. 1990).

Toch, H. (1980) *Therapeutic communities in corrections.* New York: Praeger.

Toch, H., Adams, K., & Grant, J. D. (1989). *Coping & maladaptation in prisons.* New Brunswick, NJ: Transaction Books.

U.S. Department of Justice, Bureau of Justice Statistics. (1991). *Women in prison: Special report.* Washington DC: Government Printing Office.

U.S. Department of Justice, Bureau of Justice Statistics. (1994a). *Prisoners in 1993.* Washington, DC: Government Printing Office.

U.S. Department of Justice, Bureau of Justice Statistics. (1994b). *Violence between intimates.* Washington, DC: Government Printing Office.

U.S. Department of Justice, Bureau of Justice Statistics. (1995). *Prisoners in 1994.* Washington, DC: Government Printing Office.

van Ochten, M. (1993). Legal issues and the female offender. In American Correctional Association (Ed.), *Female offenders: Meeting the needs of a neglected population* (pp. 31-36). Laurel, MD: American Correctional Association.

van Voorhis, P. (1985). Restitution outcome and probationers assessment of restitution. *Criminal Justice and Behavior, 12*(3), 414-426.

van Voorhis, P., Braswell, M., & Morrow, B. (1992). Family therapy. In D. Lester, M. Braswell, & P. van Voorhis (Eds.), *Correctional counseling* (pp. 155-174). Cincinnati, OH: Anderson.

Wallace, B. (1995). Women and minorities in treatment. In A. Washton (Ed.), *Psychotherapy and substance abuse* (pp. 470-491). New York: Guilford.

Walsh, A. (1988). *Understanding, assessing and counseling the criminal justice client.* Pacific Grove, CA: Brooks/Cole.

Ward, D., & Kassebaum, G. (1965). *Women's prison: Sex and social structure.* Hawthorne, NY: Aldine.

Warren, R. (1986). The female offender. In H. Toch (Ed.), *Psychology of crime and criminal justice* (pp. 444-469). Prospect Heights, IL: Waveland.

Weisheit, R. (1985). Trends in programs for female offenders: The use of private agencies as service providers. *International Journal of Offender Therapy and Comparative Criminology, 29,* 35-42.

Wellisch, J., Prendergast, M., & Anglin, M. D. (1994). *Drug abusing women offenders: Results of a national survey* (National Institute of Justice: Research in Brief). Washington, DC: Government Printing Office.

Widom, K. (1989). Child abuse, neglect and violent criminal behavior. *Criminology, 27,* 251-271.

Widom, K. (1991). Avoidance of criminality in abused and neglected children. *Psychiatry, 54,* 162-174.

Widom, K. (1995). *Victims of childhood sexual abuse-Later criminal consequences.* National Institute of Justice. Research in Brief. Washington, DC: U.S. Department of Justice, Office of Justice Programs.

Wilkie, M. (1993). *Sentencing women: Pre-sentence reports and constructions of female offenders.* Nedlands, West Australia: The University of Western Australia, Crime Research Centre.

Wilson, J. Q., & Hernstein, R. (1985). *Crime and human nature.* New York: Simon and Schuster.

Wooldredge, J. D., & Masters, K. (1993). Confronting problems faced by pregnant inmates in state prisons. *Crime & Delinquency, 39,* 195-203.

Wright, R. A. (1995). Rehabilitation affirmed, rejected, and reaffirmed: Assessments of the effectiveness of offender treatment programs in criminology textbooks, 1950-1965 and 1983-1992. *Journal of Criminal Justice Education, 6*(1), 21-41.

Young, E. (1995). The role of incest issues in relapse and recovery. In A. Washton (Ed.), *Psychotherapy and substance abuse* (pp. 451-469). New York: Guilford.

Zupan, L. (1992). The progress of women correctional officers in all male prisons. In I. Moyer (Ed.), *The changing roles of women in the criminal justice system* (pp. 323-343). Prospect Heights, IL: Waveland.

Zweben, J. E. (1995). Integrating psychotherapy and 12 step approaches. In A. Washton (Ed.), *Psychotherapy and substance abuse* (pp. 124-140). New York: Guilford.

Resources

ABA Center on Children and the Law
1800 M St., NW
Washington DC 20036
(202) 331-2649

Chicago Legal Aid to Incarcerated Mothers
205 W. Randolph, Suite 830
Chicago, IL 60606
(312) 332-5537

Edwin Gould Services for Children
Incarcerated Mothers Program
104 East 107th Street
New York, NY 10029
(212) 410-4200

M.A.T.C.H.
(Mothers and Their Children)
200 North Comal
San Antonio, TX 78207
(512) 270-6330

M.I.L.K.
(Mothers/Men Inside Loving Kids)
Virginians for Child Abuse Prevention
224 East Broad Street, Suite 302
Richmond, Virginia 23219
(804) 775-1777

M.O.L.D.
Osborne Association
135 East 15th St.
New York, NY 10003
(212) 673-6633

National Network for Women in Prison
Ellen Barry, Chair
c/o Legal Services for Prisoners with Children
474 Valencia St., Suite 230
San Francisco, CA 94103
(415) 255-7036

National Women's Law Center
1616 P Street, NW, Suite 100
Washington DC 20036
(202) 328-5160

Social Justice for Women
108 Lincoln Street, 6th Floor
Boston, MA 02111
(617) 482-0747

The Children's Center
Bedford Hills Correctional Facility
PO. Box 803
Bedford Hills, NY 10050

The Women's Prison Association & Home, Inc.
110 Second Avenue
New York, NY 10003
(212) 674-1163

The Neil J. Houston House
9 Notre Dame Street
Roxbury, MA 02119
(617) 445-3066

Index

Adams, K., 191
Adams, L., 26, 58
Addiction (theories of), 78-80
Adelberg, E., 101, 102
Adler, F., 13, 47
AIMS, 64
Ainsworth, M., 106
Albanese, J., 12
Alcohol, 75, 78, 79, 84
Alcoholics Anonymous, 68, 163
Anger management, 141, 154-158
Anglin, M., 74
Arbour, L., 162
Arbuthnot, J., 132, 133
Assessment, 71
Attachment, 106-107

Bagley, K., 82, 84, 92
Baskin, D., 16
Battering, 15, 19, 41, 102
Baunach, P., 105
Beck, A., 73, 79, 85, 87, 88, 121, 122, 123, 127, 128
Bedford Hills, 54
Behavior modification, 122, 126
Bloom, B., 8, 9, 10, 11, 13, 18, 24, 25, 66, 67, 74, 5, 76, 84, 97, 100, 139, 140
Blount, W., 67
Blumenthal, K., 103
Bohn, M., 61

Boot camps, 124-126
Bowlby, J., 106
Boudouris, J., 106, 114, 116
Braithwaite, J., 195
Brochu, S., 75
Browne, A., 15, 102
Brownstein, H., 15
Burglary, 13
Burke, P., 26, 58
Burkhart, K., 55
Burnout, 171-173

California Treatment Project, 62-63, 125
Camp, C., 36, 125
Camp, G., 36
Carlen, P., 194
Carp, S., 138
Catan, L., 114
Chesney-Lind, M., 8, 16, 17, 25, 40, 41, 45, 194, 201
Childhood abuse (of women), 96-100
    programs for, 98-100
Children (of women prisoners), 28, 70, 82-83, 102-108, 160
    impact of imprisonment on, 105-107
Chodorow, N., 50
Clark, D., 149
Classification, 57-65
    behavioral systems of, 64-65
    developmental level systems of, 62-63

measures of, 59-65
objective, 58
"Omnibus System" of, 65
subjective, 57
treatment, 57
Clement, M., 110, 111
Co-dependents, 32
Cognitive therapy, 86-88, 126-130
Confidentiality, 174-175
Correctional officers, 36-38
male officers, 37
"Cottage plan," 24
Coulson, G., 190
Counseling, 4-5
(in) bureaucracies, 169-170
crisis, 6-7
(and) cultural issues, 161, 163, 192, 194,
198-199
(and) dependency, 184-186
goal, 21
(and) personal security, 166-168
relationship, 177-179
resistant clients, 180-181
(and) risk taking, 170-171
success, 5-6, 21
transference, 178-179
(and) values, 168-169
"Crack babies," 82, 83
Crawford, J., 55, 102, 148
Crime(s) (of women), 11-20
motivations for, 50-53
property, 12-13, 50, 74
rates, 25
violent, 13-16, 74
white collar, 12
Crime Prevention Institute, 146
Criminology (theories of), 45-50, 52
biological, 47, 49, 52
current, 49-50
psychological, 46
Crimmins, S., 15
Currie, C., 101, 102

Daly, K., 42, 19, 195
Dawson, J., 14
Dayton, K., 37
Depression, 153-154
Diagnostic and Statistical Manual, 60
"Difference approach," 40-42
"Different voice" theory, 133
Dix, D., 54

Dobash, R., 28, 34, 54
Dobash, R., 28
Doremus, S., 54
Drug(s), 15, 18-20
abuse, 68-70
addiction, 51
and criminality, 73-75, 93
dealing, 52
effects of, 77-78
patterns of use, 74-77
subculture, 107
treatment programs, 69, 83-92

Eaton, M., 155, 159
"Economic marginalization thesis," 48
Eisenstein, H., 41, 42
Ellis, A., 129
Emory, G., 127
Employment, 144-146
Empowerment, 200-201
Enos, R., 60, 62, 64, 71, 161
"Equality approach, 40-42
Ethic(s)(al)
guidelines, 36
responsibilities (of counselor), 173-177
Evans, K., 148
Ewing, C., 15, 102
Ewles, C., 128

Fabiano, E., 128
Faith, K., 26, 29, 31, 37, 38, 169
Family murders, 14
Family programs, 108-117
Family Therapy, 109-110
Federal Bureau of Investigation, 11, 61
Feinman, C., 53
Feminism, 193-194
Feminist therapy, 197-198
Ferrero, W., 46
Flaubert, M., 121
Fletcher, B., 8, 9, 65, 66, 68, 69, 74, 75, 78,
83, 188
Fox, J., 27, 28, 29, 39
Frankl, L., 153, 154
Freedman, A., 121, 122, 123, 127, 128
Freedman, E., 54, 55
Fry, E., 54

Gaes, G., 6

Gangs (female), 16-18, 40, 51
Gaudin, J., 105
Gendreau, P., 189
Giallombardo, R., 38, 39
Gibbons, A., 54
Gilfus, M., 66
Gilligan, C., 42
Glover v. Johnson, 55, 149
Glueck, E., 46, 47
Glueck, S., 46
Gordan, J., 132
Gottfredson, M., 3, 49, 52
Grant, D., 191
Gunther v. Iowa State Men's Reformatory, 36
Gutteridge, S., 29

Hairston, C., 100, 103, 104, 106, 107
Hale, D., 102
Hannah-Moffat, K., 195, 196
Hatcher, H., 165, 188
Heffernan, R., 38
Heide, K., 14, 98, 99
Heidensohn, F., 42
Henriquez, Z., 114
Hernstein, R., 49
Hickey, E., 14, 131, 132, 135
Hirschel, J., 91
Hirschi, T., 49, 52
HIV, 77, 89
Hoffman-Bustamante, D., 47, 50
Homosexuality, 38-39, 102
Hopper House, 54
Hser, Y., 74
Huling, T., 18, 19

Immarigeon, R., 70, 116
Incarceration, rate of increase, 9, 24-26
Inciardi, J., 74, 77
Intergenerational criminality, 107-108

Joe, K., 16, 17
Jones, M., 135
Jordan v. Gardner, 36, 37

Kapsner, C., 153
Kaslow, F., 109
Kassebaum, G., 38

Kalinich, D., 3
Keeney, B., 14
Kellor, F., 46
Kendall, K., 4, 138, 197
Keny, J., 91
Koban, L., 104
Kochis, D., 85, 89
Kohlberg, L., 130, 131
Kramer, J., 49
Kratcoski, P., 4
Kuhns, J., 67

Landis, J., 25
Langley, S., 15
Lee, C., 97
Lekkerkerker, E., 38, 55
Lenhart, J., 25
Leonard, E., 114
Lester, D., 134
Levesque, M., 75
Lifeskills, 143, 152-153, 163-164
Little, S., 112, 113
Lockwood, D., 74
Lombardo, V., 129
Lombroso, C., 46
Logan, C., 6
Long, G., 68, 99
Louis, T., 189
Lozoff, B., 202

Mahan, S., 169
Mann, C., 16
Martinson, R., 5
Masters, R., 109, 114, 134, 135
McClelland, D., 33, 34, 35, 36, 43, 196
McDermott, J., 194
McGowen, B., 103
McLeod, M., 10
"Medical model," 57
Megargee, E., 61
Menniti, D., 102
Mental status examination, 59-60
Merlo, A., 82, 84, 92
Minnesota Multiphasic Personality Inventory (MMPI), 60-62
Moon, D., 8
Moral development approach, 130-134
Morris, A., 29
Moses, M., 112
"Mules," 18, 41

National Institute of Justice, 78, 92, 96, 147
Network therapy, 195
Nutbrown, V., 190

Okun, B., 162, 168, 177, 178, 179, 181, 183,
    184, 189, 190, 192, 197, 199
Oregon Department of Corrections, 24, 67,
    115
Owen, B., 8, 9, 39, 40, 97

"Pains of imprisonment," 26
Palmer, R., 6, 124, 189, 190
Parenting programs, 110-117
Personality disorders, 121-123
Piaget, J., 130
Pollock, J. (also Pollock-Byrne, J.), 3, 4, 8, 9,
    10, 11, 12, 24, 25, 37, 38, 40, 41, 45, 46,
    51, 52, 65, 66, 67, 77, 78, 80, 81, 82, 91,
    92, 100, 105, 108, 110, 120, 124, 136,
    144, 145, 155, 175, 176, 192
Pollak, O., 47
Pottieger, A., 74
Poverty, 10-11
Prestwood, D., 169
Prisons (for women), 24, 26
    autonomy, lack of, 30-32, 138
    building boom, 25
    discipline in, 33-36, 53
    historical legacy of, 24
    monotony, 32-33
    rule enforcement in, 27, 34, 35, 43
    visitation, 104-105
Prisoners (women):
    demographic profile, 7-8, 25
    education, 65-66
    family background, 9-10
    family ties, 100-102
    juvenile history, 11-12
    needs analysis of, 65-70
    privacy needs, 36
    race, 39-40
    sexual abuse, 36, 66-68
    subculture, 38-40, 43
Programs (prison), 120-142
    educational, 148-150
    elements of, 138-130, 190-192
    evaluation of, 197
    family, 108-117
    goals of, 188-189
    group, 134-135

    parenting, 110-117
    self help, 123-124
    vocational, 55, 147-152
Prostitution, 11, 46, 52, 74, 144
Pseudo-families, 38-39

Quay, H., 64

Rafter, N., 24, 25, 41, 53, 54, 55
Raeder, M., 18, 19, 103
Recidivism, 5 163, 188, 191
Reformatories (for women), 54-56
Rehabilitation, 2-4
Reed, B., 84, 90
Resnick, J., 42
Robbery, 16
Rosenbaum, J., 96
Ross, R., 128, 189
Rush, J., 127

Sandhu, H., 125
Scharf, P., 131, 132, 135
Schade, L., 138
Schroeder, S., 4
Security classifications, 26
Self esteem, 69, 144, 158-159
Self respect, 27-28
Self mutilation, 28-29
Senese, J., 3
Serial murder, 14
Shaver, L., 8
Shaw,, B., 127
Silverman, I., 67
Simon, R., 25, 47
Smith, C., 96
Smith, J., 121
Smith, R., 129
Smith, S., 50
Snell, T., 8, 9, 10, 11, 12, 25, 49, 66, 67, 70,
    74, 75, 77, 83
Socialization, 50
Solomon, E., 98, 99
Sommers, I., 16
Southern, S., 60, 62, 64, 71
Sparger, J., 189
Spencer, D., 57
Spunt, B., 15
Stanton, A., 103
Steffensmeier, 12, 13, 49

Stone, W., 145, 146, 148, 149, 151
Streifel, C., 49
Stress, 27-30, 43
    effects of, 28-29
"Structured opportunity theory," 47
Stumbo, N., 112, 113
Sultan, F., 68, 99

Taylor, C., 10, 17, 73
Therapeutic communities, 85, 135-138, 158
Thomas, W., 46
Thornberry, T., 96
Tilbur, K., 117
Timm v. Gunter, 36
Toch, H., 136

UNICOR, 146
U.S. Dept. of Justice, 1, 9, 13, 14, 23, 24, 66, 75

van Ochten, M. 37
van Voorhis, P., 109, 110, 132, 134

Walsh, A., 122, 189
Ward, D., 38
Warren, R., 62, 63, 64, 65, 70
Wellisch, J., 74, 77, 91
Widom, K., 78, 96
Wilkie, M. 59
Williams, S., 4
Wilson, J., 49
Wister, M. 54
"Women-based corrections," 42, 194-197
Women's liberation (movement), 47, 56
Women's Prison Association of New York, 54
Woolredge, J., 114
Wright, R., 188

Zupan, L., 36
Zweben, J., 86

About the Author

Joycelyn M. Pollock, PhD, JD, is Professor of Criminal Justice at Southwest Texas State University. Her published works include *Ethics in Crime and Justice: Dilemmas and Decisions* (3rd ed.), *Prisons: Today and Tomorrow* (Ed.), *Women, Prison, and Crime, Sex and Supervision: Guarding Male and Female Inmates,* and *Women, Law and Social Control* (with Alida Merlo). She has written numerous articles in the areas of ethics for criminal justice professionals, and women in the criminal justice system. She conducts training sessions for criminal justice professionals in the areas of criminology, ethics, sexual harassment, and female offenders. She has recently received a Soros Justice Fellowship to develop a compendium of parenting programs in women's prisons and design a model parenting program for female inmates.